Radio's Intimate Public

Radio's Intimate Public

Network Broadcasting and
Mass-Mediated Democracy

Jason Loviglio

University of Minnesota Press
Minneapolis • London

Published by the University of Minnesota Press
111 Third Avenue South, Suite 290
Minneapolis, MN 55401-2520
http://www.upress.umn.edu

Library of Congress Cataloging-in-Publication Data

Loviglio, Jason.
    Radio's intimate public : network broadcasting and mass-mediated democracy / Jason Loviglio.
        p.   cm.
    Includes bibliographical references and index.
    ISBN 0-8166-4233-8 (hc : alk. paper) — ISBN 0-8166-4234-6 (pb : alk. paper)
    1. Radio broadcasting—Social aspects—United States.   2. Radio broadcasting—United States—History.   I. Title.
    PN1991.3.U6L68   2005
    302.23'44'0973—dc22   2005010221

Printed in the United States of America on acid-free paper

The University of Minnesota is an equal-opportunity educator and employer.

12   11   10   09   08   07   06   05   10   9   8   7   6   5   4   3   2   1

For Anne, Benjamin, Andrew,
and in loving memory of
Michael Loviglio and Julien Mezey

Contents

Acknowledgments

It is a bit overwhelming to consider the long list of people and institutions that have provided me with valuable assistance in the conception, research, and completion of this project. I would not have undertaken the study of radio history if not for the graduate program in American studies at the University of Minnesota and the wonderful faculty and classmates who inspired and advised me. Many thanks to Joe Austin, Rachel Buff, Roland Delattre, Ed Griffin, David Hall, Elaine Tyler May, Naomi Mezey, Carol Miller, Karen Murphy, David Noble, Thea Petchler, Paula Rabinowitz, Guillermo Rojas, and Michael Willard. Lary May and Riv-Ellen Prell provided an enormous amount of insight, guidance, and constructive criticism. Andrew Seligsohn and Martina Anderson deserve big thanks for endless cups of coffee and equally boundless counsel and insight. Betty Agee and Gratia Coleman helped me over every administrative bump in the road and were unfailingly kind and patient.

The faculty at the University of Massachusetts–Boston deserve thanks as well, more for treating me (a graduate student teaching as an adjunct while finishing a thesis) with respect and kindness out of all proportion to the terrible pay and benefits of the job. Lois Rudnick, Judy Smith, and Rachel Rubin set a high standard for how to treat all fellow workers, regardless of rank. They won my lasting admiration for marching alongside me and other adjunct faculty as we pushed the administration for higher pay and health care benefits, a fight that we actually won!

I have been blessed with another set of fine colleagues at the University of Maryland Baltimore County. Warren Belasco, Kathy Bryan, Michael Hummel, Nicole King, Carole McCann, Pat McDermott, Ed Orser, Dabrina Taylor, Kendra Wallace, and Joshua Woodfork make it a pleasure to go to work. They also set a high standard for the engaged teaching of undergraduates. I am also indebted to the support of Rick Welch, Dean of the Arts and Sciences at UMBC. As department chair, Ed Orser set a tone of civility and fairness, and he has been unmatched in his commitment to our students past and present. Ed and Jo Orser made me and my family feel right at home from the beginning with frequent dinner invitations. During her tenure as department chair, Pat McDermott arranged for a semester's paid paternity leave for me, a gesture that I hope will help to set a precedent for employers of working mothers and fathers. Her constant support as a chair and colleague has been invaluable these past few years. In addition to protecting me from the endless call to service that so often bogs down junior faculty, she provided thoughtful feedback to drafts of two chapters of this book. Carole McCann took me out to lunch during the first week I was on campus and we haven't stopped talking since. Her mentorship, generosity, and humor carried me through some of the most difficult parts of this project. I would surely have perished during her well-deserved sabbatical if not for the arrival of Kendra Wallace, a wonderful colleague and friend. Carol Harmon, the department's indispensable administrative assistant, helps me every single day with so many different crucial aspects of my life as a teacher and scholar that it is impossible to list them all. Many thanks.

My students at the University of Minnesota, the University of Massachusetts–Boston, and the University of Maryland Baltimore County taught me a great deal, and in my conversations with these students I refined many of the ideas for this project. Special thanks to Dayo Akinwande, Jennifer Arrington, Abby Dagen, Alicia Gabriel, Caitlin Galligan, Saralyn Garcia, Ed Kapuscinski, Lauren Madow, Michael McLaurin, Brendan Martin, Ryan Moschell, Faith Perfecto, Phu Pham, Michael Rund, Carol Simone, Jessica Skolnik, Sutton Stokes, Hieu Truong, Matt Vasconcellos, Jackie Vreatt, Michelle Whelan, Ania Welin, and Samantha Zline.

I am grateful to David Wigdor, Les Vogel, and the entire Kluge Center of the Library of Congress as well as the American Historical

Association for research funding support in the form of a J. Franklin Jameson Fellowship in spring 2002. Thanks also to Bryan Cornell and Janet McKee in the Recorded Sound Reference Center for their expertise and patience. I am also grateful to the Library of American Broadcasting in College Park, Maryland. Michael Henry, Karen Fishman, and Chuck Howell are superb at what they do and I doubt very much I could have done much of this research without their expertise and generous support. The entire research staff at the Franklin D. Roosevelt Library and Museum deserves thanks for their helpful guidance in my many visits to their phenomenal archive. Special thanks to Mark Renovitch, Robert Parks, Bob Clark, Karen Anson, Alycia Vivona, and Virginia Lewick. I am also indebted to Alexis Ernst-Treutel at the Wisconsin Historical Society Archives Division and staff of the Boston Public Library, the Widener Library at Harvard University, the Humanities Library at the Massachusetts Institute of Technology, and the Eisenhower Library at The Johns Hopkins University.

There is a loose community of radio scholars who have discovered each other in journals, in books, at conferences, and in online networks over the past decade. These people have provided a great deal to me in the way of camaraderie, intellectual support, and inspiration. I thank all the contributors to *Radio Reader: Essays in the Cultural History of Radio* and the Radio Conference: A Transnational Forum for their wonderful work. In particular, I recognize Allison McCracken, Susan Douglas, Kathy Newman, Elena Razlogova, Alex Russo, Barbara Savage, Susan Smulyan, and especially Michele Hilmes, the dean of a new generation of radio studies. Much of the best research in radio studies today can be described as Hilmesian; if this book merits that description, I will be most gratified. Jim Cox gave me useful data at several stages of the project, and Ryan Ellet and G. Worsely generously shared hundreds of hours of recorded old-time radio programs. The Old-Time Radio Digest, an online community of knowledgeable fans and veteran radio stars, has provided me with helpful information on many occasions.

I am grateful to Felice Shore and Gregg Nass for a hundred meals and a thousand kindnesses, including some clutch child care. Stephanie Shafer, Sujata Guin, Nancy Shallenberger, Diane Hurbon, and Julie Lombardi are also in my debt for taking such wonderful care of my sons when my wife and I were working.

Thanks to Rachel Buff, Michele Hilmes, Jennifer Loviglio, Lorraine Loviglio, Lary May, Naomi Mezey, Pat McDermott, Richard Morrison (my editor at the University of Minnesota Press), Brendan O'Malley, Riv-Ellen Prell, Andrew Seligsohn, Nancy Lusignan Schultz, Judy Smith, Michael Willard, and above all, Anne Wolf, for generously reading drafts and providing valuable suggestions at various stages. I am also indebted to David Thorstad for his excellent copyediting. Rachel Buff has been for more than a decade my dear friend and a true mentor. She has generously shown by example the way to make a meaningful life in this profession while remaining committed to family, politics, and art. There are very few people whom I honestly cannot imagine doing without and she is one of them. Barbara Wilson is another; her sage counsel over the years has made possible the writing of this book and a whole lot more.

Anne Wolf's contributions to this book are impossible to quantify or repay. She read drafts of every seminar paper, conference paper, and chapter as this project wended its way toward completion. Her generosity, insight, and insistence on clarity have helped me more than she can ever know. She has taught me more about public life, private life, and the space between the two than any other person or book. To her, and to our beautiful sons, Benjamin and Andrew, this book is dedicated.

Radio's Intimate Public

Tuning In

> *I can recall walking eastward on the Chicago Midway on a*
> *summer evening. The light held after nine o'clock, and the*
> *ground was covered with clover, more than a mile of green*
> *between Cottage Grove and Stony Island. The blight hadn't*
> *yet carried off the elms, and under them drivers had pulled*
> *over, parking bumper to bumper, and turned on their radios*
> *to hear Roosevelt. They had rolled down their windows*
> *and opened the car doors. Everywhere the same voice,*
> *its odd Eastern accent, which in anyone else would have*
> *irritated Midwesterners. You could follow without missing*
> *a single word as you strolled by. You felt joined to these*
> *unknown drivers, men and women smoking their cigarettes*
> *in silence, not so much considering the President's words*
> *as affirming the rightness of his tone and taking assurance*
> *from it. You had some sense of the weight of troubles that*
> *made them so attentive, and of the ponderable fact, the one*
> *common element (Roosevelt), on which so many unknowns*
> *could agree. Just as memorable to me, perhaps, was to learn*
> *how long clover flowers could hold their color in the dusk.*
> — SAUL BELLOW, *IT ALL ADDS UP*

In memoir and popular memory, Roosevelt's Fireside Chats, like the performances of other highly popular radio figures of the 1930s, are often recalled in an archetypal account of the ritual power of radio to conjure a new social space—public and private, national and local. A pedestrian walking down a city block during a Fireside Chat hears the broadcast issuing from the open windows of every home on the street. Without missing a word, the pedestrian traverses the public space of the street, joined at once to the intimate space of reception and to the sense of shared national space evoked by the rhetoric of common purpose in Roosevelt's carefully wrought but disarmingly folksy "chats." Such accounts typically emphasize the seamlessness of the pedestrian's reception of the broadcast from dozens of individual home sets and the sense of anonymous communion uniting the city's and the nation's listeners, as if part of a single audience, a simultaneously public and private experience.[1]

In the 1920s when radio was new, families, neighborhoods, and even towns gathered around a receiving set located in a common space, such as the general store, town hall, or someone's front porch.[2] By the 1930s, the ubiquity of radio meant that for Americans in densely populated urban neighborhoods, participating in accidentally collective acts of reception became a feature of everyday life, yet one that was still somehow strange. In Ray Barfield's *Listening to Radio, 1920–1950,* memories of this type abound: "When walking home in the hot summer evenings after window shopping on Madison Street," a Chicago man recalls, "one could follow the entire progress of *Amos 'n' Andy* from the open windows." By the 1940s, even in small towns like Honea Path, South Carolina, it was possible to listen to "practically the whole *Grand Ole Opry*" as it issued out of every house on the block. "As one walked down Middletown's residential streets in 1935," the Lynds reported in *Middletown in Transition,* "everywhere the blare of radios was more pervasive than in 1925."[3]

In Saul Bellow's account, the sense of Roosevelt's words reaching listeners across traditional boundaries of public and private is enhanced by the substitution of cars for homes as the private sites of reception. Like radio and motion pictures, automobiles did much to redefine the contours of everyday notions of social space in the years between the world wars. This recollection and others like it exude a sense of nostalgia for a particular moment in the formation of a national audience, one that links the anonymous camaraderie of the urban crowds to the radio's system of centralized transmission and private reception. This historical moment was less about the disintegration of the distinct public and private spheres than it was a time of heightened interest in the advantages and perils to be gained from both transgressing and reinforcing them. Bellow's reminiscence of the quintessentially modern world of ubiquitous automobiles and radio signals evokes older themes, both urban and pastoral. His pleasure in the anonymous communion with the crowd recalls an Old World notion of urban space, a public life marked by the easy sociability among strangers, Philippe Aries's notion of "a life lived in public," Baudelaire's *flâneur*. But Bellow is not jostled by the crowd so much as he is drawn into the curiously private world of the cars parked amid a mile of green. A sense of intimacy, even domesticity, pervades the scene—men and women smoking silently in the temporarily breached privacy of automobiles. Here, amid the clover of Chicago's Midway, cars "parking bumper to bumper" with their windows and doors open, Bellow feels "joined to these unknown drivers." An American pastoral scene unfolds: in the cars, under the elms, radio, the machine in the garden, recalls old forms of public space along the fault lines of a new urban and technological landscape.

Accounts such as these emphasize radio's ritual power to transform the anonymous space of towns, cities, the nation itself into a new site of reception, a momentary extension of the private space of the family car or home. The domestic space of reception becomes more public even as feelings about its intimacy become heightened. The open doors and windows of the cars in Bellow's recollection, like the open windows of houses in other versions, mark the site where public and private have temporarily merged to form a national community, an *intimate public*. But these accounts of shared radio reception also reinforce the notion of distinct spaces, spaces whose difference becomes most apparent in moments like these, when the listener's mobility across the lines of public and private space makes the boundaries seem clearer and more porous at the same time. Network radio in the 1930s and 1940s amplified the importance of these "blurred" social spaces; in the middle distance opening up between publicity and intimacy, radio seemed to conjure a ritual of national identity.

The Public/Private Dichotomy

Broadcasting via publicly owned, federally regulated airwaves and from privately owned stations to an unlimited number of receivers, most of which were located in the domestic space of family homes, network radio seemed to offer, in its very structure, particularly difficult challenges to distinct boundaries or singular definitions of public and private. The tension between intimacy (interpersonal communication) and publicity (mass communication) was the defining feature of early network radio, its central problem and its greatest appeal.[4] The "intimate public" of this study's title refers to a new cultural space created by radio broadcasting in the 1930s that was marked by tensions between national and local, inclusion and exclusion, publicity and privacy. The mobility of radio voices across the borders between the intimate worlds of domesticity, solitude, and one-on-one conversation, and the public world of politics, sociability, and mass communication—captured nicely in Bellow's account of collective eavesdropping on the president's voice—represents "authorized transgressions." In other words, radio's intimate public generated a category of permissible crossings of the public/private boundary, leaving the larger principle of the public/private distinction intact, perhaps even revitalized.[5] This is a book about the beginnings of what would become a remarkably sustainable contradictory impulse in broadcasting and, more generally, in electronic media in the twentieth century. Radio offered listeners a new way to think about the shifting boundaries of public and private space and speech at the start of an era in which these terms had come to be understood as permanently "in crisis."

Indeed, a sense of crisis of one kind or another has been a feature of the discourse around the public/private dichotomy throughout the modern era, starting in the mid-nineteenth century, when telegraphy, the railroad, and photography introduced profound changes in the experience of social space.[6] In fact, a preoccupation with this dichotomy is itself a central feature of modernity. Endless talk about the collapse of the public world into the private one (and vice versa) functions, in a Foucauldian turn, as the discursive incantation that calls modern notions of public and private into being.[7] In other words, worrying about the blurring boundary between publicity and privacy became a central way that Americans in the twentieth century made meaningful use of public and private as social categories. And nowhere was this process more elaborate, more self-conscious, and more foundational than on the radio airwaves of the 1930s and 1940s.

Radio, this book argues, was an apparatus that helped produce a new kind of social space—the intimate public—in which the terms "public" and "private" came to represent a complex web of social performances perpetually in play rather than distinct and immutable categories. This new space promised listeners a fantasy of social mobility, even as it reminded them of the importance of social hierarchies in protecting their own relative privilege. Radio voices were thrilling because they moved with impunity back and forth from private to public modes of performance. In this founding contradiction of mass-mediated society, listeners were invited to participate vicariously in authorized transgressions of the public/private boundary, even if only to help police it.

As radio voices began to make themselves at home in a number of familiar social spaces, both public and private, anxieties about the social identities of the denizens of these new mass-mediated spaces were inevitable. One of the key features of the public/private dichotomy for the purposes of my analysis is that it "subsumes" other dichotomies, distinctions, and hierarchies.[8] In the era of electronic mass media, the terms "public" and "private" have come to constitute a kind of meta-code for understanding social power and the nearly constant struggles for it. The central question is, as Nancy Fraser has put it, "who has the power to decide where to draw the line between public and private? What structures of inequality underlie the hegemonic understandings of these categories as well as the struggles that contest them?"[9]

For the answer we turn to the usual suspects: gender, race, class, nationality, and sexuality are the central axes of identity, difference, and inequality that help to determine one's power "to draw and defend the line" between the different meanings of public and private.[10] In struggles over women's reproductive freedom and protection from domestic abuse, the key questions have had to do with deciding which areas of social life are properly to be kept private, that is, *personal* and free from the authority and surveillance of the state, and which areas require the interventions of public authority. In civil rights struggles over access to public accommodations and employment, the power to determine the scope of government authority into the private, that is, *economic,* dealings of businesses was the crucial issue. In the case of the confirmation hearings of Clarence Thomas, Fraser demonstrates how the inequalities of race, class, and gender identity played determinative roles in the public and Senate debates about whose privacy—Thomas's or his accuser Anita Hill's—was judged to be more worthy of protection. In the twentieth century, cultural debates over whose stories properly belong to the realm of public debate and whose sexual and personal lives deserve privacy were conducted in courts and legislatures but also circulated through the newspaper, radio, and television. Because of its invisible—or disembodied—voices, its ubiquity in American life, and its powerful evocation of a live national audience, network radio provided perhaps the most complicated and compelling negotiations of these struggles.

Recent scholarship has pointed to the preoccupation with the sexual, racial, and national identity of invisible, often ambiguous radio voices whose mobility through these fictive social spaces in the 1930s and 1940s made it increasingly uncertain how to maintain traditional social boundaries.[11] Radio's promiscuous mixing of interpersonal and mass communication meant that intimate questions of identity and difference became part of a national conversation. Radio's aural representations of difference provided highly complex resolutions to this problem, according to this new work. White men who "sounded black," straight men who "sounded queer," Americans who "sounded foreign," and men and women, boys and girls, who sounded like each other—all these performances evoked intense pleasure and anxiety precisely because they seemed to put fixed social identities into play in highly public ways. But ultimately, these performances, rooted in caricature, also helped to reinscribe traditional boundaries of race, gender, nationality, and sexuality, reinforcing complex rules about who is entitled to the privileges of privacy and publicity.

Using this scholarship as a point of departure, this study argues that network radio's most durable and popular performances, programs, and genres constitute a series of negotiations of the contradictions inherent in the public/private dichotomy in American social life. The preoccupation with both transgressing and policing this boundary can be found in soap operas, presidential addresses, audience participation programs, and mystery thrillers, along with other programs that take as their subject the adventures of "average Americans."

The era of network broadcasting was the historical moment in which the already blurry public/private dichotomy came to be invested with powerful meanings about national and personal identity that continue to resonate today. In this crucial period, network radio's project of representing (that is, describing and serving) a national audience played a key role in a larger set of changes in how Americans thought about the mass media, citizenship, and the public and private registers of everyday life. Listening to the radio became more than a national pastime; it became a constituent part of national identity.

In the 1920s, the first decade of radio broadcasting, the power of radio's invisible voices was often interpreted through analogies to the "supernatural."[12] Like telepathy, interplanetary communication, or talking with the dead, radio seemed to be heralding a new relationship between space, sound, and human experience. By the next decade, radio had come to seem less strange, but the challenge it posed to traditional notions of social space continued, albeit in less fantastic forms. Between 1927 and 1934, as radio became popular, profitable, federally regulated, network-dominated, and highly commercialized, questions about how to imagine its audience consumed journalists, policy makers, listeners, and broadcasters alike.[13]

Metaphors of space and place came to replace those concerned with the supernatural. Radio's ability to mimic or replace familiar social institutions was offered variously as a source of comfort and excitement, or as a metaphor for democratic participation, or as a sign of danger. Radio programs invited listeners to town halls, town meetings, highways, alleys, and sanctums. Listeners were asked to imagine workshops, taverns, ranches, caves, lobbies, barns, schools, and cafés as the place from which their favorite shows were broadcast. Hundreds of programs were named for the galleries, studios, museums, marquees, opera houses, theaters, showcases, soundstages, playhouses, schools, universities, and other cultural and educational institutions that served as sponsors or models for the programs. And, of course, radio programs were presented as another kind of *home:* many shows were named for houses, manors, chambers, firesides, kitchens, parlors, and families and family members.

The People, the Public, and the Radio

In the broadest context, of course, the imagined space for radio's new audience was the nation itself. More than any other medium, radio's theoretically universal address "seemed in its early days to lend itself to association with ideas of nation, of national identity, to 'the heart and mind of America,' its 'soul.'"[14] Radio's invisible national reach and its galvanizing universal and simultaneous address became the perfect symbol of national unity. Radio's preoccupation with the voices, reception practices, and interests of "the people" gestured toward a model of participatory democracy, a national town meeting of the air. It also became an irresistible symbol for the dangers associated with mass-mediated politics. National radio evoked fears of hypnotized audiences falling under the sway of irrational forces like fascism, communism, or even a corrupt and bankrupt capitalism.

This profound ambivalence about the kind of social space conjured by radio represents a particularly acute crystallization of the debates about the meaning of the "public sphere" in the twentieth century. Precisely because of its perceived blurring of public and private spheres, radio epitomized the concerns of Jürgen Habermas and other twentieth-century social theorists about the fate of democratic society, based as it was on the rational critical debate possible only in a distinct public sphere separate from both the authority of the state and the encroachments of commercial capitalism.[15] Indeed, Habermas, in a strange echo of Walter Lippmann's "phantom public," referred to radio and television talk shows as the epitome of the "sham public" that had replaced the authentic one that sprang up in European capitals in the eighteenth century.[16] Along with the expansion of the welfare state, mass-mediated intimacies helped to doom the integrity of the public sphere, ushering in an age in which the blurring of public and private spheres spawned hypertrophied state and corporate powers.

Since the 1989 English translation of Habermas's *Structural Transformation of the Public Sphere,* a lot of critical attention has been paid to the crisis of the public sphere, the blurring of public and private, and the role that the electronic mass media play in undermining rational-critical debate. And although these critics have found significant flaws in Habermas's public sphere as a conceptual norm and as a historical category, they have, without exception, agreed that they "cannot do without" the concept of the public.[17] For many recent critics, the key has been to consider the concepts public and private less as fixed opposites than as protean, historically contingent qualities that exist in spaces and quantities far more heterogeneous than Habermas's schema allows for.[18] In these revisions of public sphere theory, the mass media are not considered the source of a sham public but rather the site for a reconceptualization of the meanings and uses of publicity.

Jeff Weintraub emphasizes the multiple, overlapping, and protean nature of the terms "public" and "private," such that the capitalist marketplace is considered *private* in classical economics but part of the *public* world to feminists who identify wage earning as part of the public sphere from which women have been historically excluded.[19] Michael Warner argues that "the bourgeois public sphere has been structured from the outset by a logic of abstraction that provides a privilege for unmarked identities: the male, the white, the middle class, the normal." For Warner, the process of joining the public requires a process of self-abstraction, or self-negation: "No matter what particularities of culture, race, gender, or class we bring to bear on public discourse, the moment of apprehending something as public is one in which we imagine—if imperfectly—indifference to those particularities, to ourselves."[20]

Warner sees this process of self-abstraction as highly ambivalent—as a moment of "utopian universality" and as a "major source of domination." The opportunity for people to "transcend the given realities of their bodies and their status," however, depends on "the rhetorical strategy of personal abstraction," an ability that "has always been an unequally available resource." Thus, although the bourgeois public sphere purported to ignore or bracket the particularities of culture, race, gender, class, "[t]he subject who could master this rhetoric in the bourgeois public sphere was implicitly—even explicitly—white, male, literate, and propertied." These particularities were more easily "bracketed," while other forms of identity were subjected to "the humiliating positivity of the particular."[21]

In the newer, mass-mediated public sphere of consumer culture, however, "difference" is assumed rather than bracketed and access to publicity is not predicated on the paradoxical and disingenuous notion that the particularities of personal identity and body image—one's race, class, gender, sexuality—have nothing to do with one's public subjectivity.

In the era of electronically mediated consumerist discourse, the rhetoric of the bourgeois public sphere has become "complicated by other forms of publicity."[22] With the irruption of this consumer-culture counterutopia in the space formerly occupied primarily by the liberal notion of the public, Warner sees a blurring not so much of public and private but of different modes of publicity. Radio's public, forged at the intersection of an emergent consumer culture and residual notions of the liberal public sphere, combined elements of both of these modes of publicity.

Warner, Weintraub, and Fraser offer crucial insights into the debate about the public sphere in the era of the electronic mass media and my discussion of radio's intimate public. My analysis of radio performances, programs, and genres is influenced by these critics' shared attention to the enormous social and political power wielded by those who can determine where the public ends and the private begins in any given instance. I am also influenced by their shared commitment to the notion that publicness remains, despite the limits of classical liberal formulations, a crucial category for theorizing and practicing democracy.

When competing notions of public and private clashed, popular radio voices of the 1930s and 1940s narrated the ensuing complex social conflicts. Radio's authorized transgressions celebrated a new kind of social mobility back and forth across the boundaries of home and work, onstage and backstage, national policy and hearth, private citizen and public figure. At the same time, they drew attention to persistent anxieties about the ways an American public represents differences and inequalities of race, class, gender, nationality, and sexuality. If the president and the man in the street, superheroes and housewives could all mingle the social codes of publicity and privacy at will and listeners could, at least vicariously, join them in the intimate public ritual of reception, did this suggest a model of participatory democracy? If the social power to join radio's national public was an ambivalent and unequally available resource, then perhaps the cultural work of these different radio voices was more varied, ambivalent, and harder to pin down.

Competing Populisms

According to cultural historians, radio, film, advertising, popular music, theater, and various New Deal arts programs together formed the matrix out of which was born the mass-mediated public sphere of the 1930s.[23] With laborers, immigrants, and other marginalized groups composing an unprecedented proportion of the audience for these new mass media, the conflation of this mass audience with "the people" became an irresistible impulse for a wide range of competing interests. The struggle over the "competing populist rhetorics" of left and right shaped the development of the mass media in a period of mass culture, political and economic upheaval at home, and darkening clouds of another world war overseas.[24] This struggle also reflected a keenly felt ambivalence about this new populist impulse. In the case of film, for example, Lawrence Levine notes:

> Hollywood evinced a pervasive ambivalence concerning the American people, who were constantly referred to as the core and hope of the state but who were depicted again and again as weak, fickle, confused sheep who could be frightened, manipulated, and controlled.[25]

Were the mass media productive of fascism? Were Walter Lippmann and the "democratic realists" of the 1920s correct in dismissing the public of democratic theory as a mere "phantom"?[26] Did average people, with their irrational and emotional impulses, belong to the sphere of public life or should they more properly be considered private and thus not a part of political deliberations? Such questions haunted the academic, political, and popular discourses in the years between the world wars. From the New Deal's "Forgotten Man" to the competing versions of "Americanism" promulgated by the Popular Front and the Du Pont–financed Liberty League, to the portraits of "average Americans" produced and disseminated by new generations of pollsters, public-relations experts, advertisers, and political scientists, popular representations of the American people entered into a highly competitive discursive field.

Kenneth Burke, writing in the 1930s, saw the left and the right engaged in a constant process of a "stealing back and forth of symbols," and no symbol was more important to the popular and political culture of the period than that of "the people." Indeed, Burke caused a controversy at the 1935 meeting of the American Writers Congress with the suggestion that the left replace "the workers" with "the people," in effect stealing the term back from the fascists at home and abroad.[27] This stealing back and forth of symbols was most apparent in radio, where an imagined public was constituted daily, hourly, and where commercial, regulatory, and popular interests collided over how radio broadcasting could best serve the "public interest, convenience and necessity."

More than any other mass medium, network radio in the 1930s and 1940s, by addressing a national public in an immediate and intimate manner, was perfectly situated to capitalize on the era's ambivalent romance with populism. Nowhere was the discourse of "the people" more dramatically—and ambivalently—expressed than in the national radio broadcasts of the 1930s and 1940s. On many programs in a variety of genres, the voice of the people spoke in performative utterances; like opinion polls, these programs helped to create the publics they simply claimed to represent.[28] At the same time, stubborn anxieties about the public becoming simply a mob turned on key questions: Who was included and who was excluded? Which interests were public and which were merely private? And which sorts of people merited privacy and which sorts surveillance?

In the broadcasts of the early 1930s, celebrations of and appeals to "the people" abounded, inspired in part by Roosevelt's "Forgotten Man" rhetoric, the folksy populism of such pioneering radio pitchmen as Dr. John R. Brinkley, of the "goat-gland cure" for impotence, the radio and film personae of Will Rogers, and, of course, the political and economic context of those first miserable years of the Depression.[29] Like Brinkley, Roxy Rothafel and Arthur Godfrey developed a national audience with folksy chatter starting in the 1920s. In a style of broad-cast address that is still extant on late-night radio and early-morning television, Godfrey chatted about weather, announced listener birth-days and anniversaries, and read excerpts of fan mail starting in the early 1930s.

The posture of public outreach that helped to make these broadcasts so engaging was part of an intense preoccupation with understanding and shaping public opinion. This "quest for data" about the contours of national public opinion was a central feature in the development of network programming and sponsorship plans. Network strategies for determining the reach of radio signals, the size and characteristics of the audience, and the range of responses for sponsored programs ini-tially involved similar efforts to encourage listener letter writing. It has been estimated that by the early 1930s, about two-thirds of all radio programs on NBC explicitly requested listeners to write to the station. By 1931, NBC and CBS reported receiving 7 million and 12 million pieces of listener mail per year, respectively. "Father Coughlin was reported to have received 1.2 million messages in response to a single broadcast of 1930 in which he attacked President Hoover."[30]

From government-sponsored educational programming such as *Americans All, Immigrants All* and *Freedom's People* to dramatic pro-grams such as *Columbia Workshop* (which adapted Carl Sandburg's play *The People, Yes!* for broadcast) and variety programs such as *The Pursuit of Happiness* (which featured Paul Robeson's famous ren-dition of "Ballad for Americans"), "the people" was a shibboleth of the New Deal and Popular Front writers and producers working in radio. And on commercial programs such as *The People's Platform* and *We the People,* the phrase represented radio's democratic accessibility, and the notion that radio constituted its own national public sphere.[31] Programs that focused on matters of serious public debate recalled the democratic traditions of the seventeenth-century New England town meeting. To cite the most well known example, *America's Town Meeting of the Air* brought opinion leaders together across a surpris-ingly broad political spectrum to debate important public issues be-fore an often rowdy live audience that participated by hooting at and asking questions of the invited experts.[32]

Even on comedy/variety programs such as Fred Allen's *Town Hall Tonight,* the conventions of a small-town, face-to-face public space were celebrated and gently parodied as Allen bantered with fictional denizens of "Allen's Alley" and with real "townsfolk," the members of his studio audience who bravely came before the microphone. The opening of *Town Hall Tonight* mimics the sense, evoked in Saul Bellow's recollection of Roosevelt's Fireside Chat, of radio's universal reception, cutting across the multiple registers of public and private, inside and outside. All across "town," people engaged in a variety of social activities drop what they are doing because "It's *Town Hall Tonight!*" These townsfolk/listeners join in the parade to the Town Hall that kicks off each program, taking to the street to participate in a radio ritual that cleverly joins quaint notions of small-town civic pride with the decidedly urbane humor of Allen and his Mighty Allen Art Players.[33]

In every case, radio's peculiarly intimate and national address served as a metaphor for the populist sentiment that "the people" were welcome anywhere in national life. Further, the proliferation of "average" voices on the air seemed to suggest that the people, in all their simplicity, were themselves embodiments of and continuous with that nation.

At the same time, fears about radio's indiscriminate publicness were well represented on the air, too. The fear of radio's ability to mobilize a hysterical mob has been explored by many in relation to the famous *War of the Worlds* broadcast of 1938 and by Michael Denning with regard to Orson Welles's other "allegories of anti-fascism."[34] And Michele Hilmes has shown how a logic of gendered distinctions on network radio created a system in the 1930s whereby programs deemed prestigious and more worthy of the radio's "public interest" mission were broadcast during the prime-time hours, in many cases without taint of commercial sponsorship.[35] The daytime schedule was reserved as a ghetto for radio's degraded, commercialized, feminized, and thus "private" fare: soap operas.

Radio's Intimate Public examines how radio performances up and down the dial constantly negotiated the preoccupation with public and private; indeed, it argues that this negotiation became the central cultural work of network radio in its first two decades. Threats to national security, women's virtue, family happiness, and urban crowds were constantly evoked and assuaged in radio's preoccupied discourse of universal access and populism. Radio was an apparatus that dissolved and then reconstituted the distinctions between public and private and that fractured these vague terms into their often overlapping, contradictory parts. In this seemingly Sisyphean work, radio helped to create a template for mass-mediated popular culture that continues to shape popular formats on radio, television, film, advertisements, and

Web sites. Publicizing the privacy of average people continues to serve as a source of pleasure, danger, and moral outrage, and as an expression of populism and participatory democracy. Radio's insistent and ambivalent voices ushered in an era in which privacy and publicity became flexible modes of performance and the electronic mass media became central discursive institutions in shaping cultural identities.

The book is organized into an introduction, four chapters, and a conclusion. Each chapter examines a popular, enduring, or influential performance, program, or genre from radio's golden age. They include the Fireside Chats of Franklin D. Roosevelt; *Vox Pop,* a pioneering audience-participation show; daytime serials, or soap operas; and the popular mystery thriller *The Shadow.* Each of these radio forms is shaped by a preoccupation with transgressing the public/private boundary and the cultural work of redrawing it in the name of national security; traditional gender roles; racial, ethnic, and class hierarchies and distinctions; or some combination of these conservative values. Each of these broadcasts is marked by a sense of ambivalence about which is the more important impulse: transgressing social boundaries or re-creating them, challenging traditional notions of national and gender identity or reaffirming them.

Chapter 1 examines Roosevelt's Fireside Chats, and argues that Roosevelt and network radio developed into complementary and mutually reinforcing symbols of national unity. Roosevelt's mixture of state authority and folksy intimacy served as the perfect embodiment of radio's fluidity across the boundaries of public and private. But at a time of unprecedented unemployment, Roosevelt offered listeners access to a new kind of productivity: helping to produce and mobilize the favorable public opinion that he claimed for himself became a galvanizing form of cultural work for millions who were hailed as both objects and agents of the new science of public opinion. What Roosevelt sold better than anyone else was the sense that Americans shared both his responsibility and his talent for gathering, measuring, and representing public opinion and that the radio was the apparatus par excellence for doing precisely that. In his hands, radio became a tool for enlisting a mass audience of listeners for the important work of transforming itself into a highly self-conscious public, a rhetorical arsenal of mass-mediated democracy.

At the same time, taking up Roosevelt's invitation to join the national public of radio entailed a process of self-abstraction in which the private particularities of class status, national origin, and political dissent somehow had to be shed. Roosevelt's speech oscillated between the rhetoric of unity and a set of distinctions between those who belong to this new mass-mediated public and those who do not. In their letters, listeners volunteered their services as public relations agents for the president and his radio campaigns. Many of them borrowed from Roosevelt's rhetoric of shifting distinctions: celebrations of national unity almost always concluded with an echo of Roosevelt's own dark warnings of the dangers of foreigners, radicals, organized labor, isolationists, and other "selfish" interests.

The chapter concludes with a brief consideration of the largely forgotten but highly successful and influential radio career of Eleanor Roosevelt. These commercially sponsored broadcasts, targeted to a primarily female audience of consumers, addressed issues of national and international importance through the deceptively informal and "intimate" mode of women sharing chatter "over our coffee cups." The mixture of public affairs and intimate address—so powerfully effective for her husband—earned Eleanor Roosevelt widespread scorn as well as hundreds of thousands of dollars and millions of fans. In stark contrast to the Fireside Chats, the first lady's broadcasts consistently celebrated the seemingly endless differences in national identities, class statuses, and approaches to national defense that characterized the world at the start of World War II.

Chapter 2, "*Vox Pop:* Network Radio and the Voice of the People," traces the rise of one of broadcasting's most enduring genres: the audience-participation program. In particular, it explores the persistence of "the people's voice" both as a trope for radio's democratic potential and as a new marketing strategy for an endless supply of intimate commodities. On audience-participation programs such as *Vox Pop*, the voices of average people became the site for a series of negotiations about what kinds of publicity and privacy were available to men and women, natives and the foreign-born, white folks and people of color, voters and consumers. Between 1932 and 1948, *Vox Pop* helped to invent a series of compelling but ambivalent figures in mass-mediated public life as it cycled through a variety of formats: from the Forgotten Man on the streets of Houston and New York to quiz-show contestants vying for consumer goods, to military and defense workers, to postwar consumers. *Vox Pop* serves as a useful example of network radio's uneasy preoccupation with the voices of "average people" and the changing strategies for defining who these people are and what parts of their private lives should be publicized. On live broadcasts and in letters to the producers, these "real" voices could be unpredictable, even offensive at times, expressing with brutal honesty competing notions of where the public/private boundary should be drawn and by whom. Containing the explosive potential of "real voices" while continuing to profit from it required constant innovation in how the lines between public and private could be breached and redrawn, a process that continues to shape popular formats in electronic media.

Chapter 3, "Public Affairs: The Soap-Opera Cultural Front," explores the soap opera as a site where women's difficult relationship to public and private space is endlessly negotiated. Women who feel out of place in their own homes constitute the besetting problem in almost all serial drama from 1933 through the end of World War II. Although the causes of their anxiety and suffering seem formulaic—dead, missing, or unreliable husbands and suitors, ruthless female competitors, and so on—many of their solutions are surprisingly inventive. On many soap operas, protagonists respond to their intimate problems with ambivalent, often transgressive behavior that takes them in and out of hypertrophied domesticity and radical community organizing. Radio serial drama may not, in itself, constitute a hidden cultural front, but it does present a fairly compelling case that the struggle to find authentic social spaces for women and their families in between the narrowly conceived spheres of domesticity and the competitive marketplace or mothering and other forms of labor was the central motive force for the genre.

Chapter 4, "*The Shadow* Meets the Phantom Public," examines how the promise and problems of a mass-mediated urban public became the self-conscious focus of suspenseful dramatic narratives on mystery-thriller programs such as *The Shadow*. By evoking and assuaging fears of foreign invasion, mass manipulation, and the rising menace of totalitarianism, *The Shadow* emphasized the importance of maintaining and mobilizing traditional exclusions, hierarchies, and boundaries in the imagined community of the United States in the late 1930s and early 1940s. At the same time, the show seemed to insist that public life—even amid the diversity and unruliness of the city—was something we couldn't do without. The early years of the popular serial illustrate how network radio's discourse of intimate publicity could attract a national mass audience at the same time that it dramatized the dangers that such an audience posed. Following a brief history of *The Shadow*'s origins in radio and pulp fiction, and the generic and ideological similarities in other popular radio thrillers such as *The Green Hornet,* this chapter closely examines "The Hypnotized Audience," an episode from 1937, the show's first season. In this episode, the mystical threat of "Oriental culture" to white denizens of an urban sphere of popular entertainment becomes the means for dramatizing and resolving the interrelated crises of public space, mass culture, and national/racial outsiders.

The Conclusion considers the broader legacy of radio's intimate public in twentieth-century broadcasting and beyond. From *America's Town Meeting of the Air* to the recent spasm of "reality TV" programming to the phenomena of Web dating and amateur Web logs, or "blogs," the impulse to bring "average people" into contact with the latest communications technology represents one of the most enduring strategies for negotiating the powerful ways the electronic media have shaped our relationship to the notions of public and private speech, space, and performance.

If ambient listening to the radio voice of President Roosevelt—or *Amos 'n' Andy,* or Jack Benny—constituted an archetypal moment in radio's power to focus attention on the powerful and slippery boundaries of public and private, then what constitutes an analogous moment for the contemporary mediascape of the early twenty-first century? With the proliferation of media channels and technologies and the fracturing of the mass audience into many smaller niches, it is almost impossible to imagine a similar ritual of simultaneous national reception. Even so, certain broadcasts—national disasters, sporting events, awards shows—command a massive global audience. Still, despite the typically fractured audience, the impulse to watch, or eavesdrop, or lurk as "average people" perform their private selves in public continues its centrality in the American popular imagination.

CHAPTER 1

The Fireside Chats and the New Deal

> [Roosevelt] is . . . a ganglion for reception,
> expression, transmission, combination, and
> realization which, I take it, is exactly what
> modern government ought to be.
> —*H. G. Wells,* Experiment in Autobiography

Among the tens of thousands of letters and telegrams that poured into the White House in the days after Roosevelt's second Fireside Chat of May 7, 1933, one letter from a Louisiana listener included a clipping of a cartoon from the *New Orleans Times-Picayune* portraying the event. Underneath the caption, "Just Among Friends," a husband and wife sit on a comfortable pin-striped sofa, presumably their own, next to a smiling President Roosevelt. "And so," Roosevelt says (in a paraphrase of the chat's concluding lines), "with mutual confidence, we go forward!" The president is depicted as slightly oversized, handsome, and energetic, gesturing casually, a visual representation of the intimate tone that made the chats so affecting. In one hand he holds a document that reads: "Roosevelt's open way of explaining his policies to the people." The couple beam at the president as the husband exclaims, "Boy! Does this beat the White House spokesman!"

The *Times-Picayune* cartoon's central image—a smiling, reassuring Roosevelt seated in the home of an American family—had, in the first two months of his administration, already become a well-recognized symbol of these special addresses, the president's persona, and, more broadly, the public philosophy of the New Deal. Roosevelt's mail reflected the public preoccupation with this image, and the intimacy,

1

Cartoon that appeared in the *New Orleans Times-Picayune* on May 9, 1933. Courtesy of the Franklin D. Roosevelt Library.

friendliness, and "open way" with which the new president communicated via the radio. After the first Fireside Chat, a New York City man wrote: "you are more than just another President, in that your willingness to put plain facts in a plain way before the people brings you real close to their fireside, and creates a warmth in their hearts for you, such as they have for a real good friend."[1] Anticipating the "Fireside Chat" name months before Harry Butcher first used it in a CBS press release for the second Fireside Chat of May 7, this listener was not alone in imagining Roosevelt in the intimate space of the family home. "It was just like having a good friend sit down and talk your troubles over with you," wrote a man, from Sunnyside, California.[2] Describing himself as a "citizen of little or no consequence," a Brooklyn listener wrote: "as I listened to the President's broadcast, I felt that he walked into my home, sat down and in plain and forceful language explained to me how he was tackling the job I and my fellow citizens gave him."[3]

In addition to mastering radio's intimate mode of address, Roosevelt also borrowed from a centrifugal force in radio address—beckoning to listeners to leave the privacy of domestic space for a broader, wider, and more public site of reception. Saul Bellow's recollection of listening to Roosevelt's voice as it issued from the radios in a line of parked cars along the Chicago Midway provides a particularly compelling example of the power of radio—and the Fireside Chats—to transform public space. The Fireside Chats were one of the most effective ways that Roosevelt articulated the public philosophy of the New Deal: an expansion of government's role in the everyday life of its citizens and a rhetorical embrace of a broader, more inclusive public sphere. The Fireside Chats, perhaps more than any other broadcasts of the early network era, made the most of the contradictory impulses in radio's construction of its own public. In examining the popular responses to the chats, it becomes clear that Roosevelt's intimate visits in the homes of his listeners were often experienced as invitations to transform the boundaries of domestic, political, and social space in the service of national renewal. Listeners to the chats, such as Charles Johnson of Englewood Cliffs, New Jersey, appreciated the intimate yet public ritual of sitting down and talking with the president and "sixty million others too."[4]

Bearing this centrifugal force in mind, let's take another look at the cartoon from the *Times-Picayune*. On closer inspection, the living room in which the president visits the couple has some curious features. In the background, instead of furniture, we see a large, almost theater-sized curtain, drawn back just to the right of the president. The foreground is bare, except for a perfunctory table holding a book and an ashtray. Even that quintessential feature of the 1930s living-room furniture, the radio console, is missing, replaced by Roosevelt's imposing physical presence. The only seating is afforded by the sofa, so that all three figures are seated facing forward. In addition, the couple's dress is rather peculiar for an evening at home. The wife is wearing a gown with lacy trim at the neck and an elegantly cocked evening hat, and carries an evening bag. The husband is sporting a three-piece suit and a fat, expensive-looking cigar. The living room begins to bear a resemblance to a roomy balcony box at the opera or the theater. Seated, all in a row, but facing away from the drawn curtain, it is unclear whether the president and his auditors are part of the audience or part of the performance. Indeed, it appears that they are both at once.

Roosevelt's audience, as imagined in this cartoon rendering of the ubiquitous image of a home visit, was hailed not in a purely domestic space, nor in one that is uncomplicatedly "public." Instead, these listeners seem to inhabit the domestic space of the home, the "public" space of the theatergoer, and the proscenium space of a theatrical performer all at once. Roosevelt, seated next to them, seems to occupy these same spaces as well. This couple is not so much a passive audience watching Roosevelt glide elegantly into their home as they are partners with him in transcending the confining boundaries of "public" and "private." They are curious representatives of "the people" as the cartoon refers to them; in their luxurious clothes and accoutrements, they seem to be as delighted by some transformation in themselves as they are in the apparition of Roosevelt in their living room. They certainly don't resemble the haunted faces of the "Forgotten Man" invoked by Roosevelt and documented in photographs of the era. Instead, they represent a peculiarly American populist representation of the people, one in which the miracle of wealth and leisure is possible for anyone at any time.

The couple in the cartoon, dressed up for an evening at the theater but sitting in the proscenium space of their living room, is an apt figure for the complicated public performance of radio reception.[5] As this cartoon suggests, the Fireside Chats epitomized the immediacy, intimacy, and direct democracy that Americans associated with their new president and with the still-new phenomenon of national radio. Radio's installment into the family home promised an end to the circuitous routes of information through press secretaries, newspapers, and other media. The absence of a radio in the cartoon depiction of the couple's transformed living room makes clear the conflation of Roosevelt and the radio apparatus. Like Saul Bellow's account of listening to a Fireside Chat issuing from cars parked along Chicago's Midway, the cartoon connects the pleasure of radio listening to leisure, consumption, and the shifting boundaries of public and private space. The Fireside Chats invited listeners into a privileged realm of mobility that enabled them to feel as if they had crossed the boundary separating public and private, backstage and onstage. Roosevelt's audience was made to feel privy to the cultural work of defining a national identity by transgressing the border between public and private. These authorized transgressions—public speech in "intimate" spaces—were part of the unique allure of network radio.

In this chapter I argue that Roosevelt's Fireside Chats conjured a new and ambivalent social space at the intersection of these protean boundaries. Joining Roosevelt's New Deal public required a curious process of self-abstraction and self-consciousness. Listeners were invited to see themselves as objects of and agents for Roosevelt's mobilization of public opinion. Moving back and forth from these subject positions, listeners who wrote to the president alternately identified with the socioeconomic and ethnic or national identities that marked them as particularly vulnerable to the Depression and the war, and abstracted themselves from these particularities in order to help counsel the president on how best to court and manipulate the public of which they were a part.

In addition, Roosevelt presented the American public as essentially riven by a shifting set of distinctions between in-groups and out-groups, agents of his New Deal and wartime publics, neutral objects of public opinion, and, more sinisterly, counteragents or enemies of the state. The only force capable of both naming and resolving this crisis of disunity was Roosevelt's radio voice. Edward Miller has argued that Roosevelt's voice did not calm panic so much as regulate it, distributing it in order to insist upon the president's indispensability.[6] My analysis will show how Roosevelt used the Fireside Chats to enlist listeners as an indispensable corps of publicity agents during the depths of the Depression, and then as national security agents as the nation headed toward World War II. Publicity agents were responsible for the self-reflexive and self-abstracting work of identifying with and reporting on the national public opinion that the early Fireside Chats were explicit in trying to produce. Defense agents were responsible for similar work, plus the crucial task of identifying those whose "private" interests made them "enemies of democracy."

This chapter will also explore the ways that listeners made sense of this complicated new social identity in relationship to their own stubborn "particularities" in their letters to the president. Finally, it will contrast the rhetoric and politics of the chats with the broadcasts of Eleanor Roosevelt. A popular radio persona and a key New Deal and "civil defense" figure in her own right, Eleanor Roosevelt and her nearly forgotten radio career demonstrate how radio could be used to negotiate women's tenuous access to public life and the power to define where public and private begin, end, and blur together.

The Making of the Fireside Chats

It is necessary to provide some background to the production of the Fireside Chats and the context in which they were heard. From the very start, the Fireside Chats were strikingly successful performances, as radio broadcasts and political speeches, two distinct categories that would overlap during Roosevelt's presidency. The popularity of the chats has to be considered within several related historical contexts, not the least of which is the rapidly developing radio industry. The chats, like the Roosevelt presidency of which they were a part, came on the scene during the most crucial period in the development of broadcasting. Between 1930 and 1937, the percentage of homes with a radio grew from 40 percent to 80 percent.[7] A national network system was already in place by the early 1930s, and programs like *Amos 'n' Andy* and *The Goldbergs,* with national brand-name sponsors like Pepsodent and Oxydol, already commanded massive national audiences.[8]

It is important to note that Roosevelt drew on radio's already established convention of the intimate mode of address. Prior to Roosevelt's Fireside Chats, several national and regional broadcast "personalities," including "Roxy" Rothafel, Will Rogers, and Father Coughlin, won large audiences who responded enthusiastically to the informality and intimacy of their speech.[9] In the popular press, radio critics also called for a more intimate mode of address on the air. "Talk to me as if I were sitting in the room with you," one critic of the era pleaded, "not in an auditorium full of morons."[10] Even political figures like Father Coughlin and Senator Huey Long had already used aspects of this folksy mode of address for broadcasts that sought to move a national audience on pressing matters of policy and politics. Indeed, early network radio actively "trained" its listeners in the late 1920s and early 1930s to participate in a reciprocal, "two-way" relationship with radio personalities by sending letters to favorite actors, announcers, even characters.[11]

The Fireside Chats tapped into intimate modes of address established by such programs and revolutionized their political potential. From an average of about four hundred messages a day from the administration of Grover Cleveland through that of Herbert Hoover, the number of messages received at the White House soared during Roosevelt's presidency to between five thousand and eight thousand a day.[12] Listeners had as much praise for Roosevelt's tone and language as for his policies: "It was a wonderful talk," wrote one listener from Blair, Nebraska, "so lucid and in such plain everyday language that everybody could understand it."[13] The chats also tapped into the national address inherent in network radio and in presidential oration itself. As in the cartoon, the president placed himself right beside his listeners on the threshold of a new social space, the intimate public of national radio.

At least part of the popularity of the Fireside Chats can be attributed to the elaborate planning that went into the details of the broadcasts. Although fifty-five of Roosevelt's speeches were carried over the radio in his first year in office, only four of them were considered Fireside Chats.[14] Unlike speeches broadcast from public venues, the chats were delivered exclusively from the White House, that is, from Roosevelt's home. And although Roosevelt and his top staffers used radio, press conferences, newsreels, and personal appearances more than any other administration had, the Fireside Chats marked a qualitative departure from previous political uses of the mass media. Unlike most speeches carried by the networks, the chats were uniquely designed to suit the formal and ideological requirements of network broadcasting.

In addition to elaborate preparations in the writing of these addresses, great care was taken in the timing and aesthetics of the broadcasts.[15] Scholars of speech have dissected Roosevelt's impressive radio performances from a myriad of perspectives, generally concurring with Robert T. Oliver that he had "the best modulated radio voice in public life."[16] Studies of his pitch (tenor), intonation ("vibrant with enthusiasm"), pronunciation ("eastern" mixed with elements of "general American"), cadence ("measured and deliberate"), and speaking rate (a comparatively slow one hundred words per minute) and volume (great dynamics) all bear out the general scholarly, journalistic, and popular consensus that Roosevelt was a master public speaker.[17] In a study of his wartime Fireside Chats, Waldo Braden points to Roosevelt's "short declarative sentences," parallel structure, repetition, and "attractive cadence."[18] A great deal of care went into the timing of the chats as well. Nearly every one of them was delivered at a moment of strategic importance; nine were given on the same day as or within a day of an address, proposal, or proclamation to Congress.[19] Typically broadcast between 9:45 and 10:45 p.m. eastern time (often on a Sunday evening), to reach the entire nation during the prime evening hours, the chats were brief, averaging thirty minutes apiece.[20]

In these accounts and in popular historical memory, the chats came to stand in as a symbol for Roosevelt's persona, and to some extent for his physical person as well. It has often been remarked that the radio extended the president's limited mobility, compensating for his paralyzed legs and thus enabling him to reach corners of the country he could not possibly have reached otherwise. From the very beginning, the Fireside Chats were popularly figured as "intimate visits" from the president to the homes of his listeners. Roosevelt, as master of ceremonies, used the apparatus of network radio so skillfully that it seemed to disappear, leaving in its place the figure of Roosevelt himself. Clearly, Roosevelt was made for radio, right down to the special dental bridge custom-made to eradicate the faint whistling sound his voice made over the air. And, for the millions of Americans whose reception habits were being formed during the tumultuous days of the Depression and the early New Deal, radio was made for Roosevelt.

The New Deal Chats

The first chat, on March 12, 1933, came at the end of Roosevelt's first week in office, a week that began with the radio broadcast of his inaugural address. These two radio addresses together generated nearly half a million pieces of mail to the White House, launching the era of mass political mail and inaugurating Roosevelt's unprecedented mastery of the public opinion, mass media, and especially radio.[21] National audiences for the subsequent chats remained high—breaking and rebreaking records for listenership. The chats gave Roosevelt a way to create a mass public outside the reach of the nation's press, a seemingly "unmediated" national public, an incredibly sophisticated "circuit of communication," as Robert K. Merton has put it, "between the holder of political power on the one hand and both organized groups and unorganized masses on the other."[22]

The Fireside Chats proved to be the ideal medium for Roosevelt to articulate the New Deal's rearrangement of public and private spheres in American life. The national public that Roosevelt hailed in the Fireside Chats was a broad one, collapsing distinctions between state authority, economic activity, citizenship, and the social world. Roosevelt's broadcasts were an apt medium through which to explain the

New Deal's unprecedented expansion of the state's regulatory and administrative authority into the "private" economic spheres of industry, agriculture, labor, and the family.

The early Fireside Chats are remarkable in their ability to combine intimate gestures ("you and I know," "my friends," etc.) with often highly sophisticated and involved discussions of monetary policy, agricultural price controls, the history of the British welfare system, and so on. They were successful broadcasts in part because of Roosevelt's ability to translate the initiatives of and the impulses behind the New Deal into the informal patterns of radio speech. In particular, Roosevelt used the chats to explain the unprecedented federal interventions into industrial and agricultural modes of production. He also used the chats as a way to sell his audience on the paradoxical notion that a new expert class of government planners would join "the people" in revitalizing participatory democracy.

The chats were successful because of the way they conflated radio listening with national identity, inviting listeners to participate in the invention of the new public realm of radio reception from the comfort of their own homes while also collaborating in the process of national recovery. Listening to the chats, Roosevelt implied, conferred on his audience the status of amateur brain truster, an active agent in the New Deal's reshuffling of the relationship between the government and the people, labor and management, public and private. In the intimate public of radio, Roosevelt invited his audience back and forth across the boundaries of public and private, retracing in words the authorized transgressions of the New Deal. In the process, the early Fireside Chats made themselves at home in the emerging patterns of radio reception.

Roosevelt's first Fireside Chat, on the severe nationwide banking crisis of February and March 1933, at the start of his presidency, provides an excellent example of how he used radio and New Deal interventions into "the private sector" to encourage listeners to see themselves as both members of and agents for the public his broadcasts called into being. Indeed, the very nature of the banking crisis—a radical loss of depositors' confidence in the nation's banks' ability to convert savings into currency—was an ideal first test for the administration's broad approach to the Depression and for Roosevelt's use of the radio to establish an intimate but authoritative rapport with his audience. The extraordinary success of this broadcast in restoring confidence in the nation's banks has been well documented.[23] This episode is also, in some ways, an ideal one for demonstrating Roosevelt's conservative use of populist imagery to reinforce existing economic institutions. The specter of "incompetent or dishonest bankers" violating "the people's" trust becomes the setting in which the people—divided and afraid— are galvanized into unity and confidence in the system by Roosevelt, radio, and the promise of their own upward mobility.

Roosevelt's crisp recitation of the government's plan to overhaul the entire banking system, one bank at a time, eliminating the corrupt or incompetent bankers in the process, marked the first stroke in the flurry of New Deal legislative action of the first one hundred days. Rather than nationalizing the banks—or any of the other failing in- dustries—Roosevelt used government intervention to bolster the power of private corporations, lending the prestige of the activist, public phi- losophy of the New Deal to the market economy, another important way in which he was able to move easily across the borders of public and private while leaving them intact, even strengthening them.

Roosevelt begins his first Fireside Chat by distinguishing two parts of his audience: "the comparatively few who understand the mechan- ics of banking" and "the overwhelming majority of you who use banks for the making of deposits and the drawing of checks."[24] Drawing this distinction between the expert few and the uneducated many may seem an odd way to begin an appeal for national unity. But by the end of the chat it becomes clear that drawing, effacing, and redrawing dis- tinctions between members of his audience is Roosevelt's main rhetori- cal strategy for forging a national public.[25]

Roosevelt's explanation of the banking crisis begins by assigning blame to the "undermined confidence on the part of the public," part of a passage that deftly conflates bank depositors, his radio audience, and "the public."[26] This may seem an unremarkable observation, yet this move accomplishes some important rhetorical and ideological work. First, like all subsequent chats, this one, by addressing the en- tire American public, announces itself, performative-style, as a quasi- official utterance. Roosevelt speaks with the voice of the government to the nation itself. A second important elision is that which links the government of the United States to the banking industry, a mixing of public and private authority that the present emergency requires. Third, by assuming that his audience—the American public—is divided be- tween banking experts and depositors, he effectively excludes the millions of Americans too poor to own bank accounts. Participating in Roosevelt's unifying public requires listeners to abstract themselves from their own particular circumstances in order to join a larger imagined community.

By failing to understand that their deposited money was not available as currency on demand, then, this American public panicked; their runs on banks shut down virtually every bank in the country. In tones that have been praised for their warm confidence, Roosevelt then assured his listeners that the problems posed by the crisis were simple to understand and thus, to solve:

> I recognize that the many proclamations from the state capitals and from Washington, the legislation, the Treasury regulations and so forth couched for the most part in banking and legal terms, ought to be explained for the benefit of the average citizen. I owe this in particular because of the fortitude and the good temper with which everybody has accepted the inconvenience and the hardships of the banking holiday. And I know that when you understand what we in Washington have been about I shall continue to have your cooperation as fully as I have had your sympathy and your help during the past week. (12–13)

Tacking back and forth between his two audiences, now divided into another, starker pairing, "the hysterical demands of hoarders" and "the intelligent support" of the more thoughtful, Roosevelt makes clear that the integrity of the banking system, like the government's reconstruction of the financial and economic fabric, requires a new definition of the public and a new mode of communicating to that public (15). By the end of the address, the ratios of these two audiences seem to have switched: the majority seems to understand banking and their important role as faithful depositors while the "very few who have not recovered from their fear" persist in "unfashionable" hoarding (ibid.). This shift, Roosevelt implies, has been effected through the radio broadcast itself; the president, the radio, and the listeners together completed a circuit of communication in which words became performative utterances, conjuring the changes they described.[27] Understanding and helping to solve a national crisis, Roosevelt assures his audience, depends on the public's confidence in the "machinery" of government—in particular the apparatus that enables Roosevelt to "talk for a few minutes with the people of the United States" (12). In exchange for their confidence, this address seems to offer the listener an opportunity to move out of class-bound identity as an uninformed depositor, or worse, a "hysterical" hoarder, into a new position of status and trust.

In his conclusion, Roosevelt made clear the link he saw between this broad, new public—educable and unafraid—national radio reception, and national recovery: "there is an element in the readjustment of our financial system more important than currency, more important than gold, and that is the confidence of the people themselves" (16). In the case of the banking crisis, it becomes clear that the self-confidence of "the people" is the key to the recovery of the nation's banks; further, such a national spread of confidence depends on the nation's moving from the initial division of the uneducated many and the sophisticated few to the confident many and the hysterical few. In this move, Roosevelt replaces a distinction of expertise in the "mechanics" of government and industry with a distinction in a different kind of expertise: the confident and self-conscious knowledge of "the people" as the sovereign power behind national recovery and reconstruction.

Roosevelt employs this strategy of shifting distinctions again in his third Fireside Chat, when he moves from a description of the nation as divided by class—"half boom and half broke"—to a nation brought together by radio and the National Recovery Administration but divided by a new distinction: the "soldiers" of the NRA—laborers and owners, "big fellows and little fellows," are pitted against selfish shirkers, employers, and aggressive workers who "question the standard set by this universal agreement," the National Industrial Recovery Act (32, 35–36). On a Labor Day broadcast in 1936, Roosevelt seeks to unite "brain workers and manual laborers" in common recognition of the holiday, replacing the "class" distinction with the distinction between those in the know ("the average man") and the out of touch ("those who fail to read both the signs of the times and American history") (81). Here, the implication is that excessive identification with one's class status marked one as out of step with the average, and thus with history and with the nation itself.

Roosevelt's early Fireside Chats called for a unified national audience—an audience already hailed by network radio's national address—at the same time that they policed key distinctions within that audience. The rhetoric of "the people" worked to target a broad "popular elite" in his audience, the supporters of New Deal programs, as opposed to the "selfish few," "the hoarders," and "shirkers." In this way, Roosevelt explicitly invites his national audience to join in the

production of public opinion and to abandon any notion of class solidarity and the particular fears, interests, and complaints that may
have been part of that class-based identity. And although this invitation applied theoretically to everyone, rich or poor, class status was,
and still is, a particularity that is harder for working-class people to
shed in such invocations of national unity, as we shall see.

Indeed, at the end of the first chat, Roosevelt has begun to celebrate
the immediate and almost audible confirmation of this public confidence
that he seems to be able to tune into: "It has been wonderful to me to
catch the note of confidence from all over the country." He seems to
hear the music of the swelling public opinion behind him and is especially grateful for the support of those for whom "all our processes
may not have seemed clear," returning again to the original distinction
between the knowledge elite and the ignorant majority (16). This passage, with its sense of an immediate two-way electronic connection
between speaker and listeners, was echoed in the thousands of letters
Roosevelt received.[28] Some of these letters were written during the
broadcasts of the chats themselves, in a conversational style that emphasized the reciprocal nature of the interaction: "excuse me," one
woman wrote as she listened to Roosevelt's voice on the radio, "while
I laugh at that joke you just made."[29] In the course of this Fireside
Chat, the president and the nation seem to have moved from division,
confusion, and "the phantom of fear" to a stirring sense of unity and
an interesting new division of labor: "Let us unite in banishing fear.
We have provided the machinery to restore our financial system; and
it is up to you to support it and make it work" (17).

At the start of the second chat, on May 7, 1933, Roosevelt reinforced the idea that the radio is the means by which to generate the
public confidence required by the New Deal and the national economic
crisis. This chat, the first to be dubbed a "Fireside Chat," begins, as
most of the subsequent chats do, with a reference to the previous one:

> On a Sunday night a week after my inauguration I used the radio to
> tell you about the banking crisis and about the measures we were tak-
> ing to meet it. In that way I tried to make clear to the country various
> facts that might otherwise have been misunderstood and in general to
> provide a means of understanding which I believe did much to restore
> confidence. (19)

In the next several chats, the president makes it clear that the radio
is the means by which a national public can be imagined, constructed,

and galvanized. By continually letting his radio audience in on the central problem of public relations facing his administration, Roosevelt enlists their support as agents in the difficult task of generating public support for the New Deal and the market economy that it was working to save. Such a plan would succeed, Roosevelt insisted, "if our people understand it" (33).[30]

In the 1935 chat introducing the Works Progress Administration, Roosevelt calls upon the "eternal vigilance of the American people themselves" in making the WPA "the most efficient and the cleanest example of public enterprise the world has ever seen" (69). He follows up this appeal with another invocation of the two-way communication that radio has established with his national audience. More than anything else, the Fireside Chats were rituals designed to celebrate the principle of participatory democracy. "If you will help," Roosevelt promises, "this can be done" (ibid.). As Sussman points out, Roosevelt invited feedback from his radio audience by making it clear in the chats that he actually read listener mail and attended to the opinions expressed therein.[31]

In the fourth Fireside Chat, of October 22, 1933, Roosevelt returns again and again to the concept of the "average citizen" to assess the successes of the New Deal and to explain to his "friends" the limits of the recovery. "[I]n every step which your government is taking we are thinking in terms of the average of you—in the old words, 'the greatest good for the greatest number'" (38). Once again, the president's speech is marked by key distinctions, as he notes the conflicting interests of the farmers versus the speculators "who had never seen cotton growing," and the small businessmen loyal to the NRA codes versus "the chiselers" with "a private axe to grind." Roosevelt moves from divisiveness to unity; using the new words "the average of you" to mediate between the conflicting interests (40–41).

In the following Fireside Chat, of June 28, 1934, Roosevelt responds to his critics and appeals to his audience in a deft movement back and forth between statistical and intimate representations of the people. Roosevelt boasts of raises in average weekly pay, the value of farm products, and the demand for durable goods, but smoothly changes gears, counseling his audience to look for more intimate signs of the nation's well-being. "The record is written in the experiences of your own personal lives" (49). Here, "personal lives" are posed against the cold calculations about "the average American," a shift in meanings from the previous chat's distinction between the great American "average" and those consumed by "private" interests.

This oscillation between the negative and positive connotations of the concepts public and private, average and personal, demonstrates Roosevelt's rhetorical dexterity but also the multiple and slippery meanings of these terms. Instead of merely blurring these categories, rendering the public/private distinction null and void, Roosevelt confidently shifts between different versions of "public" and "private" to suit his needs at any given moment. First, he contrasts the privacy of greedy profiteers with the public-mindedness of the average Americans who support measures to save banking and stabilize prices. Next, he privileges the privacy of family life in opposition to the coldly mathematical notions of a shared "average" national experience. In the chats of this era, defining public and private was a continuous process, one that Roosevelt mastered while still making overtures to his audience as necessary collaborators, whose new status replaces class-bound notions of identity.

The Arsenal of Democracy

"The development of our defense program makes it essential that each and every one of us, men and women, feel that we have some contribution to make toward the security of our nation" (62). So begins the Fireside Chat of May 26, 1940. By early that year, the Fireside Chats had become part of a broader mobilization for war. Hailing a national public for "active duty," these wartime chats enforced conformity and discouraged "difference" by making the most of the link between listenership and citizenship. By celebrating the mass production of public opinion as a kind of "arsenal of democracy," these chats also helped to shape the contours of the public's opinions and participation, subordinating democratic processes to the exigencies of national emergency. In the process, a contradictory version of "the public" became ingrained both in the political culture and in the idea of broadcast reception; this public was intimate and national, sovereign yet passive, theoretically all-inclusive and yet sharply bounded by traditional exclusions.

Along with the shifting play of distinctions that characterized the earlier chats, the wartime chats articulated sharper, more fixed boundaries between "citizens" and "friends," on the one hand, and "enemies of democracy," "foreign agents," and "fifth columnists," on the other.

Radio listening became, in the rhetoric of the chats, a component of a broader media mobilization that preceded the United States' entry into the war by more than a year. The chats of this period regarded radio listeners as the cultural equivalent of military and industrial defense workers, creating through their production of a unified public opinion a cadre of defense agents.

The Fireside Chats of December 29, 1940, and May 27, 1941, were, in many ways, the most dramatic expressions of Roosevelt's masterful invocation of "the people" as part of a nationalist mobilization. These two chats, which marked the most decisive steps toward American war mobilization and distinct material aid to Britain, were the most listened to radio broadcasts in the history of radio, garnering 59 percent and 70 percent of the total radio audience, respectively.[32] These were unheard-of ratings on radio, even in radio's golden age, when top-rated shows were thrilled to get 35 percent of the audience.[33] Roosevelt, more than any other broadcaster of his time, utilized radio's intimate, national address to create a ritual moment of nearly universal reception. The *New York Times* reported sharp increases in electricity usage and precipitous drop-offs in theater attendance during these two broadcasts. The day after the May 1941 chat, heard by 65 million Americans, the *Times* observed, "[f]or almost an hour, a whole nation here stilled itself to listen to his words."[34]

The "Arsenal of Democracy" chat of December 1940 announced the lend-lease plan of direct military aid to Britain, making official U.S. involvement in the Allied effort. The following chat, of May 27, 1941, marked another significant step toward outright participation in the European war, as Roosevelt assumed broader powers over both military and private economic spheres with the proclamation of un-limited national emergency. But even before this, by mid-1940, the pressure on the radio and film industries to cooperate with the federal government's war mobilization program had begun to yield results. In response to investigations of monopoly violations started in the late 1930s, both industries participated in circulating the administration's views on the war in both formal and informal collaborations.[35] Hav-ing threatened the networks with drastic reforms, Roosevelt's admin-istration found them willing partners in telling the story of the war in ways that pointed toward the inevitability of U.S. involvement.

The Fireside Chats of 1940 and 1941 epitomized Roosevelt's mas-terful use of radio to galvanize the American people around powerful nationalist imagery, during a period of unprecedented need for indus-

trial production. Roosevelt's vision of a productive, unified people laying aside all particular notions of identity (labor allegiance, pacifism,
isolationism, etc.) is at the heart of his call for "a great arsenal of
democracy." It is an arsenal, Roosevelt makes clear, in which the people produce not just war matériel but also an idealized version of
themselves, a unified national public.

In these chats, Roosevelt explicitly connects this national mobilization to that of the New Deal, reversing the more familiar "analogue of
war" used to describe federal responses to the Depression.[36] In the
"Arsenal of Democracy" broadcast of December 1940, Roosevelt begins with a memory of how he had imagined "the American people"
eight years earlier, when he gave his first Fireside Chat on the banking
crisis. "I saw the workmen in the mills, the mines, the factories; the
girl behind the counter; the small shopkeeper; the farmer doing his
spring plowing; the widows and the old men wondering about their
life's savings" (164). Roosevelt's portrait of his 1933 radio audience,
remembered in 1940, evokes potent images of "the people" that would
gain national currency throughout the war years. But it is a curious
memory to claim from 1933, when at least a quarter of the nation's
workforce was out of work. Images of the unemployed factory workers and farmworkers became archetypal during the Depression and
dust bowl days. Images of a happily and diversely employed labor
force evoke Norman Rockwell's propaganda posters of the 1940s,
with their homogeneous cast of stalwart folk. This imagined America
serves as a prelude to a speech that pits the productive power of Americans against "the threat to America's independence" posed by the
expansionist Axis powers (ibid.).

Roosevelt invokes this idealized vision of an industrious American
people, united by productive roles in the economy and a shared her-
itage, as the solution to both the domestic crisis of 1933 and the international crisis that was fast proving to be unavoidable. By linking this
chat to his first, and revisiting this remembered image of "the people,"
Roosevelt stresses the similarity between the two crises, but he also
makes clear a sense of continuity in the rhetorical strategies of the
Fireside Chats through the years. In the face of a national crisis that will
require unprecedented industrial productivity and staggering human
sacrifice, Roosevelt's first move is to appeal to an already-existing
source of strength, the productive "people," extending back eight years
to the happily employed folk of his first chat, and even further, to the
Anglo-Protestant historical and ancestral roots of "Jamestown and

Plymouth Rock" (165). In a chat from the previous spring, Roosevelt locates "the promise of America" in similar ancestral and historical foundations of "the people" and their productive capacity: "For more than three centuries, we Americans have been building on this continent a free society" (162).

The broadcast from May 1941, which Roosevelt concludes with a proclamation of unlimited national emergency, focuses on the increasingly precarious international situation and emphasizes the link between national defense and a unified public opinion. Idealized images of a productive people are subordinated in this chat to more dire imagery in which the people, the government, and the nation have merged to form a "common defense" (185). In calling for a heightened—if vague—commitment to defending against Nazi incursions on national security, the terms "our people," "the government," "the nation," and "the citizens" are used interchangeably. Although Roosevelt was unable at first to decide on a bureau for war morale and information, he calls on his audience to form itself into an ad hoc bureau of public information responsible for "the use of a greater common sense in discarding rumor and distorted statement," and for "recognizing, for what they are, racketeers and fifth columnists, the incendiary bombs in this country at the moment." Roosevelt emphasizes that "defense means," among other things, producing a national morale, distinguishing between truth and rumor, and, above all, identifying the foolish, the blind, the naysayers—in short to police the domestic boundaries that divide "the overwhelming majority of our citizens" from "the enemies of democracy" in our midst. This is "the common work of our common defense" (ibid.).

In both chats, Roosevelt makes the point that popular reception of the chats was key to the national defense and to understanding distinctions between those who fall within the borders of the national public and the "trouble breeders" and "foreign agents" who do not (168). In these chats and several others from 1939 and 1940, Roosevelt urges his listeners to not blind themselves to these crucial distinctions and tutors them in how to spot "secret emissaries," "spies," "saboteurs," and "traitors" (161, 168, 179, 185). Indeed, he offers a virtual taxonomy of the different kinds of internal threats and how to spot the differences between foreign agents ("Trojan horses within our gates") and their witting and unwitting American accomplices. Again and again, Roosevelt links dissent to illegitimate forms of expression and disloyalty: "[s]ound national policies come to be viewed with a

new and unreasonable skepticism, not through the wholesome political debates of honest and free men, but through clever schemes of foreign agents" (168).

In these constructions, the nation trumps every other individual
and collective form of identity or alliance. In both of these prewar chats,
Roosevelt makes clear that labor–management struggles, strikes, and
lockouts cannot be tolerated within the bounds of this national public. Indeed, he says that "the nation expects and insists" that these differences be resolved within the new state "machinery" he has set up to
handle such disputes (171, 185).[37] In addition to explicit exclusions,
this national public proved to be remarkably resistant to invocations
of national unity on behalf of a range of interests and associations
that were relegated to a residual category of "private concerns."

The May 1943 Fireside Chat dedicated to putting down a strike
among the nation's coal miners was perhaps the most explicit drawing
of this boundary. This broadcast took place during a time when labor
unrest among various defense-related industries from San Francisco to
Detroit threatened to shatter the December 23, 1941, no-strike, no-
lockout accord between labor and management. The situation in the
bituminous coal-mining industry, however, was particularly volatile.
Four hundred thousand bituminous coal miners, led by John L. Lewis's
United Mine Workers (UMW), struck for higher pay and more safety
equipment four times in 1943. On May 2, Roosevelt took to the airwaves, to address, once again, a split audience: "the American people,"
and "those of our citizens who are coal miners" (249, 251–52).

Although this one broadcast did not end the labor conflict in the
mines, Roosevelt masterfully won the political contest with his adver-
sary Lewis by invoking the language of "the people" to unite this split
audience. Linking striking mine workers to the men fighting overseas
and to the men and women working in other defense industries, Roosevelt reasserts the essential unity of the American people by refusing all
other categories of identity, including class. Using a logic of equiva-
lences, he appeals to the strikers as members of the national family
involved in producing for the war effort. His appeal to the "essential
patriotism of the miners and to the patriotism of their wives and children" is an invitation to join "we Americans—135 million of us" in
the war effort, an invitation backed up with a threat: "I know that the
American people will not tolerate any threat offered to their government by anyone" (251–52, 256). This same strategy worked to mute
the claims of black soldiers, workers, and families who fought for the

double V (victory over the Axis abroad and Jim Crow at home), often without even token support from the administration.[38]

The nation emerges in these broadcasts as a historical actor, both an expression of popular will and the centralized force dictating how it is to be mobilized: "the nation expects," "the nation has a right to expect," "the nation will expect," and "The American people will not tolerate" (171, 187, 256). This version of the nation connected the will of the people with the authority of the state and the industrial capacity of the market economy.

Listener Response

In her widely syndicated "My Day" column, Eleanor Roosevelt provided an interesting model for the process by which "private" citizens came to participate in the national public commanded by the Fireside Chats. Seated in the front row in the East Room of the White House for the National Emergency broadcast of May 1941, Roosevelt describes her feeling of alienation from the proceedings. Surrounded by diplomats from several South American republics, Mexico, and Canada, the first lady felt "strangely detached, as though I were outside.... I represented no nation, carried no responsibility." Out of this sense of public alienation, via her husband's words, comes a sense of belonging. Detached from the affairs of state and the goings-on in her own home, the first lady suddenly understands herself as "a part of the general public." From this vantage point, she is moved by the sight of her husband's face and the sound of his voice to a new sense of patriotic mission. "In my capacity of objective citizen, sitting in the gathering, I felt that I wanted to accept my responsibility and do my particular job whatever it might be. I think that will be the answer of every individual citizen of the U.S.A."[39]

Alienating and isolating on a personal level, her husband's radio address becomes irresistible to the extent that she can adopt the subject position of "objective citizen." The first lady, like the rest of the 65 million Americans who listened to Roosevelt that night, had to be recruited from some residual private space into the self-consciousness and self-abstractedness of the national public of the Fireside Chats. The Fireside Chats, more than any other broadcasts of the period, made explicit the personal and political significance of the transformation from private person to citizen/listener.

Eleanor Roosevelt's frank account of her own response to the broadcast illustrates an idealized version of the process of becoming a member of the radio public. It also illustrates some of the ways her public persona came to represent a significant model of citizenship in the context of the contradictory demands of mass-mediated democracy. Her own radio persona, composed in several different commercially sponsored series of "chats" on a variety of national and international policy issues, represents a response to her husband's much more celebrated one.

Scholarship on the letters written in response to the Fireside Chats has tended to emphasize the powerful ways Roosevelt's audience responded to his rhetorical appeals for national unity. Letters thanking the president for his intimate visits also celebrated a new sense of national belonging. Borrowing from his rhetorical style, they even mimicked his shifting use of pronouns, to effect either a wider sense of national community or an anxious uncertainty about inclusion into this community. It has also been well documented that these listeners appealed to Roosevelt in large numbers for a regular, even weekly, program of presidential chats as a way to maintain a spirit of national unity and hopefulness.[40] Finally, it has been widely observed that letter-writing listeners, swept up in this new spirit, volunteered "to do [their] particular job, whatever it might be," in the first lady's words. We can see from the responses to the early New Deal and later wartime chats, which echoed the president's shifting definitions of the role of the public, that she had accurately read the mood of the letter-writing public at least.

Often, that job seemed to consist of providing the president with local opinion polling results on the effectiveness of his broadcasts: "I spoke to lawyers, barbers, elevator men, doctors, janitors and the comment is the same in all quarters concerning your talk on the banks. All say fine, just fine."[41] "In the past 24 hours," a New York City man wrote, "I have made it a point to ask everyone I have happened to come into contact with how he liked your radio broadcast on the bank situation last night. Without exception, some 29 different individuals have all answered 'it was wonderful. Just exactly what this country has been waiting for. . . real leadership!' and many other comments to the same effect. . . . You have the public with you."[42] Like the couple on the sofa in the cartoon, and many others in Roosevelt's radio audience, these listeners repositioned their own domestic reception into a more public space, the site from which they report both their own responses and those of "the people."

In other cases, listeners portray themselves as incarnations of "the voice of the people": "I but voice the confidence of the great majority of the people of Minnesota when I say we heartily approve of your program."[43] A woman from Chicago wrote: "I listened last night to your message Mr. President and a voice within me kept repeating over and over again: 'the heart of the nation is speaking.'"[44] Transformed from the particularity and isolation of individual reception practices into something more, these listeners presented themselves as average private citizens, unconnected to any group and yet crucially important to the work of the New Deal and to the circuit of communication initiated by Roosevelt himself: "Although not being the mouthpiece for any specified group of our commonwealth, I feel I can speak for a large body of our citizenry, whose sentiment very seldom finds expression in public utterance."[45]

The most striking quality of the letters I have examined is the excitement and self-consciousness about the transformative power of the ritual of radio reception in the lives of letter writers and "the people" who make up the mass audience. Listening in to the chats represented a process of conversion or transformation for many listeners—like Mrs. Roosevelt—in which the particularities of party, region, and class were replaced by a larger national spirit. From the Hotel Duluth, a guest reported on the "eager, almost pathetically serious" faces of "the average man" she observed during the broadcast of the president's second chat in the hotel lobby. "You talked to *them*—not over their heads—in direct simple words. A change came over them—a feeling of confidence, of hope, *we* all belonged, if you know what I mean."[46] The use of both *them* and *we* in this letter is evidence of Joy Hayes's observation that many letter writers used both *them* and *we* to talk about the new national community created through the chats. This author in particular seems to move from the outside of this group to the inside, even as she describes the transformation of the "average man" from "pathetically serious" to a state of confidence, hope, and belonging. This mobility, from outside to inside, from detached observer to public citizen, mirrors the movement described in Eleanor Roosevelt's epistolary "My Day" column.

Many letters captured the feeling of the editorial cartoon featuring the couple entertaining the president in the transformed space of their living room. "I can see you seated in the big armchair in my living room, pipe in mouth and talking on the crisis that confronts us all."[47] Others linked this sense of intimacy to the unifying power of a public gathering:

It was very cosy and friendly and cheery to have you with us last
night. We invited some friends in "to meet the President," not forget-
ting to place an easy chair by the fireplace for the guest of honor....
There were eight of us, all voters, four women and four men. Some
Republicans and some [D]emocrats, but, for the first time in our lives,
unanimous, and all for you.[48]

Like the first lady, many of these letter writers emphasized their
own personal transformation as a symbol for the larger one that had
turned the radio audience into a unified national public. "I feel more
like an American should feel thanks to your talk," enthused J. M.
Curran in a telegram after the May 1941 broadcast.[49] For Robert Reid,
of New York, listening to the June 1934 Fireside Chat transformed
him, quite literally, from alien to citizen:

I am an alien. For over ten years I have remained deliberately so, having felt all along that there could be no security in this country with so
much corruption and selfishness. Now, before the week is over, I shall
apply for citizenship, determined to be among the millions of proud
and privileged people you address as "fellow citizens and friends,"
determined to help, if only spiritually, to ease the gigantic burden
you so gamely and ably struggle with in order to make America
truly God's country. For like millions of others, I now feel secure.[50]

Many others wrote in to describe their own transformation from par-
tisan foes of the president at the start of the broadcast to loyal supporters or, in the words of a sixteen-year-old girl from New Hamp-
shire, "just an American" by the end of it.[51] "I frankly confess that I
have seldom seen eye to eye with you as President," began Alfred Cookson. However, he vowed after hearing the May 1941 broadcast to
stop touring the nation with his massive "Symbolic Elephant of the
Republican Party," and replace it with a symbolic eagle "as large as
traveling will permit with safety," in a bid to spread the message of
unity.[52]

Indeed, many reported that the mood of the entire public world
had changed overnight. "There was a tremendous lift of spirit all over
the country the morning after your speech," wrote a New York man.
"We are all catching the spirit of your courage and optimism," added
a man from Chicago. "People have been going around with lighter
steps, brighter smiles, happier voices for the last ten days," agreed
another listener.[53] For many, the truly miraculous unseen spectacle

was not Roosevelt but the radio listeners who had been united in the national ritual of reception:

> If you could see the bright smiles and hear the words spoken of the forgotten man from the Atlantic to the Pacific, from the Great Lakes to the Everglades on March 14th, 1933 of the new deal spoken by one of the greatest Presidents of these United States, it would be the happiest moment of your life.[54]

Representing the public was the kind of cultural work that changed one's status, conferring on even "humble citizens" the new social mobility made available by speaking in the intimate public arena opened up by the Fireside Chats. An April 1938 letter signed by dozens of men and women began, "As staunch believers in your interpretation of the American Way, we the undersigned feel it to be our duty to leave the vast ranks of the inarticulate and give voice to our approval of your humane program."[55] "The distinction between the inarticulate masses and the articulate few recurs frequently. "I hope your secretary lets this letter get to you," wrote another, "for I think it tries to express what thousands of the common people are thinking."[56] Many saw the intersection of the national broadcasts and the New Deal as an opportunity to collaborate with the president and his expert advisers: "I do not wish to compete with the Brain-Trusters of Washington D.C.," a Garfield, New Jersey, man wrote, "but if you should need further plans, ideas, reforms, and programs concerning recovery, I will be glad to furnish them upon request."[57]

Many of these listeners picked up on Roosevelt's rhetoric, extolling national unity while pitting "true Americans" against the selfish, the corrupt, the inarticulate, the hysterical, and the foreign. The sense of community evoked in these letters is not always egalitarian, nor is it unambivalently unified. Instead, it appears that these listeners have learned well from Roosevelt's contradictory rhetoric: appeals to national unity became the occasion for a reimposition of distinctions and hierarchies policing the boundaries of the national public. A popular construction of this split audience in the response to the first chat pitted the many "thinking people" who understood Roosevelt against the few "who failed to understand." Also referred to as those "not endowed with all their faculties," "those who would still ride in horse cars," "the few who persist in continuing to fear," the "selfish," "the morons and illiterates so abundant everywhere," and "the foolish."[58]

Making sense of their combined roles as citizens and radio listeners, listeners also policed this vast invisible public for signs of trouble and dissent. If Roosevelt regulated panic so as to insist on his own necessity, as Miller has argued, these letter writers' attention to stubborn pockets of foreignness, ignorance, and selfishness reinforced the importance of their own vigilant public-opinion work.

Hoarding disappeared in Cleveland, Ohio, thanks to the same broadcast, according to a man there, "except in the case of non-English speaking radicals."[59] The transformation swept across the country, where "avaricious financiers and businessmen," "cutthroat manufacturers," "organized minorities…and selfish or corrupt politicians," "the foreign element," and "the special pleading of selfish interests" represented the holdouts to the national unity that Roosevelt called for.[60]

Despite what has been described as a remarkable heterogeneity across class lines in the letters to Roosevelt, some patterns of reception and response do seem to have broken down along class lines. In my own modest random sampling of responses to the first chat, those who seemed to be professionals or upper-middle-class tended to avoid using terms like "the people" or "the masses" to describe themselves, using such language at a rate of less than 15 percent, compared to apparently working-class respondents, who used such terms almost half the time. Also, letters from higher-income listeners were five times more likely than those of working-class writers to use rhetoric emphasizing sharp distinctions between those who belonged in Roosevelt's radio public and those who were too simple, selfish, or corrupt to be included.

In a random sampling of the responses to the Fireside Chats of December 1940 and May 1941, I found that the rhetoric of "the people" had been replaced altogether by the language of "loyalty" and "Americanism." In response to the December 1940 broadcast, of those writers using telegrams; stationery identifying them as executives, professionals, or business owners; or fancy monogrammed personal stationery, more than 20 percent expressed a tension between loyal Americans and "traitors," "foreigners," or "fifth columnists" compared to less than 5 percent of those using plain stationery and penny postcards.[61] In the May 1941 broadcast, which proclaimed unlimited national emergency, and which used even more polarizing language, I found an increase in the rate of this rhetoric across all respondents, reflecting perhaps the heightened state of war mobilization across the dial and the nation, as well as the cumulative effect of Roosevelt's rhetoric. "Every working man . . . and all red blood Americans are behind you to the limit."[62] The linkage between dissent and disloyalty was hard to miss, as was the emphasis on lockstep unity in thought and deed: "Our thoughts are the same as all loyal Americans, and we would like to have you know that your thoughts and actions are ours."[63]

Many of these letter writers linked their patriotism—or status as "true Americans"—to their support for broader executive powers in managing the economy, aid to Britain, and suppression of dissent. "We as true Americans appeal to you, the one having our care in your keeping to use ALL THE POWER YOU HAVE for our mutual protection in this Great crisis."[64] These listeners targeted foreigners: "[Your speech was] a tonic to all unhyphenated Americans"; the unpatriotic: "Every real American will follow you"; and isolationists: "[those] of their mentalities, ought to be arrested and tried for treason" as crucial dangers to the nation and advocated increased government power to suppress their influence.[65] "All Americans with whom I have talked," began one characteristic response, "want . . . the Communist and foreign elements eliminated from the working personnel in our defense program. The PUBLIC is 'fed up' on unnaturalized foreigners dictating the labor polices of the United States."[66]

Unions came in for intense criticism as well:

We people demand that strikes stop. Our boys are getting $21 a month and working their heads off, gladly. Labor has not the right to ask for big wages and shorter hours. If it doesn't cooperate, there should be only government-run factories. We're sick of strikes and we want them stopped. We have promised Britain help and we cannot let a bunch of laborers make us break our promise.[67]

Also, in the responses surveying broader public reaction, widespread support was expressed negatively, in terms of the *lack* of dissent, rather than in positive terms, (e.g., "We are all with you!"), as was the case in the earlier broadcasts. Thus a telegram from May 1941 assured the president, "TOLEDO VISITOR HEARD NO DISSENTING VOICE FROM BELLHOP TO BIG WIG."[68] Strikingly, in the relatively few letters expressing real dissent to the president's interventionist moves, there was an appeal to the older New Deal rhetoric of jobs and democracy for "the people." Indeed, many referred to their own status as Republican voters ("I am one of the 22 million")[69] to remind the president of a massive constituency he had, perhaps, taken for granted. Others took exception to Roosevelt's subtle linkages between domestic dissent and the enemy, as in a letter, on plain stationery, from Tarrytown, New York: "It's the same old stuff—a vote for Willkie will please Hitler very much! Oh, my. Do you honestly think that you alone are always right?"[70]

Taken together, the letters Roosevelt received in response to the Fireside Chats demonstrate that listeners sought to participate in a new sense of public life by working to define who and what that public encompassed. Roosevelt's correspondents find the chats compelling not because they blurred the boundaries marking off private and public space, but because they revealed the tremendous political and social power that his rhetorical transgressions of these boundaries seemed to effect.

Eleanor Roosevelt

Eleanor Roosevelt was a popular and well-paid radio personality in the 1930s and 1940s. Her commercially sponsored programs for Ponds Cream, Arch-Preserver Shoes, Sweetheart Soap, and the Pan-American Coffee Bureau garnered the first lady unprecedented money, sway, admiration, and criticism. Along with her speaking engagements and nationally syndicated column, "My Day," which she wrote continuously for more than twenty-five years, Eleanor Roosevelt became one of the most popular and influential figures in the Roosevelt administration and in American public life. In 1940 alone, she earned $156,000 for her sponsored radio work alone, making her one of the highest-paid performers on the radio and making her a lightning rod for criticism about impropriety.[71] Curiously, most of this criticism stemmed from a perceived sense of the first lady violating traditional gender roles, rather than from questions about conflicts of interest, politicizing commercial speech, and so on. She used her radio platform to air these criticisms and to respond to them, including a letter from a woman taking her to task for being out in the public eye so much that she was neglecting her husband at home.[72]

Mrs. Roosevelt's public persona was too feminine, too intimate, for at least one male reporter, who felt like "he had blundered into the powder room" when covering one of her press conferences.[73] Henry Morgenthau III faulted her for failing to make proper distinctions between national, public broadcasts and the informal social settings at the White House.[74] The very distinctions that her husband was praised for blurring, in other words, drew down on Eleanor the wrath of the son of the secretary of the treasury, among others. Still another critic found her "My Day" column nauseating in its promiscuous combination of social tidbits and gruesome war news: she "spoke of cake and legless men and tea and concussions of the brains and the seeing of the new grandchild and miles of suffering human beings and too much lunch, all in the same jolly breath."[75] And, of course, she was criticized for her voice: for its high pitch, uncertain delivery, nervous giggles, and patrician accent.[76]

Despite this relentless criticism, Mrs. Roosevelt forged a public persona that was influential and popular. In opinion surveys, her approval ratings were much higher than her husband's and cut across all sectors of the nation, but they were especially high among women. On the strength of this persona, she was offered a five-year renewal deal on her United Features contract for "My Day," early in 1940, before anyone had an inkling that her husband would challenge tradition and seek a third term, proof that her appeal extended beyond her status as a sitting first lady. Her considerable clout was demonstrated in the fall of 1940 when she took to the podium at the Democratic convention to persuade the delegates to support Henry Wallace as vice president, an address that her husband and millions of Americans heard over the radio. That same year, she received more than a million pieces of mail. Tacking back and forth between Victorian codes of noblesse oblige and wifely duty, on the one hand, and liberal politics, on the other, Eleanor Roosevelt was able to insulate herself from critics while projecting a powerful model for women's participation in public life.[77]

Along with several soap-opera heroines, "women in the street," and other unlikely allies whom we will meet later, Mrs. Roosevelt challenged the gendered logic of network radio that consigned women's voices to a purely private realm of domesticity, consumerism, and emotional relationships. That her contributions to radio have been largely forgotten says more about the continued power of such gender discrimination and perhaps the general amnesia that clouds over nearly all of our historical memory of radio.[78] Eleanor Roosevelt's media reputation was made chiefly in her syndicated "My Day" column. Here too, however, her work has been remembered, if at all, for its chatty, even trite, intimacies rather than for its contribution to public discourse.[79]

Sponsored by makers of soap, hand lotion, shoes, and coffee, and encouraged to discuss recipes, and forced to donate all proceeds from her work to charity, Mrs. Roosevelt was, in many respects, cast into a stereotypically feminine role on the broadcast dial. In her 1940–41 program, she was introduced as the Coffee Bureau's "charming news analyst" and her discussion of domestic and international current events took place "over our coffee cups," evoking the metaphoric space of the home, even, more precisely, the kitchen, where women gab rather than debate. However, what she actually said on that program provides a fascinating example of one of the myriad ways women on the radio negotiated gendered boundaries of public and private discourse. In addition, her work on this program provides a fascinating contrast to the president's use of the radio, in its embrace of a radio public in which the particularities of national and religious differences, political disagreement, and, above all, class struggle are acknowledged and affirmed as necessary to a democratic society. Also worth noting is the striking way that the commercial system of radio provided so many opportunities over the years for Mrs. Roosevelt's progressive voice. Public-service broadcasting, in contrast, tended to treat women, and politically minded women in particular, as if they did not exist at all.[80]

Her radio career began in the latter part of 1932, before her husband's inauguration, with her delivering commentary on child rearing and family relations. The job quickly exposed her to the particularly bizarre challenges of the job of first lady, a public role, which she likened to being in a fishbowl, but which required her to tread carefully outside of any but the most domestic sorts of activities. Criticized for using her name "for commercial purposes," and for an unguarded on-air comment in which she seemed blasé about the drinking habits of teenaged girls, Roosevelt conceded: "I suppose I have made some mistakes."[81] In friendly articles written by her friend Lorena Hickok, she indicated that she would donate her salary to charities and that, upon completion of her contract with Pond's, she was finished with radio work.[82]

By 1934, she was back on the air, earning five hundred dollars per minute, compensation reserved for only the highest-paid stars in radio.[83] Sponsored by a roofing company and then by the Simmons Mattress Company, the first lady delivered weekly news commentaries. A short series on education, sponsored by a shoe company, followed shortly thereafter. In 1935, she broadcast a program focusing on "life in the White House," which tended to highlight the amusing, glamorous, and mundane aspects of the Roosevelts' daily life, as many of her "My Day" columns did.[84] Through it all, Roosevelt fended off criticism that she was too highly paid, that she unfairly benefited the commercial prospects of one company over another, that she failed to disclose the precise details of her donations to charity, and in general that she brazenly transgressed the propriety of public and private modes of speech and conduct. And, of course, she was criticized by intellectuals and industry insiders for the triteness of her commentary and the shrillness of her voice, respectively.[85]

In 1937, she was back on the air with Pond's once again her sponsor, and once again the topic was "A Typical Day in the White House." Her compensation, three thousand dollars for each of thirteen broadcasts, was donated once again to the American Friends Service Committee. In April 1940, Sweetheart soap sponsored a twenty-six-week series of her talks, at the same rate of pay, on the White House, the domestic arts, politics, and travel.[86]

Throughout the 1930s and into the early 1940s, Mrs. Roosevelt's radio broadcasts tended to focus on traditional women's issues relating to domesticity: child rearing, wifely duties, and the social duties of modern debutantes. The titles of some December 1932 broadcasts of the *Pond's Program*—"Are We Going Back to Chaperones?"; "Keeping Your Husband Happy"; "The Girl of Today"—capture this emphasis on stereotypically feminine chatter.[87] The commercial dictates of daytime broadcasts sponsored by soap, lotions, and other household consumer items, and the controversies swirling around the first lady's active working life, worked together to make such topics the safest and most successful. But because of her own status as a working, dynamic personage, many of her broadcast topics tended to stretch the definition of domestic affairs to embrace questions about traditional women moving into public life—the very boundary that Mrs. Roosevelt transgressed. The *Pond's Program* featured programs on the topics "Married Women Working" and "Woman's Career vs. Woman's Home."[88] With the *Pan-American Coffee Hour*, Mrs. Roosevelt began to take on more consistently serious matters of politics and policy. Although there were occasional digressions into lighthearted homemaking tips, the seriousness of the times seemed to have enabled her mobilization on behalf of New Deal programs and civilian defense, which she saw as inextricably connected. And although this would prove to be one of the most controversial periods in the first lady's tenure and evoked the most heated opposition to her transgression of the public/private boundary, it also produced some of the most impressive radio broadcasts of her career.

After her husband's death and her return to civilian life, Eleanor Roosevelt maintained an impressive media presence, picking up her "My Day" column after only a four-day hiatus at the time of the funeral in May 1945. In 1948–49, she and daughter Anna teamed up on a daytime talk show that covered important international affairs as well as show-business news. "Although the program was dropped for lack of a commercial sponsor," Maureen Beasley observes, "it drew critical acclaim." *The Eleanor Roosevelt Show* premiered in October 1950, featuring her son Elliot and interviews with people of note. This program sparked controversy as anticommunists protested Eleanor's liberal views, J. Edgar Hoover fumed at her criticism of the FBI, and distaste for Elliot's eagerness to exploit his mother's fame in the name of commercial sponsorship caused uneasiness for coworkers and ridicule in the press.[89]

What followed was more than a decade of appearances on radio and television programs such as *Meet the Press*, and briefly her own television program, in which she interviewed world leaders using the conceit of a "tea party."[90] Drinking tea or coffee, on radio or TV, she was able to blend the social codes of domesticity with a stunning array of public and international affairs programming. On the television program, Mrs. Roosevelt, now a widow living outside of the "fishbowl" of first lady status, embraced consistently serious topics: "What Should Our Future Policy Be in China?" "Pakistan Looks to the Future," and "America's Role in Germany," to name a few.[91] Importantly, these hard-hitting episodes were not leavened with others focusing on child rearing, debutante etiquette, and so forth. The following paragraphs examine the radio program in which she first moved boldly out of the traditional realm of domesticity, a program that aired, significantly, at nighttime, and during the ominous months leading up to U.S. participation in the war. Following on the heels of the wartime chats, Eleanor's broadcasts, sponsored by the Pan-American Coffee Bureau, provide a striking set of contrasts to those of her husband.

Over Our Coffee Cups, a weekly Sunday evening program aired from September 1941 through April 1942, a season in which the nation moved from the sidelines to the center of the global conflict.[92] If this period was marked by the president and others in the administration as a time to circle the rhetorical wagons around an increasingly narrow definition of Americanism, Eleanor Roosevelt moved in a starkly different direction. In her first broadcast, she emphasized the warm relations between the United States and the nations of Central and South America, many of which constituted the Pan-American Coffee Bureau, her commercial sponsor. Americans, she observed, composed "twenty-one separate and individual nations, each with its own particular interests and individualities, each holding the same loyalties to their particular country that we hold to our United States."[93]

In her gently chiding way, Roosevelt accused her countrymen of using terms like "Pan-Americanism" "rather meaninglessly" and cautioned that "we cannot generalize as freely as we've done."[94] This move, away from meaningless generalizations and toward a multiplicity of differences among people, words, and countries is characteristic of her broadcasts from this period. Her emphasis on the importance of differences stands in stark contrast to the tendency, in 1940 and 1941, of the president to emphasize unanimity and to warn against the dangers of dissent. Throughout the autumn of 1940, she returned again and again to the "thousand different meanings" of the word *defense*.[95] For her, the term became an invitation to talk about a broad range of social problems and their solutions, which were as crucial to national defense as guns and soldiers. The rising cost of living, the dangers of wage controls, the quality of government-run homes for the aged, equality of opportunity—these became central issues in her expansion on the meaning of defense. And, while staunchly supporting the administration's growing interventionist positions, she did not shy away from the uncomfortable juxtaposition of her proposals for civil defense and the massive mobilization for military defense:

> The word *defense* is often confusing too. Because in its military sense it often means the subordination of the kind of service we have talked about above, in order that we may be able to meet a mass attack of force with a trained mass defense. And yet, in a truer sense, defense is something that is built by real service in peacetime in the way of daily living. Real defense is making day by day a way of life which we would gladly die to preserve. And this will call for the highest type of service from every citizen in every nation.[96]

Just as she defines America in "twenty-one separate and individual" ways, she acknowledges that defense has "a thousand meanings," and that the civic duty of citizens extends to "every nation" in the world. *Democracy* is another word whose confusing meanings she sets out to parse with remarkably catholic breadth. Arguing against the notion that the word is synonymous with the United States, she insists that democracy's purchase anywhere is tenuous and that democracy itself is fundamentally dynamic:

> It does not have to be frozen in any one pattern. It may grow with the changing point of view of mankind.... We must not forget that a form of government and a way of life ... only remain democratic because the people retain in their hands the one real democratic instrument: freedom of expression in thought, word, and deed.[97]

Roosevelt's embrace of "particularities," dissonance, and change extends even to opponents of the administration's support for England and the Soviet Union, most of whom she describes as sincere idealists, whose pursuit of peace is "misguided" by a failure to recognize the interconnections that join the peoples of the world. In a more sharply nationalist and divisive passage, she does rebuke American fascists as those "who for personal and selfish reasons ... advocate a course which would destroy us as a nation." But, for the most part, she works to undo divisive rhetoric, as when she debunks an anti-Semitic conspiracy theory sent to her from one of her listeners, or when she defends Hollywood writers and producers against congressional investigations into their patriotism, or, most strikingly, when she acknowledges a listener's complaint about the very distinctions her husband has employed so effectively to marginalize dissenters: "A letter has just come to me from a correspondent who is much upset because the word *traitor,* she says, is applied to everyone who opposes the administration's foreign policy." Although she responds by pointing out that "the word *warmonger* is applied to everyone who champions" the administration's policies, she also concedes that "this type of name-calling is never confined to any one side."[98]

This last example is marshaled as part of her advocacy of free speech, a strikingly sophisticated discussion, replete with quotations from Justices Brandeis and Holmes. Throughout the series *Over Our Coffee Cups,* Eleanor Roosevelt drew on lengthy passages from Thomas Wolfe, Abraham Lincoln, the *Antioch Review,* and other scholarly and literary sources.

In one remarkable broadcast in October 1941, she advocates for continued armed support of merchant ships in the North Atlantic, emphasizing the bravery, ethnic diversity, and Americanness of the lost crew members of a tanker recently sunk by a German submarine. Her support for arming or escorting merchant ships is deftly delivered through intimate details of the family lives of some of the sailors who perished aboard the tanker: Jewish parents praying for their missing son, dutiful brothers setting aside life-insurance money for impoverished siblings, reluctant sailors who took to the sea to escape the toxic zinc chromate fumes of factory work.[99] Next, she stresses the importance of economic planning on a global scale in the postwar world, arguing that "fair dealing for all countries . . . is the only possible groundwork for future peace." After that, she notes with approval the benign effects of a new "Labor" government in Australia, the promise of a new program for "free medical care" in New Zealand, and the success of a theater in Abingdon, Virginia, run entirely on a system of barter. In the bit on the barter theater, the story of a single pig, producing (and reproducing) enough hams to pay royalties and to feed the theatrical troupe rings with a utopian optimism, a fable of abundance that resonates with an almost biblical moral authority. Her accounts of the social-welfare programs in Australia and New Zealand sound a similar tone. It is the most passionately ideological of the broadcasts, combining the most progressive impulses of the New Deal and the war mobilization.[100]

These images of an enlightened social-welfare state infused much of her talk about civil defense and about her hopes for a postwar world "we would gladly die to preserve." The Roosevelt White House was well aware, in the latter part of 1941, thanks to exhaustive studies of public opinion, that the American people were already worried about the state of the *postwar* life in the United States, the return of high prices, and low wages. Summarizing their findings as a "portrait of gloom," Elmo Roper hypothesized that the pessimism of the average American about postwar life might have something to do with "his lingering reluctance to do what he knows must be done."[101] Visions of a progressive, egalitarian, and affluent postwar world became central to the propaganda strategies of the Office of War Information and related agencies. In her broadcasts, Eleanor Roosevelt often gave voice to the sense of gloom of the average Americans who wrote to her and made their economic struggles the center of her work on civil defense:

> Tonight I want to talk to you about something that I feel is of vital importance to defense because it touches everyone in their homes and that is the increased cost of living. I received a letter not long ago from a young woman whose husband has been working in one of the defense industries and whose income has gone up considerably. Bitterly she said that she had no more in the way of comforts than she

had before and no chance to save because the extra money which her husband earned was all swallowed up in the increased cost of living. It is true that in industry wages lag behind the rise in prices. There is an increase in wages, however, but white collar and retirees don't have any rise in their salaries or savings.[102]

Eleanor Roosevelt's controversial appointment as codirector of the Office of Civil Defense reflected the important insight that Americans shared her uneasiness about a wartime defense that ignored domestic spending to improve the lives of working people. The fact that she was forced out of the position rather quickly says more about the tremendous difficultly of maintaining her tricky public persona as first lady. Talking about civil defense over her coffee cup, and projecting a "motherly concern for oppressed peoples everywhere," was one thing.[103] Working as associate director of a federal agency was quite another, drawing upon her the ire of conservatives in Congress who had been waiting for a chance to attack her in ways that would score political points. The attacks centered on the appointment of friends of hers—Melvyn Douglas, an actor with controversial liberal activist credentials, and Mayris Chaney, a dancer hired to teach children to dance as part of Mrs. Roosevelt's emphasis on physical fitness as a component of civil defense.[104] Attacks in Congress and the press focused on the disparity between these wasteful "boondoggles" and the lack of proper compensation for soldiers or emergency equipment for civilian use in case of attack. Accused of "flitting in and out" of her government post, and hiring a "fan dancer" for defense work, Mrs. Roosevelt fell victim to a coordinated campaign of attack designed to bring into high relief the inevitable contradictions between her public persona, her political work, and her essentially domestic figurehead role as first lady.

One letter demonstrated the power of this attack to reinscribe powerful gender boundaries that silence women's voices when they dare to speak outside of narrow channels of private discourse: "Mrs. Roosevelt, you would be doing your country a great service if you would simply go home and sew for the Red Cross. Every time you open your mouth the people of this country dislike and mistrust you more."[105] In her response to these attacks, Mrs. Roosevelt resigned her post at the Office of Civil Defense. In her weekly broadcast for the Pan-American Coffee Bureau, however, she struck back sharply at her critics, employing to very powerful effect the rhetoric of war to define an irreducible distinction between the values of "privilege or equality."[106] Instead of seeking common ground through a shared recognition of the diversity of meanings and positions, Roosevelt makes clear that some distinctions cannot be eased or transformed through the rhetoric of unity, nor through the blandishments of radio oratory. Unlike President Roosevelt, the first lady does not seek to transform class and ideological divides into something more convenient and manageable; instead, she recognizes the attacks on her as the last front in "the age-old fight for the privileged few against the good of the many." She continues:

> There is not now and never will be in this country or anywhere else in the world unity between these two groups. Perhaps we must all stand up and be counted in this fight, the virtuous Westbrook Peglers [a conservative newspaper columnist and one of her chief critics] on one side, the boondogglers, so called, on the other. This is not a question of Republican or Democrat but privilege or equality. But if there has to be a fight, I'm glad I'm enlisted as common soldier with the many. There is nothing that matters in the least to me which those who have raised this hue and cry can give me or take away from me. What makes this country in the long run a better place in which to live for the average person, what makes us strong to win the war and the peace, because our needs are met and because we are given a sense of security. That matters. For that I intend to fight.[107]

At the conclusion of the Pan-American Coffee Bureau program's season in April 1942, Eleanor Roosevelt did not broadcast on her own commercially sponsored program for the duration of the war. However, she continued to speak over the air as a guest on other programs, or as part of ad hoc presentations concerning vital wartime issues, on several dozen occasions over the next three years. And, loosed from the restrictions of her official post in the Office of Civil Defense, she felt freer "to speak my mind as private citizen," and thus her broadcasts featured controversial topics such as "Negro Rights" and "New York City Diversity," both in 1943, as well as a "Report on War Work of American Women" and the "Purchase of War Bonds" in 1944.[108]

Remarkably, as Maureen Beasley has noted, Mrs. Roosevelt received virtually no criticism for taking a paycheck from a consortium of foreign governments during a war. Also remarkable, by contemporary standards, is the rather crude way the Pan-American Coffee Bureau plugged its product as "America's necessary drink in these busy days," ideal for keeping the nation "alert" in times of war, and for making "good neighbors" at home, an unmistakable reference to President

Roosevelt's "Good Neighbor Policy" with the Americas. These commercials were woven into Mrs. Roosevelt's spirited, policy-minded addresses by the unctuous announcer, Dan Seymour: "For remember: coffee is the drink of friendship as well as the drink which gives us the energy, the extra-steady nerves we need in these difficult times."[109]

For all her success and popularity on the radio, in print, and in her personal appearances, Eleanor Roosevelt remained deeply ambivalent about her status as a public personage, insisting that "I only like the part of my life in which I am a person." Longtime friend Lorena Hickok was similarly ambivalent about the transformation of the first lady from a person into a personage. Precisely because that transformation was always in process, and always in doubt, Eleanor Roosevelt was a powerful symbol for women's uncertain perch in public life in the 1930s and 1940s. In her movement from Victorian wife and mother urging women to stay at home, to her bold public criticism of legislation that would have restricted married women from working, she became adept at creating a personage at the intersection of domesticity and politics, while holding on to a sense of herself as essentially fractured between person and personage. "It is less difficult," she reflected in 1960, "for a woman to adjust to new situations than it is for a man."[110]

Franklin and Eleanor Roosevelt each used radio to construct unprecedented political personages. In creating a nationalist discourse in the folksy strains of commercial radio speech, Franklin emphasized unity both as an ancestral given and as the never-ending work of the New Deal and wartime publics he hailed. In almost diametrical opposition, Eleanor's radio voice insisted on the "thousand meanings" that swirled around the words, people, and concepts of the administration, the nation, and the world. She addressed not "the nation," nor "the people," but instead "those who listen to my broadcast,"[111] a humbler sense of audience, which reflects the marketplace realities of commercially sponsored programming and her own marginal place in the national discourse. Emphasizing diversity and the often uncomfortable juxtaposition of military and civil-defense goals, Eleanor Roosevelt's radio public—ridiculed and forgotten—provides an alternative legacy for radio's potential as an apparatus for negotiating the shifting grounds of public and private performance on a national and international stage.

CHAPTER 2

Vox Pop: Network Radio and the Voice of the People

You've been asking for something different
in radio, and here it is . . . an unrehearsed
program that gives you a cross section
of what the average person really knows—
and what he thinks about.
—*First network broadcast of* Vox Pop, *from
Columbus Circle in New York, July 7, 1935*

By 1935, millions of American radio listeners did seem to be re-
sponding to "something different in radio." All across the dial,
the untutored voices of average people could be heard matching wits
on quiz shows, warbling popular tunes for *Major Bowes' Original Amateur Hour,* and piping up from the audience at public forum programs
like *America's Town Meeting of the Air.* As the networks consolidated
their dominance over the airwaves and as professional broadcasters—
crooners, comedians, commentators, politicians, and pitchmen—mastered forms of address suited to radio's curious blend of interpersonal
and mass communication, radio listeners turned to the sound of voices
very much like their own.

The popularity and commercial success of audience-participation
programs during the network era reveals, more clearly than in any
other format, the self-consciousness with which network radio and its
new mass audience came to think about the role that radio should play
in national life. By reflexively turning the microphone onto members
of the listening audience, these programs made this new national audience an important part of radio entertainment. Further, audience-
participation programs accelerated the process by which the new mass
audience of radio came to stand in for the nation in general and "the
people" in particular.

As stated in the Introduction, "the people" was a shibboleth of the New Deal and Popular Front writers and producers working in government-sponsored educational radio. At the same time, on hundreds of amateur-hour, quiz, and human-interest shows, the voices of "the people" articulated more complicated and ambivalent meanings as populism, consumerism, and patriotism collided with each other and the production imperatives of live radio. "The popularization and commodification of transgression," Wayne Munson has argued, has its origins in *Arthur Godfrey's Talent Scouts,* where the balance of risqué material and conventional chatter proved enormously successful.[1] Programs such as *Meet Joe Public, Paging John Doe, The People's Platform, We the People, Americans at Work, America's Most Interesting People,* even *Major Bowes' Original Amateur Hour* drew an analogy between participatory radio, participatory democracy, and a new culture of consumption.[2] On these commercially sponsored programs, "the people" were represented primarily as consumers, as recipients of radio's magical windfall of free cash and merchandise prizes, and as holders of a common stock of shared knowledge that somehow confirmed their status as "real" Americans, or, as Lizabeth Cohen has argued, as members of an emergent "Consumer's Republic."[3]

Radio fan magazines, meanwhile, were encouraging audiences to see themselves as potential broadcasters. In 1933 and 1934, *Radioland* asked its readers, "What chance would you have in radio?" and "Will you be one of radio's future greats?" (Sammis, 16, Bisch, 18).[4] Articles on the important role played by fan letters in the lives of radio stars and in the production of programming itself echoed this same theme of the central role that listeners' voices played in radio. In 1936, *Radioland* changed its name to *Radio Mirror,* reinforcing the sense that radio's appeal resided in its ability to reflect back to audiences images of themselves.

More than any other show, *Vox Pop* exemplified network radio's preoccupation with the voices of the "average people" that composed radio's unprecedented national audience. And throughout the course of its sixteen-year run, its protean and ambivalent uses of the voice of the people also exemplified the "competing populisms" that characterized the emerging mass-mediated public sphere of the 1930s and 1940s.[5]

Between 1932 and 1948, *Vox Pop* helped to invent a series of compelling but ambivalent figures in mass-mediated public life using a variety of formats: in 1932, the show turned its attention to the "Forgotten Man in the Street."[6] By the mid-1930s, *Vox Pop* helped to invent the network "quiz-show" format, posing questions of "spectacular un-importance" to "the men and women who build America"; in the war years, *Vox Pop* pioneered the traveling human-interest and defense program. Searching for "the people" at the intersection of military service and consumerism, *Vox Pop* rewarded the men and women in uniform with fabulous merchandise prizes for their tricky negotiation of unstable social roles. During its short postwar run, *Vox Pop*'s version of "the people" changed again. Reflecting the postwar values of consumerism and conformity, the show became a traveling public relations machine, flacking for Hollywood premieres, corporate celebrations, and other "pseudo-events." *Vox Pop*'s longevity, popularity, and format make it a good example of changing network strategies for hailing "the people" as a central—and contested—notion in radio and in mass-mediated American life.

What are we to make of *Vox Pop*'s restless search for "the voice of the people"? This process was a complex and vexed one, marked by tensions and conflicts about the nature of this mass-mediated national public, whom it included, whom it excluded, and its relationship to democratic reform and the rise of a postwar culture of consumption and consensus. With its national reach, network radio broadcasting played a pivotal role in circulating the idea not only that radio was the best way to reach the American people, but that its programs were national rituals that helped to constitute a revitalized sense of national identity. Network broadcasts featuring the voice of "average Americans" provided a series of compelling performances of who "the American people" were, what they sounded like, and what they believed in.

Audience-participation programs like *Vox Pop* tapped into this process by blurring the line between audience and broadcaster. The changing sounds of the voice of this format over time, and the competing accents and tensions within these voices at any given moment, echoed the larger uncertainty about radio's relationship to public and private life in the 1930s and 1940s.

The strange career of *Vox Pop*—from political interviews with men on city streets during the worst years of the Depression to wartime pageants of consumerism and patriotism—at first appears to follow precisely a trajectory common to many cultural histories of the 1930s: the left populism of a popular form or mass movement becomes co-opted and disarticulated by the increasingly dominant culture industry in league with an increasingly statist national government.[7] And indeed, there is an undeniable shift of emphasis away from the leftism of the early New Deal and toward the politics of wartime consensus. It is nearly impossible, after all, to tell the story of radio broadcasting during this period without acknowledging the steadily increasing dominance of the networks and advertising agencies and the government's heavy-handed influence on broadcasting during the war.

But, on closer inspection, *Vox Pop*'s changing representations of the public tell a far more complex story, one that gets to the heart of the contested and contradictory discourse of "the people" in the popular and political culture of twentieth-century America. Radio's turn to the "voice of the people" was part of a broader set of preoccupations, alignments, and debates about the new media of communication and entertainment and the traditional political and social structures that they were threatening and promising to reform.[8] In its general political trajectory, *Vox Pop*'s history is highly ambivalent. Each distinctive phase of the program mixed sharply incompatible definitions of "the people"—in each instance, a rather faithful representation of the larger confusion and debate circulating through popular, political, and scholarly discourses. For example, *Vox Pop*'s early fascination with the man in the street combined a New Deal vision of participatory democracy with the "democratic realism" of Walter Lippmann and other intellectuals who saw in the mass audiences of radio, journalism, and politics an irrational and easily fooled mob. As a quiz show, *Vox Pop* retreated from the political potential of average people's voices even as it emphasized the analogy between audience participation and participatory democracy. During the war years, in an attempt to represent an inclusive and unified national defense, the show juxtaposed sharply incompatible ideas about the role that women, African Americans, returning veterans, and other groups should play in national public life.

This ambivalence stems in part from the multiple, overlapping, even contradictory meanings that both public and private can assume in different contexts. The conflation of different notions of public when imagining radio's mass audience posed particularly interesting problems for *Vox Pop*. On it and similar programs, the liberal public sphere of political theory collided with the "commercial public" of mass media.

The merger of political and commercial publics is key to radio's powerful discourse of the people in the 1930s. Radio's installation into both politics and mass culture came at such a moment in American history that it was impossible for most observers to see it as an extension purely of one or the other. In order to merge the two into one national public, commercial radio had to accommodate the competing demands of unity and difference, inside and outside. Audience-participation programs epitomized the networks' self-conscious efforts to finesse and ultimately to define the 1934 legislative mandate to "serve the public interest" by tapping into the overlapping and contradictory populisms of the New Deal, the Popular Front, Hollywood, and Madison Avenue.

Audience Participation

In its search for the always-changing sound of the public voice, *Vox Pop* helped to create the new sound of audience-participation radio, inventing several broadcasting formats that continue to be popular on radio and television today. Under the savvy direction of Parks Johnson, the show's creator, producer, and star for its entire run, *Vox Pop* pioneered the "man-in-the-street" format, in which an interviewer conducted a remote broadcast from a busy city sidewalk, asking random passersby their opinions on a range of public issues. It was also among the first of the quiz shows and the first to give away cash prizes for correct answers. During the 1939 New York World's Fair, *Vox Pop*—now a human-interest program featuring interviews with "typical Americans" and workers with "interesting" jobs—became the first regularly aired, half-hour commercial television program. In 1940, it became the first network program to give away merchandise prizes and to dedicate itself completely to boosting military morale, traveling from training camp to defense plant to veteran hospital for more than four years.

The story of *Vox Pop*'s continuous record of innovation in audience-participation radio (and briefly television) has as much to do with the proliferation of rival programs laying claim to some version of the "voice of the people" as it does with the creative and commercial tension between Parks Johnson and the network and advertising executives with whom he collaborated. Throughout the late 1930s, Johnson waged a protracted and ultimately fruitless legal battle for sole ownership of the phrases "*Vox Pop*" and "The Voice of the People," which were ubiquitous in the popular discourse of the period. An NBC executive finally urged Johnson to give up, pointing out that "the term 'Vox Pop' is in such constant use generally, by the public, for the purpose of describing events in which the voice of the public is heard." Johnson was also constantly battling with the network and the advertisers over how much of "the people" to use on the air. The search for a fresh approach to audience participation was thus shaped by commercial as well as artistic and ideological considerations.[9]

Audience-participation programs proliferated across the radio dial during the 1930s and 1940s because "the average person" had become a compelling figure for network radio's producers and audiences alike. As Warren Susman and Michael Denning have pointed out, the popular culture of the 1930s was marked by a profound concern with representations of "the people." In the mid-1930s, programs featuring "the voice of the people" increased dramatically. By 1935, quiz shows, human-interest programs, talent contests, and public-affairs programs were becoming increasingly popular on local stations as well as on the networks. The first two network quiz shows hit the air in 1934. By the following year, there were at least twenty-six on the national airwaves. Dozens more followed over the next several years, and within a decade there were more than 250 audience-participation programs on the radio. The high-water mark of the quiz format was the postwar, pretelevision era when hundreds of quiz shows appeared on network and local radio, featuring ever-larger cash and merchandise giveaways.[10]

Most of the early quiz shows followed the format established by the first two, *Uncle Jim's Question Bee* and the *Ask-It Basket:* contestants were solicited from a studio audience or from the "street" and asked questions submitted by the listening audience. Others combined network radio's highbrow and popular impulses, pitting the home audience's questions against a panel of "experts." One of the most popular of this kind was *Information Please,* which ran from 1938 to 1948, featuring such guest panelists as Orson Welles, Dorothy Parker, Alfred Hitchcock, Lillian Gish, Carl Sandburg, and H. V. Kaltenborn. *The Answer Man,* which ran from 1937 to 1956, featured Joe Chapman as the lone eponymous expert answering dozens of questions every day for nearly twenty years. Listeners provided the questions, sending in as many as 2,500 questions a day and the Answer Man provided the answers, one after the other, in a "deadpan" delivery. Many of the early quiz shows, like *Professor Quiz* and *Vox Pop* itself, evolved from a local man-in-the-street format. Questions designed to gauge public opinion eventually developed into questions that tested the public's knowledge of geography, spelling, history, and trivia.[11]

This period also saw the emergence of network-run, "sustaining" (i.e., unsponsored) "public forum" programs designed to fulfill network radio's avowed educational mission and to allay criticisms about the commercial nature of the "American Plan" of broadcasting, which was codified in the Radio Act of 1927 and the Communication Act of 1934.

These programs focused on contemporary issues and, to varying degrees, sought to include the voice of the "average American" in public debate. *America's Town Meeting of the Air* was one of the first and most successful of the "public forum" programs to originate in this period. The program typically featured several guest speakers representing different positions on a contemporary social or political question. By encouraging fiery debate among panelists, and between the panelists and the audience, the program's moderator, George V. Denny, sought to represent "all points of view." On its debut program, representatives of the four ideological positions took up the question "Which Way America—Communism, Fascism, Socialism or Democracy?" The show received as many as four thousand letters a week during its heyday and more than one thousand local debate and discussion clubs were formed to debate the issues covered on the broadcasts.[12] *The American Forum of the Air,* which ran from 1934 to 1956, another panel discussion among experts fielding questions from the audience, presented a more tightly controlled version of "public debate." *The American Forum*'s host curbed the more boisterous outbursts from the audience, and banned communists from the panel. According to John Dunning, "transcripts of the show were reprinted verbatim in the congressional record: it sparked many floor debates in Congress as lawmakers continued on Monday the discussion they had heard on the Sunday broadcast." *The People's Platform* (1938–52) combined the panel format with audience participation, bringing together "one big name individual, one expert on the subject at hand, a woman and an average man." On *The People's Rally,* which aired in 1938, debate on topical issues was combined with the quizzing of audience members.[13]

By 1937, *Vox Pop* had begun to move away from the quiz format and in the direction of interviews with "interesting people." "Human-interest" programs like *We The People, America's Most Interesting People, Americans at Work, America's Hour,* and *America Calling* proliferated in the mid-1930s. Many of these programs focused on the themes of patriotism and diversity, the American worker and the American Way. Like most of the programs, *Vox Pop* found these interesting people at work. In their emphasis on the American worker as the heart of radio's inclusive "public" and in their affirmation of an often narrow vision of "Americana" that included hostility toward "radical" solutions to the nation's ills, these network programs mediated conflicting visions of "the people."

On patriotic human-interest programs in the mid- to late 1930s such as *America's Hour* and *Americans All, Immigrants All,* the documentary presentation of Americans at work and at home functioned as more compelling evidence that radio was in fact the ideal medium for speaking to and for an unprecedented national public.[14] Comedy, variety, and talk programs throughout the 1930s and early 1940s also registered the widespread fascination with the voice of the people and with representations of radio's power to constitute a new form of public community, a "town meeting of the air." Fred Allen's *Town Hall Tonight, The National Amateur Night,* and *Major Bowes' Original Amateur Hour* were the first network showcases for the talents of "average Americans," starting in 1934. Within two years, *Major Bowes' Original Amateur Hour* was one of the most popular programs on the air, posting an extraordinary 45.2 in the Hooper ratings. The show remained in the top ten for most of the decade and spawned many imitators, including *Arthur Godfrey's Talent Scouts* and *NTG and His Girls* (1935–1936), which combined the amateur show with the plot of a Hollywood musical, each week picking several young women out of the chorus line and giving them a chance to be stars. Morning talk programs such as *The Breakfast Club,* which ran from 1933 to 1968, relied on informal, unscripted chatter of the sort pioneered by Will Rogers, Arthur Godfrey, and Roxy Rothafel. By 1938, *The Breakfast Club* had devoted a quarter of its airtime to unrehearsed interviews with members of the studio audience.[15]

In order to consolidate their ideological hold over this vast new resource, Robert McChesney argues, the networks and other for-profit broadcasters waged a sustained campaign throughout the 1930s to make their programming epitomize service to "the public interest, convenience, and necessity." The turn toward programming that featured the voice of the people, along with other forms of public-service broadcasting, can be seen as part of their campaign to prevent any rival definitions of "the public interest" from threatening their advantageous regulatory and market position. The meaning of this regulatory phrase, borrowed from nineteenth-century public-utility statutes, was never more vague than in the context of radio broadcasting, where the identity and interests of its "public" were so hotly contested.[16] Cultural edification, commercial profit, national security, and the often loosely organized interests of various interest groups all advocated for distinctly different versions of "public service."[17]

The turn toward programming that featured the voice of the people along with other representations of radio's public service (in fictional, documentary, and "public forum"–type programs) was part of the commercial broadcasters' campaign to corner the market on the "public interest," and thus to foreclose any rival definitions from threatening their advantageous regulatory and market position.

Commercial considerations also played a role in the development of these audience-oriented formats. With the economic crisis of the 1930s came a crisis in cultural values that was rather quickly registered, Lary May argues, in the popular tastes of audiences. May identifies this process in Hollywood during the first years of the Great Depression and argues that it helps to explain the spectacular success enjoyed by Will Rogers, who spoke in his films "exactly like the man in the street":

> The producers catered to audiences' rejection of foreign formulas in favor of talking films that dramatized a counternarrative of "Americanism" emerging from the bottom rather than the top of the social order. In addition, instead of isolating the revolution in morals to the private domain, the carnival spirit of mass art and modern amusements entered the center, altering both in the process. Nowhere was that more clear than in the rise of Will Rogers from the urban world of vaudeville and the penny press to become the top male box-office attraction of the era.[18]

A similar phenomenon occurred on network radio, where the emphasis on perfect enunciation, vaguely British-sounding voices, and highbrow musical programs is accompanied, in the early 1930s, by a new emphasis on "the language of the street." As the audience for network radio grew, radio producers began to pay closer attention to what listeners responded to most. Incorporating the listening public into the show itself made for compelling radio and was an innovative way to do market research on its growing but still dimly understood audience.

The Forgotten Man in the Street

In 1932, *Vox Pop* helped to invent one of broadcasting's most enduring figures: the man in the street. As part of a broader cultural climate that produced popular images of "the people" as iconic representations of democracy and reform, *Vox Pop* drew heavily on the analogy between the voting polls and the open microphone. *Vox Pop*'s origins are inextricably tied up with the election of Franklin D. Roosevelt and his galvanizing rhetorical invocation of the "Forgotten Man" as inheritor of a revitalized democratic government and a more unified nation. Inspired by an election day 1932 broadcast in which voters were asked on the air to talk about who they were going to vote for and why, Parks Johnson and Jerry Belcher, two advertising agents in Houston, Texas, developed a show around a "sidewalk interviews" format.[19]

Dangling a microphone on a long wire out of the window of radio station KTRH in downtown Houston, the hosts stopped unsuspecting passersby and peppered them with questions—live, uncensored, and on the air. The show was the first to dedicate its entire format to the voices and opinions of "the people" in such a direct way. With its sense of unrehearsed immediacy, background street noise, and the halting, untutored voices of men and women in the street, *Vox Pop* captured the feel of an inchoate radio public still becoming acclimated to the national significance of the new mass medium. The show presented "the voice of the people" as part of the spontaneous, unruly, and heterogeneous sounds of urban life. Posing a dizzying array of questions seemingly designed to measure everything from political orientation to psychological makeup to IQ, *Vox Pop* compiled a weekly clearinghouse of data about an amorphous and mysterious public. Although mysterious, unrehearsed, and urban, the public interviewed by *Vox Pop* was exclusively white, American-born, and for the most part, male. Women interviewees were asked questions from a different list, one that emphasized private relationships, the differences between the sexes, and domestic chores.

Here is an excerpt from early 1935, right before the show was picked up by NBC. In this excerpt, Parks Johnson is interviewing Wilburn Gladsby of Houston about the trial of Bruno Hauptmann, kidnapper and murderer of the Lindbergh baby.

> JB: Mr. Gladsby, from what you've read in the papers, have you formed any opinion as to the guilt of Hauptmann in the matter of the murder of the child?
>
> WG: I have.
>
> JB: What's your opinion?
>
> WG: In my opinion, Hauptmann is guilty.
>
> JB: He's guilty. Now, why do you say that?
>
> WG: That's just the idea that I draw from the newspapers.

JB: From the newspapers. Could you give any definite reasons why you have formed that opinion?

WG: Well, from seeing his picture on the [newsreel] screen, he looks like a man that would be capable of such a crime.

JB: In other words, you judge him by his looks.

WG: That's right.

JB: How about the testimony? Would that indicate that he was guilty of murdering the child, in your opinion?

WG: Not necessarily, no.[20]

What follows is an increasingly fast-paced series of questions seemingly designed to plumb the political, intellectual, and psychic depths of Wilburn Gladsby, man in the street: "Do you think the soldiers should get their bonus?" "Is a yellow dress still yellow in the dark?" "Describe an elevator to me as if I'd never seen one."[21]

Other interviewees were asked series of questions such as What causes love? How does it feel to feel important? What famous man's first name is Benito? What do you think about section 7a of the National Industrial Recovery Act, giving labor the right to collective bargaining? Who is the Forgotten Man? What's the first word that comes into your head when I say the following?[22]

These interviews also seemed designed to measure the success of local advertising campaigns and the radio public's receptivity to advertising in general. Johnson and Belcher, both admen by trade, asked an enormous amount of market-research–type questions. Some of these questions (word associations, brand-name and slogan identifications) sounded much like the standard "quiz"-type questions, designed to test quick thinking and topical knowledge. Other, more open-ended questions (e.g., Which radio stations do you tune in regularly?" "Name four weekly magazines," "Do you feel any obligation to the sponsor of a radio program which you enjoy very much?") made more overt appeals for information about the consumer mind.[23]

Equal parts quiz show, opinion poll, market-research survey, and psychological examination, the *Vox Pop* interview, taken cumulatively, reflected a world of discontinuous and arbitrary demands. The men interviewed in this manner frequently sounded confused, but good-naturedly so, uncertain about the technical and aesthetic requirements of the new medium, but free with opinions on just about any topic.

Vox Pop questions reflect, in an appropriately jumbled fashion, the juxtaposition of contradictory ways of thinking about the concept of "the public," then current among radio producers, audiences, academics, politicians, and advertisers. Presented as a stream of non sequiturs, the early *Vox Pop* interview functioned as a kind of aural Rorschach test for both the interviewees and the listeners at home. What version of "the people" do *you* hear emerging from this amorphous interrogation? A democratic public? A phantom? An unruly mob?

On the one hand, political questions, particularly those that touched on the legislation and rhetoric of the New Deal, seemed to hail a politically engaged public, a reflection of the New Deal embrace of the Forgotten Man in the street as the central figure in a politics of democratic reform. Questions such as "Who is the Forgotten Man?" and "What do you think of child labor?" reflected the new political common sense that mass-mediated public opinion had, to an unprecedented extent, become a crucial part of the momentum behind the New Deal. This political orientation was borne out most famously in the massive success of Roosevelt's Fireside Chats. As Roosevelt's own masterful use of radio to chat intimately with "average Americans" had proven within the first week of his presidency, the radio public was an enormously important political actor in the early days of the New Deal.[24]

On the other hand, the show asked questions designed to emphasize the limits of listeners' education and the private and irrational nature of their experience of politics. *Vox Pop* presented these people as confused bystanders to public life, stumbling over questions on arithmetic and current events, and judging defendants' guilt by how they look on the newsreels rather by the merits of the testimony. These voices evoke the "phantom public" made famous by Walter Lippmann and elaborated on by other "democratic realists" in the 1920s and 1930s.[25] Like the notorious army IQ tests, and the behaviorist and Freudian studies of the effects of propaganda on the irrational mass mind conducted by social and political scientists, the *Vox Pop* interview revealed a public mind overwhelmed by the blooming, buzzing confusion of public life and ruled by essentially private, psychological motivations. The manifest public—the man in the street—was, by itself, inscrutable. Solving the riddle of public opinion required the use of radio, a cultural apparatus that gathered "the people" together into an unprecedented national audience and then gave it a public voice. Munson described the quiz show as "multivalent, an amalgam: a 'real'

Vox Pop hits the streets, hotel lobbies, and train stations of New York City in 1935. Courtesy of the Library of American Broadcasting.

person with a name and a job but also a comic role-player, consumer and commodity."[26]

These conflicting notions—the public as the arsenal of democratic reform and as a phantom—actually seemed to merge in the notion of the radio audience: immense, immediate, and united, yet also vulnerable, passive, and irrational.[27] *Vox Pop* hailed a public whose shadowy features only began to become clear in its capacity as a "mass audience," an entity whose suggestibility and accessibility together promised profits and the hope of national renewal.[28] Simultaneously hailing two distinct groups—a rational political public and the irrational audience of mass culture—*Vox Pop* echoed one of the central tensions in radio's early efforts to carry out its complex and, at times, contradictory mission of serving the public interest and selling goods.

The tension between radio's public-service mission and its commercialized, mass audience, Hilmes has shown, was partially resolved in the early 1930s by employing the masculinist liberal logic of distinct gendered spheres. Thus the networks consigned women's programming—chiefly soap operas—to the daytime hours. Prime time, mean-

while, was reserved for more prestigious, public, and thus more masculine programming, such as variety shows and "prestige dramas."
Early audience-participation programs like *Vox Pop*, however, did not
always fit neatly into these gendered schedule distinctions. Seeking to
give voice to radio's entire public, and scattered all over the radio
schedule, these programs were hybrids, working to represent and contain the contradictory audiences hailed by radio's national address.[29]

On *Vox Pop*, this tension was exacerbated by the show's afternoon
time slot, presumed to reach housewives only, and its almost exclusive
use of American-born men as the voice of the people. Although the
occasional (white) woman was asked questions about food, shopping,
and child rearing, women's opinions on most issues, and thus their status as "the people," were largely ignored. People of color and recent
immigrants were not heard at all. Such a narrow conception of the
people's voice made sense politically, but not commercially on a daytime program in which an audience of housewives was assumed and
the importance of engaging it with the show and the sponsor's product
was paramount. In this case, the sponsor was Fleishmann's Yeast and
cakes of it were given away free to the brave citizens who stepped before the *Vox Pop* microphone.

These exclusions and distinctions are evident in the extant early
recordings of the broadcasts themselves, as well as in Parks Johnson's
meticulous notebooks, in which he recorded the name, sex, race (if
other than white), and some other salient features of each interviewee.
In his notes on the January 11, 1935, broadcast, Johnson writes: "No
current events questions for women." And in his collection of interview
questions from the network era, he has a separate category, marked
"Women—Questions for," that focuses on matters of child rearing,
nutrition, the differences between the sexes, and so forth. It is not
until the late 1930s that he makes any record of "Negro" interviewees
at all.[30]

Johnson's approach to the gathering, categorizing, and asking of
questions reveals the extent to which this problem shaped the program's
early years. Johnson compiled thousands of questions, each written on
a 3 × 5 index card, organized into categories, each with its own coded
markings scribbled at the top of the card. Three wavy lines indicated a
"loosen-up," a question designed to get the interviewee and the crowd
of onlookers to relax and laugh for the microphone. "Hook...trick,"
the largest category, consisted of questions designed to catch people off

guard, usually with a play on words (e.g., Is it possible for a man to get intoxicated on water? On a boat!). "Opinion" questions were divided up into "heavy" and "light" and there were far more of the latter than the former. Whereas "heavy" opinion questions took on issues of class, politics, and the distribution of wealth, questions for women were, in one way or another, of the "hook . . . trick" variety, designed to make them seem silly in stereotypically feminine ways (e.g., "Women are usually pleased when referred to as 'kittenish' but get fighting mad if they are referred to as 'catty.' Is this an example of inconsistency?"). The separate category designated "Women's questions" was relatively small, indicating the segregation of women's opinions from men's, and the general sense that the normative interviewee was a man.[31]

However, the man in the street had to be handled properly in order to preserve the tension between the democratic notion of the rational citizen and the irrational (and feminized) "herd" of mass culture. In early interviews, Johnson mixed questions from different categories with the precision of a chemist, being careful to start off with a "loosen-up," followed by some "general information" questions, and then perhaps a "hook . . . trick." In numerous notations made by Johnson on the cards and in his notebooks, he makes it clear how concerned he is to make men comfortable playing the fool. Part of this strategy depended on the mostly silent figure of the irrational woman, who was the topic of many of the questions posed to the man in the street.

In its efforts to enact its own logic of distinctions based on gender, race, and national difference, this early version of *Vox Pop* hailed a somewhat vexed public: white male citizens cast as an irrational mass-mediated daytime audience, a role typically reserved for women, immigrants, and racial and ethnic "others." The show's humor, suspense, and novelty derived from the inherent incompatibility of "the people" and the increasingly sophisticated means of communication that were enabling them to be reached as a mass audience. "Contrast and incongruity," Munson argues, "are at the root of the humor."[32] Because the producers understood "the public" within the framework of masculinist assumptions, however, they were unable to fully exploit the figure of the irrational female consumer, or of the ill-educated immigrant "masses." The figure of the man in the street as a self-conscious representation of radio's feminized mass audience proved too awkward as the gendered logic of day and night audiences became increasingly predominant. A new public, a mass-mediated public that embraced these contradictions more gracefully, was required.[33]

Quiz Show

The still-new quiz-show format was the perfect solution for *Vox Pop*'s dilemma. Like other man-in-the-street programs of the mid-1930s, *Vox Pop* began to ask very different questions of its live, unrehearsed, amateur audience. By the summer of 1935, when NBC brought *Vox Pop* to New York City for a national hookup, all questions of a political or controversial nature had been banished, along with the exclusive focus on men. The show emphasized instead the show's impromptu, unrehearsed encounter with people on the street. Announcer Ben Grauer began each show by promising that "Nothing is planned in advance" and "Nobody knows who will be interviewed, or what will happen, not even the boys themselves."[34] Within weeks of its debut, however, the show fled the noise and unpredictability of the sidewalks for the more respectable environs of hotel lobbies and train stations. Soon after, the show graduated from daytime broadcasts for the more lucrative and prestigious evening time slot.

Reinvented as a quiz show, network radio's first to award cash prizes for correct answers, *Vox Pop* turned its attention from the "man in the street" to a broader, less political conception of "the people." The new version paid homage to "the Great American Average," a concept increasingly common in ad campaigns, the new science of public-opinion polling, and the Fireside Chats of Roosevelt. The less controversial new format was a nonnegotiable demand on the part of Ruthrauff and Ryan, the advertising agency representing Fleischmann's Yeast, the show's first national sponsor. Johnson records his first conversation with the head of J. Walter Thompson's radio department: "At first conference with Reber he said—"Here are your sponsors—Fleischmann's Yeast . . . here's your spot on the air, between Jack Benny and Major Bowes. . . . Stay off politics and religion and otherwise, run the show to suit yourselves."[35] Despite the turn away from politics, religion, and "heavy" opinions of any kind, the network version of the show now billed itself grandly as an expression of patriotism, populism, and participatory democracy. The show now touted interviewees as "the men and women who make America," a decidedly populist turn of phrase, echoing, however obliquely, the support for organized labor circulating through both the popular and political cultures.[36] "The moment-to-moment unpredictability" was the source of anxiety for broadcasters and sponsors of all audience-participation programs in the era of live broadcasting, but also a source of their tremendous appeal.[37]

The network version of *Vox Pop* incorporated elements of the interview, quiz, and human-interest shows, creating a format that gestured both vaguely and insistently toward the centrality of "the people" in the national experience of radio listening. As the workplace roles and consumer habits of the people took center stage and politics receded, the voices of women and the occasional immigrant became audible as part of the chorus of a new mass-mediated public. And although women were still marginalized through a special list of questions concerning domestic matters, the content of their speech—the central issue of *Vox Pop*'s man-in-the-street years—now seemed less important than the sound of their voices. The breezy exchange of questions and answers about matters of little consequence proved the ideal format for showcasing and containing the many voices of the mass-mediated public. Gone were the men in the street with their ill-informed political opinions, along with the awkward calculus of how many "light" and "heavy" opinion questions to combine with the "loosen-ups" and "hook . . . tricks" in any given interview. The people on *Vox Pop* were no longer interesting as citizens but as contestants—that is, consumers of both trivia and the Fleischmann's Yeast that the sponsor generously provided to them along with a brief word on its beneficial effect on the complexion.

At the same time, contestants were rewarded for their correct answers with crisp one-dollar bills, an apt representation of the way the voice of the people had become another exciting commodity.

Almost immediately, Johnson began to embroider a bit on the concept of a straight quiz show, encouraging listeners to send in questions of their own and adding interviews of "interesting people" and scavenger-hunt contests for bits of "Americana." In the mid-1930s, *Vox Pop* celebrated the Great American Average, enlisting the audience in searches for cigar-store Indians, old-time grist mills, covered bridges, the widest main streets, the smallest towns, and other items symbolic of Anglo-Protestant, small-town American life.[38] Even during breaks between contests, Johnson received between 750 and a thousand letters a week from listeners with suggestions, corrections, and compliments.[39]

Executives at the new advertising agency Ruthrauff and Ryan pressed for a pure quiz format with prescreened contestants, arguing that it was a fast-paced, profitable, compelling format in which the voice of the people could be heard without the risk of controversial or dull interviews. Increasingly, the program eschewed the elements of risk associated with chance encounters with people on the street for a more polished presentation of "characters" who would perform well before a microphone. In a 1939 memo, Nate Tufts, the Ruthrauff and Ryan advertising executive who handled the program for Bromo-Seltzer, urged Johnson to take great care in how representatives of the public were presented on the show: "John Q. Public interviewees...should be selected far enough in advance so that we eliminate as far as possible the chance of 'dud' interviews."[40] In other memorandums from that year, Tufts strongly urged that "the voice of the people" should be heard only "when it seems advisable," rather than every week.[41]

By 1939, the program, which had begun by boasting of its totally unrehearsed encounters with the public, began to schedule special guest interviews with a new generation of people who were both "media-ready" and "average." *Vox Pop* interviewed a New York City doorman who had once been a prizefighter, an eyewitness in a celebrated murder case, the president of the Mother-in-law's Association of America, and countless other "interesting personalities" who combined ordinariness with a guaranteed "human-interest" value. Other changes quickly followed. Increasingly, celebrities came on to be "*Vox Pop*ped," that is, quizzed and interviewed. The show began to travel around the country in the 1940s—setting up microphones at regional celebrations, local festivals, on board the "Silver Meteor" train bound for Washington, DC—part of a developing trend in audience-participation shows for remote broadcasts.[42]

As a consequence of these developments, *Vox Pop* increasingly became a vehicle for creating publicity for the institutions, events, and individuals featured on the program. It also became increasingly concerned with using interviews with Americans as a way to represent the nation itself. Nowhere were these trends more clear than during the summers of 1939 and 1940, when *Vox Pop* broadcast from the New York World's Fair. Conducting shows from Billy Rose's Aquacade, the exhibits of RCA and AT&T and countless other spectacles of corporate and show-business promotion, the show wove together elements of the quiz show, the human-interest interview, and the fair's celebration of "the people" and "the American Way. *Vox Pop* helped to promote the fair's "World of Tomorrow" theme when it broadcast the first commercially sponsored, half-hour television program in history from the fairgrounds during the summer of 1939.[43] These two concepts were joined in the notion of "the plain American citizen," to whom many of the exhibits were dedicated. As Warren Susman has argued, the fair emphasized a rather narrow and consumerist vision of "the people."[44] The *Vox Pop* of this period immediately prior to U.S. involvement in World War II combined the patriotism, consumerism, and populism circulating through the fair in particular and the popular culture in general. Interviews with the public tended to celebrate the absorption of individuals into the large national institutions of the day as workers, shoppers, and citizens.

War

At the end of 1940, with the threat of war looming, *Vox Pop* refashioned its quest for the voice of the people again, part of the networks' dramatic commitment to the war effort. By July, the show had converted to full-time war mobilization, traveling every week between military bases and defense plants, conducting personal interviews with servicemen and -women, black and white, of every stripe, and from many backgrounds. The voice of the people, first assumed to reside in the randomness, then in the "averageness" of the people, now was sought in the exemplary "Americanness" of those working for the nation's defense. Heard on the Armed Forces Radio Service as well as on network radio, *Vox Pop* became an important link between the home front and soldiers abroad.

In friendly chatter vetted by military censors, the voices of soldiers, sailors, and defense workers took on a quasi-official status. Wartime security concerns required advance scripts, and government officials recommended that audience-participation shows become less spontaneous. Despite broadcasting's wartime mobilization, and partly because of it, the voices of women occupied an increasingly central, but uneasy, place in *Vox Pop*'s national public. With the stakes raised, the tensions in *Vox Pop*'s appeal to "the people" became both more important and more difficult to resolve and contain.

During the war years, human-interest, documentary, and audience-participation styles converged in numerous programs designed to give voice to the men and women in military service and defense work. Many established network programs altered their formats for the duration, traveling nationally and internationally to military camps. These programs hailed a national audience of soldiers, defense workers, and patriotic citizens as equally vital components of Roosevelt's "arsenal of democracy." The conflation of "the people" with those fighting the war was part of the broader political and popular culture of the period. But *Vox Pop* made this relationship vivid through interviews carefully divided into segments on wartime experiences and postwar dreams. In this format, the patriotic sacrifices of military service were made coherent within the context of the postwar consumerism that would be its eventual reward and rationale.

Under not too subtle pressure from the federal government, which brought an antimonopoly suit against them in 1938, the networks agreed to disseminate the messages coming out of the Office of War Information (OWI) and other government agencies. Fearing a repeat of the World War I government takeover of the airwaves or some other incursion into their profitable hold on most of the North American airwaves, the networks worked closely with OWI and other agencies starting as early as 1940 to create programming sympathetic to administration interests. Most often, these programs featured the voice and active participation of soldiers.[45]

Vox Pop was the first program to turn its attention to the war effort and to the voice of defense workers, soldiers, and servicewomen. Parks Johnson, the father of a marine and a former marine himself, responded as much to his own sense of patriotic duty and his unerring knack for finding commercially compelling formulas for presenting the voice of the people as to government pressure. *Vox Pop*'s attention to women in uniform and women defense workers made it a particularly interesting example of this format. Programs such as *American Women* (1943–44) focused exclusively on the contributions of women to the war effort, but tended to be short-lived and not nearly as popular as *Vox Pop*, which soared to its highest Crossley ratings during the war years.[46]

As the imperatives of defense work and war morale muted traditional exclusions from public life, the voices of *Vox Pop* echoed both those traditional exclusions and the new challenges to them. The private chatter in these interviews frequently generated public uneasiness, as women expressed their desire to work postwar and postmarriage, as black and white soldiers shared the microphone, and as the ritual gift giving drove home the relentless desiring that postwar life would entail. Listener mail increased dramatically during these years, as more people weighed in with their hopes for the postwar place of women, returning vets, and African Americans, and for the place of their own public voices in the consumer culture permeating the airwaves.

Interviews with servicemen and -women concluded with the presentation of lavish merchandise prizes—another *Vox Pop* innovation. These gifts were carefully chosen by the *Vox Pop* staff after extensive clandestine research into the postwar needs and desires of the guests.

Taken together, the prizes doled out during the war years amounted to a catalog of postwar consumer culture: home appliances, clothing, vacations, even intimate apparel. In the ritualized discussion of wartime service and postwar dreams, followed by the presentation of merchandise, the show became increasingly preoccupied with the sound of women's voices.

The following is an excerpt from a 1943 broadcast when *Vox Pop* visited Penn State in recognition of the school's transition to war mobilization: Here host Warren Hull interviews a Miss Frances Chandler, studying aeronautical engineering in preparation for her work at the Curtis Wright defense plant. After a stolid description of the school's war work, Hull pursues more personal information about "Cadette" Chandler:

WH: What's this deal you have with Curtis Wright?

FC: Well, we go to school here for ten months and study all the subjects that go with aeronautical engineering and they pay us board and tuition and ten dollars a week.

WH: Well, they sort of keep you on the run, don't they? Pretty busy girl?

FC: Yes, we have eight hours of classes a day. With a little off for lunch.

WH: And homework?

FC: Plenty of it.

WH: Well, how do you girls ever have any dates?

FC: You could be surprised by what a girl can do. (laughter, whistles from audience)

WH: What's the most fun in your course?

FC: Well, I think the shop work is.

WH: Oh, that's right. I heard you have to learn to weld, rivet, and everything else.

FC: Foundry. It's wonderful.

WH: What are you planning to do after the war?

FC: I think I'll keep on with aeronautical engineering. It's a good field.

WH: Well, what does the future "Mr. Chandler" feel about that? (laughter from audience)

FC: He agrees with me.

WH: He agrees with you?

FC: Sure.

WH: Ah well, that's good. You know, Frances, we found out, our own private G-2, that you were going to get the knot tied soon. So Bromo-Seltzer has a surprise for you. We went to the Penn State girls' favorite store, Sklose, and we got you a going-away outfit. A three-piece ensemble of 100 percent wool imported green and red hound's tooth Scotch plaid (that's a mouthful), with a pearly white Joan Kennelly jabot blouse, a smart red felt hat by Dobbs, a stunning purse to match—the latest thing made of plastic. And so you can see what it looks like on, Mr. Sklose sent over a charming young lady to model it for you.

How do you like that?

FC: Marvelous.

(cheers, wolf whistles from audience)

WH: And Frances, Frances. And to make you an extraspecial bride, two pairs of lovely nylon stockings.

FC: (screams with delight)

(audience gasps, then cheers)

FC: Thank you!

WH: Thank you very much and good luck to you. May you live long and prosper and be very, very happy. Curtis Wright Cadette Frances Chandler.[47]

Cutting against the grain of the program's scripted interviews, the merchandise giveaways became the most emotionally compelling part of the program, eliciting screams of delight from guests, roars of applause from the live audience, and bags of mail from overwrought listeners. It is hard to convey in print the intensity of emotion conveyed by Chandler's scream, the gasp of the audience, and the general air of celebration that greeted the presentation of the nylons. The eruption of the private voice of consumer desire into the public one of national defense proved a potent combination, giving a dramatic boost to the show's ratings. In the compelling broadcast ritual of the merchandise giveaway, *Vox Pop* celebrated the postwar return to consumerism and traditional social roles as an extension of national service.

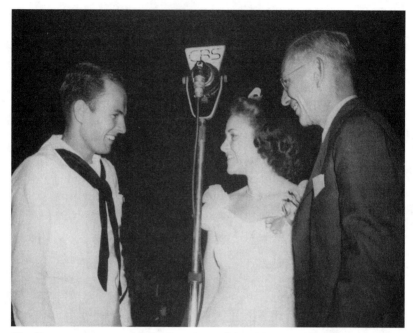

Vox Pop goes to war, 1943. Courtesy of the Library of American Broadcasting.

To drive this point home, GIs and WACs were occasionally married on the air at the end of interviews and showered with presents; one lucky bride was surprised by the appearance of Kate Smith—whose voice epitomized the wartime conflation of patriotism and femininity—as her matron of honor. Soldiers were rewarded for their service with on-air telephone interviews with prospective employers, women in service with clothes and home appliances.

The cultural work accomplished by *Vox Pop*'s embrace of a public sphere organized around shared dreams of consumer goods and marriage at first seems easy to determine. Consumer desires, in the case of Cadette Chandler's new outfit, seemed to reposition the traditional gender roles temporarily destabilized by the exigencies of the war effort. The presentation of the blouse, suit, and nylons, complete with an attractive model to show Chandler how it's done in case she had forgotten, and the approving wolf whistles of the mostly male crowd, are dramatic partially because of the powerful social meanings conveyed by this ritual. In her emotional response to the gifts, Chandler is recognizable as a conventionally nubile young woman, an irrational consumer of mass culture, and the privileged subject of radio's national public.

And indeed, there is much to support this reading. The nameless, voiceless, fashion model literally stands in for Chandler, fulfilling the traditional role of woman as consumer and sex object. The wolf whistles that attend her appearance, and the collective gasp and approving cheers that accompanied the presentation of the nylons to Chandler, all function as aural reminders to embody Chandler's untraditional, disembodied voice within the frame of mainstream postwar femininity.

However, the eruption of private desire into national service also meant that the public significance of the personal was up for grabs. Cadette Chandler—speaking of her technical training, attraction to heavy foundry work, fondness for dating, unbridled enthusiasm for fabulous prizes, and determination to work postwedding and postwar—joined a chorus of wartime voices articulating a complex set of expectations and desires of postwar life. In the context of *Vox Pop*'s dramatization of the personal, these voices composed an unpredictable mass-mediated public. Chandler has also challenged the expectations of the show's host, whose wisecrack about "the future 'Mr. Chandler'" hints at the anxious and reactionary posture of postwar masculinity in mass-mediated public life.

Chandler's emotional response to the nylons—she screams—speaks to the intensity of consumer desires and the power of her voice to make those desires public, all of which exceeds the show's ostensible focus on national service, just as her desire to work outside the home, like that of three-quarters of working women surveyed in 1944, has exceeded the requirements of the war effort.[48] These excesses—extra meanings and sounds—force our attention back to Chandler's voice and the intense subjectivity she brings to her part in this highly formatted program.

Allison McCracken has examined the unique power of women's voices on the radio to elude the typical objectification that film theorists have identified in the masculinist gaze of the camera lens. In particular, she argues that the power of the deviant woman to "undermine postwar norms of gender" resides in her disembodied voice, which can be scary, irritating, but also sympathetic, even familiar. The voice of the people—in this case the woman who wants her job and her nylons, her foundry and her husband, her body and her voice—emerges as a public figure to be reckoned with and, thanks to radio's intimate address, to be identified with.[49]

Vox Pop's tightly scripted merger of public and private during the war years proved to be the most popular, and, to judge by the quality and quantity of audience mail, the most emotionally compelling format of the program's entire run. The home audience responded in record numbers to *Vox Pop*'s clever marriage of wartime service and the intimate world of consumer desire. One self-described "tough old geezer" and veteran of World War I confessed to shedding "real tears" when listening to the presentation of gifts to servicemen and -women. It wasn't so much the actual merchandise he found so moving as it was the "dad-gummed snooping into their personal lives to find the one thing that will make them happy."[50]

Listeners also wrote in to the show asking for merchandise prizes, being careful to link their requests to the larger mission of the war effort, specifying the need for consumer goods necessary to mend marriages and thus restore the fighting spirit of their families. A woman from Cambridge, Massachusetts, asked for a "sheer black nightie and negligee," on behalf of her sailor husband, whom she follows from one stateside naval base to another, "trying to keep up [his] morale." Citing her long, intimate acquaintance with *Vox Pop* ("I grew up with your show and the products you sponsored," and "darn it, I feel I know you") and the importance of maintaining her husband's spirits, this listener understood perfectly the link between national service, intimate relations, and consumer goods that drove the program during the war years.[51]

The show relentlessly mixed private meanings with those relating to national defense, at times making explicit the connection between the emotional life of "the people" and the health of the war effort. The show played on the emotional impact of homecomings, impending weddings, and the optimism with which people talked about their future. For many listeners, especially those with loved ones fighting, missing, or killed overseas, the show's blending of intimacy, publicity, and national service made for emotionally compelling radio.

But this wartime merger of public and private proved to be as controversial as it was popular. As Hilmes points out, network radio's wartime embrace of previously excluded voices in the name of unity had the paradoxical effect of "ripping the cover of complacency off everyday practices and revealing the lack of unity and the violation of 'natural' democratic precepts that lay beneath the surface." Previously excluded groups, especially African Americans, "were not slow to respond to the openings produced by such strategies, and pressures quickly began to build to allow previously unheard voices a space on the public airwaves, telling their own stories in a context of newly invigorated inclusiveness and redrawing social boundaries."[52]

On *Vox Pop*, the representation of African American soldiers during wartime revealed this belated effort at racial inclusiveness while also demonstrating, in distressingly frank terms, the abiding racial exclusivity at the heart of network radio's construction of a national public. At the same time, the atmosphere of inclusiveness promulgated by the networks and the federal government, and *Vox Pop*'s producers and wartime sponsor, Bromo-Seltzer, opened the door for an increasingly critical and engaged form of reception among African American listeners at home and in the armed forces.

This complex set of phenomena arose in several occasions during *Vox Pop*'s interviews with African American and white soldiers. In a March 23, 1942, broadcast from Fort Knox, Kentucky, Wally Butterworth interviewed Corporal Morris Harris, an African American soldier assigned to the mess, one of the "service" jobs to which black soldiers were restricted.

The interview, though ostensibly a symbolic effort at including African Americans into the *Vox Pop*'s wartime public, bore a strong resemblance to the kinds of minstrel representations, like *Amos 'n' Andy*, that had played such a foundational role in building radio's national audience:

> WB: How long have you been in the army and tell us how you got here?
>
> MH: Seven months Saturday. Well, I tell you truthfully, I was walking down Seventh Avenue one day and a black cat crossed my path and I woke up the next morning inducted.
> (laughter)
>
> WB: Well, now tell me the truth. I'd like to talk a little about you personally. Have you ever been in a pawnshop?
>
> MH: Now listen, Mr. Wally, if I had a nickel for every time I've been in pawnshop, I'd be a multi-millionaire.
> (laughter from WB, audience)
>
> WB: Have you got a girl, Morris? Or should I say, have you any *girls*?

MH: Oh yes, naturally.
   (laughter)
WB: Where are they?
MH: New York *and* Louisville.
   (laughter)
WB: Morris, now frankly tell me: how do these Louisville
   girls compare with the Harlem girls?
MH: Now, wait a minute. There are girls listening in New
   York and there are girls listening in Louisville, so
   I'm going to say it's about nip and tuck!
   (laughter)[53]

Harris was also one of the founding members of the Ink Spots and, with a little encouragement, he and several other black soldiers treated *Vox Pop* to an a cappella version of "Wham re bop de boom bam." The crowd of mostly white servicemen howled at the minstrel act and cheered the song, but in his notes on the broadcast, Johnson records a sense of remorse ("The interview is a bit racist") tempered by his acquiescence to the essentially conflicted nature of radio's program for racial inclusion ("but it could be worse"). The song, on the other hand, was "Fantastic!"[54]

On other occasions, bitter controversies erupted over the use of racist language by white servicemen in reference to their African American fellows. In often heated language, members of the army and of the public weighed in on whether a white marine lieutenant had said "Negro" or used a more offensive term in a 1945 interview when describing a black sailor who had performed heroically during a particular battle. Congressman Charles M. LaFollette weighed in on the controversy in defense of the white officer. LaFollette hoped that the show's public recognition of "Negro heroism" would be an important step in the direction of a more unified military effort. Black servicemen and audience members, however, were less impressed. A group of twenty-five African American soldiers, to cite just one example, signed a letter calling for the elimination of "such humiliating expressions" on future broadcasts.[55] African Americans at home also expressed their displeasure. Echoing the sentiments of the March on Washington movement and anticipating the civil rights movement to come, Mrs. L. B. O'Neal of Long Island City, New York, wrote:

> Please make it a point in the future to rehearse such programs because
> I believe if such a thing continues there will be a terrific war over here

between the white and colored men.... "The colored man and woman" will not take in the future what they have suffered in the past.[56]

Similar controversies erupted in the late 1930s, as when Governor Carl Edward Bailey of Arkansas described his family on the air: "Five sons, one daughter, one daughter in law, three niggers, two horses and a wife." Parks Johnson's response was, "Well, that's fine!"[57] Although NBC received a great deal of mail about this incident, it seemed not to register with the same kind of intensity for Johnson as wartime incidents would. The problem of adequately representing African Americans as part of the war effort and as part of "the people" seemed to become more heated as the war neared an end and Americans began to look toward the shape of postwar American society. In a March 1945 letter, James L. Stuart, an African American second lieutenant in the army, wrote to complain about the lack of attention paid to black contributions to the national defense:

> Did it occur to you that of the more than 700,000 Negroes in the Army, alone, over 75% are in some theater of operations? I hate to think of this as an error of commission. But I can hardly conceive of a program for which arrangement had to be made across numerous continents being presented without the thought of bringing in all of our citizens. So, I must decide that this omission was deliberate.[58]

The show's blending of intimacy with military service resonated strongly with many family members of servicemen and -women. Letters poured in from families of soldiers begging to hear their voices when the show traveled to their training camp, barracks, or hospital. Families of soldiers who had been reported missing in action used the program's interviews with soldiers and sailors recently returned from overseas as a kind of broadcast bulletin board. Using *Vox Pop* as a middleman to contact servicemen who might have some information about what had become of their loved ones, these listeners turned the show's format into a network for communicating across the lines of official secrecy.[59]

However, many listeners were alarmed by *Vox Pop*'s ability to publicize things that were meant to be private. The show's marriage of intimate chatter, merchandise prizes, and interviews with military personnel was the source of a good deal of conflict, as competing interests collided. Many feared that national security was threatened by *Vox Pop*'s probing. Questioning soldiers and defense workers about the color of U.S. submarines, the number of rounds a particular weapon can fire, and the details about other military ordnance, and then rewarding them for their answers with fabulous gifts—this process struck many as downright treasonous, prompting several complaints to the Office of War Censorship and a subsequent federal investigation.[60] Listeners also objected strenuously to incidents in which interviewees displayed sympathy for the enemy, particularly in cases where discussion lingered too long on Japanese casualties.[61]

Letters like the one from James L. Stuart epitomized the risk of combining live radio and the voices of amateurs, that is, the people. By war's end, *Vox Pop* had moved to safer ground, shilling for postwar corporations, chambers of commerce, and the Hollywood film and television industries that would play such a huge role in shaping the culture and politics of the 1950s. In its final years, *Vox Pop* broadcast from the premieres of blockbuster movies, from grounds of regional festivals, and from the campuses of the gigantic automobile plants that were moving into postwar operations. *Vox Pop* once again became a roving publicity-generating machine. With its connection to the "voice of the people" increasingly attenuated by the turn to corporate publicity and "pseudo-events," and the loss of the sense of unified purpose that the war had evoked, the show lost steam and was canceled in 1948.

In this climate of consumerism and Cold War anxiety, radio's preoccupation with the people underwent a dramatic change. Audience-participation shows featured average Americans as consumers of postwar appliances and as private people involved in intimate relationships. The postwar years were the heyday of the quiz show, with bigger and bigger jackpots matching the stirrings of the consumerism and economic prosperity that would characterize life for millions of Americans over the next decade. ABC's *Stop the Music,* with its outlandish twenty-thousand-dollar jackpot, became such a hit in its debut year of 1948 that it pushed NBC's popular *Fred Allen Show* out of its Sunday-night time slot and off the air for good.

Taking advantage of radio's intimate address, audience-participation programs in the postwar period forsook images of public life and turned toward the most personal parts of their audience's lives. Programs like *Queen for a Day* (1945–57) combined the competitive format of the quiz show with the increasingly prurient impulse of the human-interest program. The show invited listeners into the private problems of women, rewarding personal miseries with material gifts.

Bride and Groom (1945–50) interviewed couples on their way to and from the altar. On *The American Women's Jury* (1944–45), average women told their stories of marital woe to a panel of twelve members of local women's clubs who offered advice in the form of a "verdict." *The Lonesome Gal* (1941–mid-1950s) offered its mostly male audience the pleasures of parasocial intimacy. In between spinning torchy ballads, the show's sultry host purred into the microphone, professing her loyalty to her "lover," the listener, and pushing pipe tobacco and other sponsors' products.[62]

During this postwar era, disillusioned veterans wrote Johnson to register their disappointment with the postwar American life that radio in general, and *Vox Pop* in particular, was promoting. For some veterans, the promise of postwar life proved elusive and they wrote to Parks Johnson merely to have their voices added to the program's public record. A young woman recently discharged from the WACs wrote comparing *Vox Pop*'s format to a "widespread peace program" that involves "education in the ways, beliefs, and occupations of peoples all over the earth."[63] A successful and decorated air force major who had been interviewed on the show in August 1945 wrote to Johnson several times after the war, relating to him his frustrations with the materialism, corruption, and hollowness of public and private life in postwar America: "I just can't think in terms of the values that the so-called 'normal' person is today. . . . this kind of thinking does nothing but put us overseas again." This veteran blamed the rampant greed and corruption in postwar society for his lost bid to elective office, the breakup of his marriage, and his inability to find a meaningful place in society.[64]

A group of young veterans writing from Saint Petersburg, Florida, echoed this sentiment, bitterly complaining about the town's refusal to help recently discharged GIs find adequate housing. The group had been devoted listeners to *Vox Pop* during the war and were alarmed to find that the show was planning to visit the town at the invitation of the chamber of commerce to promote the city's economic growth and tourism: "When they had a chance to let servicemen rent homes and apartments, they went ahead and advertised and brought the [non-veteran] people in here in droves, and now we have VETERANS living in cars, garages, etc." These veterans, keenly aware of *Vox Pop*'s postwar power to generate publicity for municipal, regional, and corporate entities, but also aware of the space opened up for them by the program's

ostensible commitment to the voice of the people, were part of a growing number of listeners who rejected an emerging postwar social and
cultural status quo.[65]

In its wartime convergence of consumer desires, national service,
and the voice of the people, *Vox Pop* could barely contain the unpredictable voices of its public. And with war's end, *Vox Pop*, like network radio itself, would have its hands full speaking for a public that
had grown accustomed to the sound of its own voice. *Vox Pop*'s evo-
lution from the man in the street in the New Deal era to women in
uniform during World War II to a mere roving publicity circus at the
dawn of the television age is only one story out of thousands in
the history of broadcasting. But it is a story that traces with remarkable accuracy the larger trajectory of network radio's complicated
representations of its national audience, an audience that grew both
in sheer numbers and in cultural and political significance over this
sixteen-year period (1932–48).

Throughout the war years, *Vox Pop* hailed desiring subjects of all
sorts as the imperatives of defense work and war morale worked to
mute traditional exclusions that were constitutive of the political public
sphere. The private chatter of these public interviews became increasingly unruly, as women expressed their desire to work postwar and postwedding, as African American listeners objected sharply to officers'
casual use of racial epithets, and as the ritual gift giving drove home
the relentless desiring that postwar life would require.

For sixteen years, in widely divergent formats, *Vox Pop* exemplified
network radio's preoccupation with finding and defining its own national audience and conflating that audience with the nation itself. In
the process, *Vox Pop* did much to spark radio's preoccupation with
the national implications and private motivations of the new mass audiences tuning in to the new medium. In the process of redefining radio's
public in terms of consumption rather than politics, *Vox Pop*'s public
lost its democratic-sounding voice but learned to speak in the language of desire, where the personal is sometimes political and always
compelling.

From the wildly successful *Stop the Music* in the late 1940s to the
quiz-show scandals on television in 1958–59, quiz shows were essentially the only national radio broadcasts featuring the voices of average Americans. On local blues, country, and rock-and-roll stations,
however, a new set of populist accents was beginning to take advantage of the void created by the networks' turn toward television. In the

1960s, the radio call-in format emerged as the heir to the audience-participation impulse. By the 1970s, talk radio had come into its own as Americans began tuning in the voices of average people talking politics and mediated by professional "hosts." With the return of untutored voices like Wilburn Gladsby's to the airwaves, the strange career of the voice of the people had, in some ways, come full circle.

The preoccupation with the voice of the people continues today on radio, television, and the overtly "interactive" media technologies of more recent vintage. Each innovation in "reality programming" brings with it another spasm of popular ambivalence as the voices, faces, and bodies of the people saturate the media landscape. Perhaps the larger cultural work of this decades-long process has been to make way for a culture where surveillance itself becomes the most popular and economical form of mass entertainment and where public and private denote kinds of performance rather than discrete places.

CHAPTER 3

Public Affairs: The Soap-Opera Cultural Front

When these busybodies were gossiping
about our private affairs, they couldn't really
hurt us—because no one could say for sure
if the rumor was true or not, but this—
this is something public.
—*Jane, speaking to her domestic, political, and
business partner Judy, in* Judy and Jane

Soap operas come so heavily drenched in the suds of previous cultural criticisms and assumptions that the task of attempting a fresh critique is daunting. The term "soap opera" is so laden with negative connotations that it has become a free-floating term of abuse, handy for dismissing any cultural production that appears excessively maudlin, commercialized, or that focuses interminably on the intricacies of human relationships at the expense of subtlety or taste.[1] "Speaking of soap operas," to borrow a phrase from Robert Allen, inevitably means speaking about women and their place as members of and symbols for the mass-mediated audience. It also means speaking about the importance of home as a site of reception and as a symbol of the social organization of modern life. How interesting, then, to discover in the earliest years of serial drama on the radio a wide world of dynamic and highly ambivalent stories about the inventive ways that women (and a handful of maternal men) reorganize the social boundaries of their homes and their larger communities.

Almost from the inception of the daytime serial format, it has been axiomatic for critics to focus on its uniformly and intensely domestic character. It has also become axiomatic to focus on the mostly female audience and the essentially female mode of reception that soap operas called into being—or resurrected and translated from print-based forms of melodrama.[2] For more than seventy years, corporate sponsors such as Procter & Gamble have been self-conscious and overt in their pursuit of an atmosphere of woman-centered domesticity in which to sell their wares and, just as important, the domestic ideal that would require an almost endless need for such wares. Critics have been quick to point to the social and political ills of such an atmosphere. The plush, almost claustrophobic interiors, the nearly exclusive focus on the goings-on of a handful of families, the emphasis on dialogue, close-ups, and emotional crises—it is impossible to imagine the soap opera in terms other than those most evocative of the domestic sphere. As Rudolph Arnheim has put it, "the world of serials is quite clearly a 'private' world in which the interests of the community fade into insignificance.[3] James Thurber captures the essential domesticity of the soap opera vividly in his Soapland essays, from 1948:

> Since the problems of the characters are predominantly personal, emotional, and private, affecting the activities of only five or six persons at a time, the basic setting of soap opera is the living room. But even the living room lacks the pulse of life; rarely are heard the ticking of clocks, the tinkling of glasses, the squeaking of chairs, or the creaking of floor boards. Now and then, the listener does hear *about* a hospital, a courtroom, a confectionary, a drugstore, a bank, or a hotel in the town, or a roadhouse, or a large, gloomy estate outside the town limits, but in most small-town serials, there are no signs or sounds of community life—no footsteps of passersby, no traffic noises, no shouting of children, no barking of dogs, no calling of friend to friend, no newsboys to plum the evening papers against front doors.[4]

What are we to make, then, of the soap-opera heroines who become United States senators *(The Story of Mary Marlin)*, city council presidents and tax assessors *(Judy and Jane)*, presidents of companies *(The Life of Mary Sothern)*, crusading attorneys *(Portia Faces Life)*, doctors *(Joyce Jordan, MD)*, private investigators *(Kitty Keane, Inc)*, defense workers *(Stella Dallas, Front Page Farrell, Kitty Foyle, One Man's Family)*, owner operators of lumber mills *(Ma Perkins)*, and community leaders in the establishment of countless hospitals *(Young Dr. Malone, The Right to Happiness)*, free clinics *(Big Sister, Life Can Be Beautiful, The Life of Mary Sothern, Young Widder Brown)*, orphanages *(Hilltop House, Pepper Young's Family)*, and neighborhood parks *(The Second*

Mrs. Burton)? What are we to make of the nearly ubiquitous presence of community-reform movements, headed by women, to combat unemployment *(The Life of Mary Sothern, Judy and Jane)*, crumbling tenements *(Portia Faces Life)*, illegal gambling *(Judy and Jane, Lorenzo Jones, Portia Faces Life, The Life of Mary Sothern)*, and juvenile delinquency *(The Guiding Light, Life Can Be Beautiful, Judy and Jane)*, espionage *(Portia Faces Life, Ma Perkins)*, and various fraudulent schemes *(Lorenzo Jones, Ma Perkins)*? What are we to make of soap-opera plots in which the most severe crises of the intimate sphere—illnesses, problematic pregnancies, marital discord, and unruly children—are inextricably linked to the machinations of corrupt businessmen and politicians and for which the only resolution is community-wide collective action? What do we do with male characters like Papa David in *Life Can Be Beautiful*, Curt Bradley in *Pepper Young's Family*, Bill Davidson in *Just Plain Bill*, Danny Stratford in *The Life of Mary Sothern*, Reverend Ruthledge in *The Guiding Light*, and Paul Barbour in *One Man's Family*, who often function as maternal figures in their unorthodox families? Finally, how do we explain the ubiquity of class tension as the single greatest obstacle to romantic love—that is, to the happily-ever-after that is the quarry of all melodrama?[5]

Perhaps a small part of the explanation for this gap lies in the change over time in the sound and feel of serial drama between the early 1930s, when they begin in earnest, and the early and late 1940s, when Arnheim and then Thurber set themselves the tasks of listening to and writing about them. Even Thurber concedes that some of them "began as authentic stories of small-town life" before caving inward on themselves in the face of the "interminability" of the serial format.[6] But the notion that realistic serial drama of the 1930s naturally gave way to the hermetically sealed interiority we have come to recognize as *true* soap opera exaggerates the extent of this shift while providing nothing in the way of a historical explanation for the profound popularity and unprecedented staying power of this genre. Also, it reinforces the myth of 1930s exceptionalism, which confines radicalisms of many kinds to a single decade, a magical and unsustainable moment, for which we can only feel nostalgia.[7] Thurber's analysis is significant for how perfectly it captures the dominant view of soap operas from their first appearance in the early 1930s to the present day. For radio researchers, journalists, and wags, washboard weepers of the 1930s and 1940s were almost uniformly dismissed as domestic drivel for neurotic, home-bound housewives. For regular listeners, however, it is likely that they meant something quite different.

This chapter argues that the exclusive emphasis on soap operas' domesticity obscures as much as it reveals. Radio soap operas, like the other radio genres and performances considered thus far, are intensely focused not on domesticity per se, but rather on the public/private dichotomy in American social life. In particular, the radio soap operas that I have examined from the late 1930s and through World War II call attention to the limits of this dichotomy as a way to understand local community, relations between the sexes, and, most surprising of all, the political economy of the United States. Soap operas sound, at first hearing, like a world of hypertrophied domesticity—virtuous, stalwart women rescuing feckless, inconstant men, and leading families through a never-ending series of trials. Under close examination of hundreds of scripts, recordings, and correspondence, the soap operas of the late 1930s and early 1940s depict a world preoccupied with but highly ambivalent about the real-life consequences of sharply separated spheres.

From the early days of the "hypodermic theory" of mass communications to the present, critics of soap operas and other mass-mediated melodramas have called attention to the phenomenon of audience members who seem to confuse fictive worlds of their favorite shows with the real world. Seen in this light, the parasocial intimacy forged between "truly human" soap-opera characters and their listeners provides more evidence for the critique of mass culture as the spread of irrationality and gullibility to the mass-mediated audience.[8] And given the assumption of an exclusively female audience for soap operas, this critique reinforces the notion that the irrational, mass-mediated audience is essentially a feminine one. Seen in light of the larger discourse of "average Americans" heard on *Vox Pop* and in the Fireside Chats, however, the claims to realness on serial dramas—and the corresponding intimate connection felt by some listeners—require a more nuanced critique, along with a closer examination of the texts of these dramas in the context of their production and reception.

Although rhapsodic paeans to the pleasures of domesticity were de rigueur in the serial dramas of the period, the solution to most domestic crises required the messy and unorthodox blending of the home, the marketplace, city hall, and some broadly ineffable sense of national community. The plots moved inexorably toward linking—often in highly stylized ways—the personal happiness of the "typical Americans" depicted in the soaps to the economic fortunes of the community in which they lived, and often of the nation itself. In particular, the resolutions of intimate crises were almost always linked to a collective solution to a public dilemma. The discourse of home became the code through which factories were built, mill workers were represented, and community health care needs of the under- and unemployed were guaranteed.

Hilmes has demonstrated how auteur Jane Cruisinberry was tightly constrained by network and sponsor executives who demanded that story lines for *Mary Marlin* be neither too public nor too private. "Yet these strictures were constantly challenged and violated."[9] Women's strength and heroism derived not simply from their mastery of domestic affairs, but also from their ability to take advantage of the porous boundary between the home and the larger social and economic community of which it is a part. Men's unreliability as lovers and breadwinners sometimes made them more available as parents, guardians, and nurturers of children.

This seeming contradiction between domesticity with a vengeance, on the one hand, and the highly stylized wedding of public and private affairs, on the other, can be understood best by examining two closely interrelated tropes at the center of nearly every soap opera from this period: the "truly human" story and the home in crisis. The first trope derives from the controversial appeal of "real-life," "true-to-life," or "truly human" stories, which, serial drama announcers promise, many listeners respond to, and critics deride. If domestic insularity is the most common complaint about serial drama, then the lack of "realism" runs a close second. In particular, soap operas have been mocked for pacing so slow it borders on the surreal: seventeen days to go through a revolving door in one extreme example.[10] In a narrative structure where dialogue, emotional distress, and mundane domestic activities stretch out to fill days and weeks of "action," social and economic realism seems to be neglected. *"There is no case,"* Arnheim concludes in a passage so important that he placed it in italics, *"of a factory worker, a miner, a skilled or unskilled laborer, playing an important role in any of the 43 serial samples."*[11] "Gainful employment," Jim Cox observes more recently, "simply wasn't a priority for most serial characters," leaving them free to obsess over emotional, rather than financial, crises.[12] Arnheim lists occupations that were reserved almost exclusively for men, which neglects the predominance in serial drama of women characters, women's work, and the often incommensurable class status—and precariousness—of women compared to men.[13] And although the diegetic action of most serials occurred outside the workplace, gainful employment was, as we shall see, at the center of the often emotional scenes between characters.

And, of course, the outlandish intensity and frequency of disaster, illness, and intrigue in the plots of the serials were a source for serious criticism. Dr. Louis Berg, a psychiatrist, found that listening to soaps caused anxiety and high blood pressure.[14] Soaps were also a source of endless parody, of which Bob and Ray's "Mary Backstayge, Noble Wife" was a particularly popular example.[15] Although critics howled at the outrageous story lines, audience research from the period suggests that listeners felt strongly about the emotional truths that linked their own lives to those of their favorite characters. As we will see, emotional expressions of social dislocation, however exaggerated, were key to the sense of realism for audiences. As in the controversies surrounding *Vox Pop*'s wartime mobilization of "average people," unruly populist and feminist impulses were in conflict here with concerns about upholding aesthetic standards, as well as traditional family configurations and gender roles.

Anxiety about social dislocation is also at the center of the second trope, that of the home in crisis. The centrality of home, as setting, as object of desire, as sinister character, as source of moral danger or refuge, abounds in the radio soaps. But incessant talk of the virtues of home provides cover, in moments of crisis, to talk about the limits of the traditional family home and the promise of ideal institutions beyond the domestic sphere, including the promise of a revitalized national community. As Wendy Kozol put it in her analysis of the 1940s photo-essays in *Life* magazine, these "narratives . . . aligned domesticity with nationalism."[16] The tension between the good home, which was always small, and the bad home, which was always big, became a compelling way to talk about class divisions and about the limits of the family home as fulfillment for the desires and potential of women. In the small, even cramped, homes of soap opera, traditional family structures were rare. Instead, heterogeneous gatherings of outcasts, orphans, and companions were cared for by powerful maternal figures, most of whom were women. And, in many cases, the responsibilities of mothering required these women and men to move in and out of domestic space both rhetorically and physically. In the elaboration of each of these interrelated tropes, we will see that the domestic sphere as portrayed in radio soap operas was, above all, the place where the problem of separate spheres became most powerfully evident. It also became the site where women characters were best positioned to reveal this problem and to reimagine a new social organization.

It is necessary to pause here briefly to mention some of the unique characteristics that distinguish the radio daytime serial from its television offspring. In my introductory remarks I have not bothered with this distinction, referring, for instance, to the "suffocating interiors" and "close-ups"—features that, Thurber observes, have their aural origins in radio serials, but that have since become more vividly associated with the newer, visual medium. Radio soaps conveyed the sounds of domesticity and interiority through the placement of microphones close to actors' mouths, the virtual lack of environmental background noises, the announcer's omniscient narration, complete with descriptions of domestic interiors, and, of course, the diegetic preoccupation with the goings-on of "family life."[17]

Michele Hilmes has pointed to the censorship and gendered logic of networks and sponsors that severely restricted the political and artistic possibilities of radio soap-opera writers and producers.[18] Although these restrictions were regularly challenged, it is hard to deny that they helped to shape the intensely interior, domestic, and intimate sound of the soap opera. These insights help by directing us to look beyond the individual work of art or artist and to understand soap-opera conventions as a mediated form shaped partially by the demands of the audience and partially by a set of restrictions and assumptions placed on it by sponsors, producers, and network censors. These were responded to and occasionally resisted by writers, actors, and listeners.

Robert Allen has encouraged an approach to soap operas not in terms of their aesthetics but instead in terms of their poetics, that is, the generalized conventions that shape a particular genre.[19] In this way, he draws attention not just to the plot where things seem to move at a snail's pace—or a revolving door's pace—but also to the associational depth that ties a large number of characters together. Actions occur seldom, but when they do, we get to understand them from many perspectives, each one marked by a complex historical past that provides additional layers of meaning for the most engaged and devoted members of the audience. This point seems to be relevant primarily in discussion of the television serial, with its larger casts, Byzantine plots, and exaggerated reliance on the shot–countershot framing of conversation between two principals. But this emphasis on associational depth is also useful in understanding the world of the radio serial and the persistent tropism for community. With its smaller ensemble casts, slow pacing, and emphasis on multiple intersecting relationships, the radio soap offers a slightly different example of Allen's notion of paradigmatic structure.

As we return to consider the central tropes at the heart of the radio serials of the 1930s and 1940s, it is important to remember Hilmes's point about the essentially contested ground on which the production of serials for women stood; also we must bear in mind Allen's argument that the serial plot's meaning takes shape in its circulation through an interpretive community. The stories—contested, vetted, often outrageous—serve, ultimately, as vehicles for the sustenance and elaboration of communities.

Typical Americans
Perhaps the most reliable cliché in the soap-opera oeuvre of the 1930s and 1940s is the announcer's introductory promise of a "real-life," or "truly human," story about "typical Americans." Like *Vox Pop* and the other audience-participations programs of this period, the serial drama promised a "true-to-life" account of human experience that served the commercial interests of advertisers while echoing the New Deal–tinged politics of populism and participatory democracy. And, like the Fireside Chats, soap operas were self-consciously framed as an intimate address to an "average" American listener. Soap operas' claims to realness are the boldest of all, however, promising to deliver through formulaic melodrama "a living, breathing reenactment of the day-to-day activities of typical American people."[20] Critics are quick to deride the routine resurrection of dead characters and the elaborate romantic entanglements as damning evidence of a mass-mediated break from reality and rationality. The phenomenon of fans writing to soap-opera characters—rather than to actors, writers, or producers (i.e., "real people")—is cited as further evidence of this break.[21]

Soap operas encouraged a closeness between listeners and characters that would come to be called "parasocial intimacy" by academic critics in the postwar period. *Pepper Young's Family* began each broadcast in 1941 with an invitation to "join your friends, the Youngs." The introduction to *Young Widder Brown* in this same period promised "life as we really live it." *Portia Faces Life* is described as "a deeply human story," *Stella Dallas* as "the moving drama of true life and mother love," *The Right to Happiness* as "truly human," and on and on. The announcer for *The Life of Mary Sothern* identifies himself as just another highly invested witness to the real-life events on the show. He frets about the imminent dangers posed to the principal characters: Max's old brain injury, Mary's troubled pregnancy, and so forth.[22]

The soap-opera promise of "truly human" and "typical American" experience derives its credibility from the emotions shared in common by fictional protagonists and their audiences. Powerful expressions of love, loss, and uncertainty about the immediate future are at the center of that shared emotional experience. And the main conflicts that evoke these feelings center on the experiences of women who inhabit a problematic social location: despite highly conventional familial mores and desires, they lack a stable and legitimate social identity. These heroines' struggles convey a sense of *being out of place.* The introductory epithets, such as "a truly human story," are frequently followed by an explanation of the particular predicament of social placelessness that provides the protagonist with her heroic struggle. In *Portia Faces Life,* the heroine is a widow, a mother, and also a lawyer. Her "deeply human story" describes her as "a woman forced to make her way in a man's world." Widows struggling with the incompatible roles of breadwinner, lover, and often mother—while fending off custody-seeking in-laws and unwanted suitors—featured in a large number of serial plotlines. *Young Widder Brown* was introduced each week as "The story of life as we really live it for a romantic young woman with two fatherless children." *Portia Faces Life, Judy and Jane, The Romance of Helen Trent,* and *The Life of Mary Sothern* represent other notable examples of this same dilemma.

Orphans adopted by, but ill adapted to, new families played central parts in *Life Can Be Beautiful,* as well as in *The Guiding Light* and *Today's Children.* Orphans or abandoned children play major roles in *Our Gal Sunday, Judy and Jane, This Is Nora Drake,* and *Vic and Sade.* By far the most common situation for soap-opera heroines was to be out of place within their own marriage in terms of social class. *Stella Dallas, Our Gal Sunday, Mary Noble, Backstage Wife,* and *Lora Lawton* are just a few of the most popular in this vein. The difficult role of stepmother was another highly popular device for emphasizing the "real-life" experience of displacement within the family. Such tensions were at the heart of *The Second Mrs. Burton, The Romance of Helen Trent,* and *The Carters of Elm Street* and played a smaller role in the plotlines of *Stella Dallas* and *Pepper Young's Family.* Other forms of social displacement abounded. Older immigrant men, alone in a new country, struggled to make their own hybrid families *(Life Can Be Beautiful, Judy and Jane)*. The earliest nexus of story lines on *The Guiding Light* concerned a Jewish teenaged girl whose scandalous affair with her married WASP boss leaves her ostracized from her tradition-bound immigrant community; the show also featured a mysterious itinerant artist who refers to himself as "Mr. Nobody from Nowhere," and a young boy abandoned by traveling, scam-artist parents and taken in by a kindly minister.

Because radio soap operas generally have smaller casts of characters than their television descendants, the struggle of the lone protagonist to succeed despite some form of displacement was often the only, or at least the central, story unfolding day after day, year after year. Also, the intractability of these problems of social displacement was so clear, and the feelings of sympathy they evoked so universal, that they generated an endless supply of stories. For these reasons, a soap opera could announce the same central tension at the start of every broadcast ("Can this girl from a mining town in the West find happiness as the wife of a wealthy and titled Englishman?") and perform daily variations on it indefinitely, or at least for decades.[23]

Although very few listeners could boast a dilemma identical to that of *Our Gal Sunday*, audience research conducted during the early 1940s suggests that the emotional pain caused by such dislocations struck listeners as "true to life." As the announcer for *Lorenzo Jones* said of the working-class Jones family, "Their struggle for security is anybody's story."[24] Herta Herzog, a researcher with the Office of Radio Research at Columbia University, reviewed all the audience surveys available by 1942. She found that the top three "listening gratifications" listeners gave to explain their tuning in to soap operas—emotional release ("a chance to cry"); commiseration (it "made them feel better to know that other people have troubles, too"); and as "a source for advice" about their own problems—all lent credence to the idea that listeners found the stories (or at least the emotional pain the stories evoked) "realistic." Indeed, a third of these listeners offered their own suggestions for soap-opera plotlines that would dramatize—and solve—their own domestic problems. Some of the more common examples include being forced to live with in-laws as a condition of marriage; parents demanding the entire contents of the pay envelope of a working daughter; the sudden transformation of husbands into gambling, adulterous wretches; and the broader problem of coping with "racial and religious differences."[25]

These suggestions reveal a broad interest in soap-opera solutions to various kinds of uneasiness in the domestic sphere. Again, researchers assume an exclusively female audience, despite the fact that unprecedented numbers of men found themselves at home and out of work during the day in the 1930s. This assumption, along with those about the education, morality, income, and intelligence of the audience, limit our ability to understand the full range of listener response. Hertzog found little correlation between listening to soaps and income, involvement in public affairs, emotional distress, or education.[26] A 1947 poll of the congregations of "almost all Protestant churches in the United States" found that four of the ten radio programs that "most faithfully portrayed American life" were soap operas.[27]

Soap operas' claims to realism are based in their explorations of various types of domestic uneasiness: the problem of feeling out of place at home. Taken together, they call attention to the staginess and melodramatic impracticality of an idealized, private sphere of domesticity. Soaps have been heavily criticized for their atmosphere of perpetual worry, crisis, and impending doom, exacerbated, no doubt, by the endlessness of the serial form. But such an atmosphere may be the inevitable result of characters talking to each other constantly about the failures of private life, without ever being allowed to make an explicitly political critique of the unsustainability of rigidly gendered spheres.

Irna Phillips, soap-opera *auteur extraordinaire,* was outspoken in defense of the daytime serial's claim to realism, particularly her own, in response to a *Variety* piece that mocked *The Guiding Light*'s "dubious setup of a spinster who wants to have a baby and is apparently going to adopt the unwanted infant of a young mother."[28] Phillips responded: "I am a proud spinster who adopted two children in their infancy, and there is nothing dubious about such a setup."[29] Elsewhere, Phillips asks, "Is there one of us that doesn't live a serial story? Such stuff is life made of."[30] She cites her experience of teaching the craft of serial writing to students at Northwestern University: "It was not surprising to me, after reading ten [autobiographical] manuscripts, to find that in the short period of twenty-odd years, illness, death, suicide, divorce, adoption, the problems of stepmother, stepfather—yes, of unrequited love—had all taken a hand in shaping the destinies of these young people."[31]

In her outline for the story line of *Painted Dreams,* widely considered to be the first daytime serial, Phillips makes clear the commercial rationale for dramas about domestic displacement and instability. Describing the story of Mother Moynihan as "a direct sales agent" to the prospective sponsor, Montgomery Ward, Phillips explains how the forfeiture of the Moynihans' house, the taking in of an orphan, and the ambivalent run-up to a daughter's marriage would create several new homes for the Moynihan clan and thus provide endless promotional possibilities for the sponsor's household products.[32] The soap opera's formal, ideological, and commercial givens make for an endless supply of truly human crises. The promise of family intimacy untouched by the divisions of social class, ethnicity, religion, and unequal gender roles is routinely reaffirmed and just as consistently undermined, a perpetual and profitable drama whose ideal stage is the family home.

Lynn Spigel argues brilliantly in *Make Room for TV* that early television situation comedies drew attention to the essential theatricality of postwar domestic life in plots and sets that revealed the performative and staged aspects of new ideas about domesticity. She links these programs to the nineteenth-century tradition of putting on plays in the parlor of the middle-class home.[33] The missing link in this chain of popular entertainment structured around the ideology of the middle-class home is the daytime radio serial. If the archetypal soap-opera dilemma is feeling out of place, then the inevitable—if Sisyphyean—task at the center of these dramas is the making and remaking of homes and the communities that sustain them.

Another major source of dislocation was, of course, World War II, and soap operas were one of many radio genres pressed into service by the larger cultural mobilization. The loss of fathers (to war) and mothers (to work) was a source of anxiety on the airwaves and in the off-microphone battles among sponsors, networks, and producers. The awkwardness of the returning veteran, especially the disabled one, figured in several serials. Phillips was eager to incorporate such characters into her cast of misfits on soaps like *The Guiding Light* and *Woman in White,* according to research by Horten.[34] But these story lines did not represent a break so much as a continuation, as the soaps adapted their thematic preoccupation with displacement to the specific displacements wrought by the war.

A key wartime subplot on *The Guiding Light* focuses on Claire Marshall, a single, urban journalist and adoptive mother. Claire's series of articles on juvenile delinquency focus on community-wide responses to changes in family life in the tenements of Five Points owing to the extraordinary labor demands of the war effort. Conflicts with her fiancé, a returning army veteran, over work and family roles figure as troubling first signs of the isolation she will soon face when marriage takes her out of her own apartment and into the suburbs and threatens her relationship to her adopted son Ricky. Tim Lawrence, a divorced army captain, is indifferent to Claire's crusading journalism and, when she calls him on this, responds with scorn to the idea of community and national responsibility for the well-being of wayward children. Ed Prentiss, *General Mills Hours*'s omniscient host of *The Guiding Light* (who also plays Ned, one such neglected youth), makes clear that these early spats foretell danger to Claire's home and family life.[35]

In an example of the fluidity with which advertising messages merged with the serial story lines, Prentiss begins this broadcast by alluding to the "struggle . . . in this time of war" of "every head of household—at home and abroad" to provide for his or her family. This affirmation of the war's displacement of father's bodies (*not* their authority as heads of households) stands in contrast to the sympathetic portrayal of Claire's struggle to maintain her status as the head of her own household and to her journalistic investigation into the collapse of patriarchal authority over "juvenile delinquents." "Every real wife and mother has but one goal," Prentiss continues, "her home and children." Here again, Claire's enthusiasm for other people's homes and children, as a social-minded reporter and as an adoptive mother, stands in stark contrast to Prentiss's prescriptive speech. Prentiss follows not with the predictable promise of Wheaties' wholesome goodness but with the offer of the family-centered goodness of the programs that comprise *The General Mills Hour: The Guiding Light, Today's Children,* and *The Woman in White*. The shows themselves, he seems to suggest, provide some help in the struggle for decent family life. He concludes with a promotional offer for ready-to-fly model airplanes ("to curb juvenile delinquency," Prentiss intones, requires "wholesome activities for youthful energies").[36]

Although such conservative themes as juvenile delinquency and mother and father's traditional roles abound during soap-opera broadcasts in 1944, they receive widely different treatment in the diegesis of the *The Guiding Light* and in the advertising chatter that formed the connective tissue of *The General Mills Hour.* Ed Prentiss was not merely the master of ceremonies during this hour, he also played tragic misfit Ned Holden, a victim of a recklessly absent father, on *The Guiding Light*. His shifting roles add to the sense that the stories were uneasily connected to each other, to the advertising messages, and to some larger national conversation with real women on the status of the American family.

Soap operas utilized many of the same rhetorical appeals to the great American "average" that characterized presidential addresses, audience-participation shows, and all manner of commercial broadcasts. On at least one occasion, Prentiss addressed his pitch for Wheaties and *The Guiding Light, The Woman in White,* and *Today's Children* to a "Mrs. Billingsley," whom he described as a composite of all the housewives listening to the noontime NBC broadcast.[37] In addition, Prentiss, like the announcers for other serial dramas, frequently read aloud letters from what were said to be "real" listeners; in one remarkable instance, Prentiss appeared to field a live telephone call from a "Mrs. Smith," an enthusiastic listener calling to praise the real-life quality of the *General Mills Hour* serials.[38]

The figure of the imaginary "typical" listener reappears during the diegesis of the serial dramas that form the center of *The General Mills Hour.* On *The Guiding Light,* Reverends Ruthledge and Gaylord deliver sermons at the start of some wartime episodes, directed simultaneously to the congregation of the fictitious Five Points Church and to the national listening audience, both of which celebrate the safe return of the troops and pray for those who won't be coming home.[39] During the summer of 1944, *Today's Children* concerned itself almost exclusively with "the murder trial of Bertha Schultz," broadcast before a live studio audience invited to play the part of the jury, along with the listeners at home who voted by mail on her innocence or guilt. Throughout the summer, members of this audience/jury were asked to speak on the air, live, about the proceedings of the trial, the veracity of testimony, and so forth. As with the audience-participation shows, the realness of these interviews is unmistakable, thanks to the halting, unprofessional speech of the audience members who make their way to the microphone, and even more convincingly, to those who, struck dumb at the last moment, refuse to say anything and scurry away despite the pleading of the interviewer/announcer.[40] Further, episodes featuring real people—public officials and so forth—"playing themselves" provided an additional layer of authenticity to the broadcasts.[41]

Homemaking

Talk of homes—good ones and bad ones—is ubiquitous in the soap operas I have examined from the 1930s and 1940s. What is most surprising is that, across the board, the good home is not defined by adherence to traditional gender roles and an "intact" nuclear family but rather by its size. *Vic and Sade,* for example, takes place in "the small house halfway up in the next block," a phrase that captures with admirable economy the habitus of the Gooks—Vic, Sade, and the adopted Rush: lower-middle-class, everyday folks who live in a community marked by its warm, informal sense of place and middle-American ordinariness.[42]

These small, good homes are often crowded with eclectic and nontraditional family groupings. In *Life Can Be Beautiful*, a runaway teenaged girl named Chichi finds a home with a deeply religious old Jewish man, Papa David, and a bitter but idealistic young lawyer confined to a wheelchair, Stephen. None of them are related to each other and yet theirs is perhaps the most morally exalted of all families in the soap-opera canon. They live in cramped quarters above the Slightly Red Bookstore in a gritty urban neighborhood plagued with criminals like Gyp Mendoza, who has designs on the lovely Chichi. The home she has made with Papa David and Stephen is the only bulwark she has against such threats to her virtue. Not content to let this domestic arrangement implicitly call into question traditional norms, Donald Bixby and Carl Becker, the show's writers and creators, contrive a kidnapping in which Chichi is delivered into Mendoza's hands by none other than her own biological mother![43]

Orphans, along with children of poverty and parental neglect, are brought into these small soap-opera homes in adoptions of varying degrees of formality and legality. Casual, temporary, official and unofficial, these adoptions, along with marriages of convenience and families broken and blended by divorce and remarriage, demonstrate that the good home of the soap opera is both fluid and heterogeneous. During the Depression, children bunk temporarily with other families while their fathers look for work out of town, as in *Pepper Young's Family;* or they become absorbed into the show's central family when their parents abandon them for lives of crime, addiction, and poverty, as in *Life Can Be Beautiful* and *The Guiding Light*. Sometimes, in their complexity, they appear to be travesties of the conventional family structure to which the announcers, advertisers, and central characters pay such homage. In *The Guiding Light*, Claire Marshall adopts Ricky, who is, unbeknownst to her, the biological son of her scheming fiancé, Captain Tim Lawrence, and his ex-wife, Nina Chadwick. When Claire and Tim marry, he becomes Ricky's adoptive *and* biological father, a doubly potent claim to patriarchal power that he marks by renaming the child twice, first "Rusty" and then "Tim Lawrence Jr." The small urban apartment in the "melting-pot neighborhood" of Five

Points where Claire lives alone with Ricky is portrayed as the good home in contrast to the rambling, isolated house they move to "out in the boondocks" of the suburb Riverdale after she marries Captain Lawrence.[44] Cut off from the city—and her job—by trains that run infrequently and the domestic demands of a larger home, Claire is out of place, in her home and in her own family, in which she is the only biological outsider. Like *Vox Pop*'s Cadette Frances Chandler, the defense worker who wanted to marry and keep her job, Claire confronts an emerging postwar reassertion of traditional domestic roles with some ambivalence.

Adults as well as children are taken into soap opera's hybrid families and cramped homes. In *Portia Faces Life,* Portia, a widow, lives with her son Dicky and her best friend, Katherine, a nutritionist. *Judy and Jane* features two women whose devotion to each other as business partners, as political allies, and as domestic life partners proves to be strong enough to weather a range of malicious intrigues designed to split them up. They share "the little white house" in a town outside of Chicago, which their Petticoat Party runs, with Jane's two children and Jerry, a business partner and sometimes suitor to Judy. In early 1937, they take in Ben Feinstein, a bankrupt and homeless immigrant movie producer, whose generosity, idealism, and lack of business sense were exploited by "greedy bankers" who ran him out of Hollywood. On *The Guiding Light*, Ellis Smith, also known as "Mr. Nobody from Nowhere," offers a romance-less, sexless marriage and home to Ruth Kransky, to protect her from the shame of a widely publicized sex scandal and the ostracization from her tightly knit immigrant tenement neighborhood in Five Points. In *The Romance of Helen Trent,* Gil Whitney chastely pitches woo to Helen in a series of fraught domestic settings, despite the machinations of Cynthia Carter Swanson Whitney, his "wife in name only."[45]

The homes in these soap operas are sites where related tensions about nation and family are negotiated. The constant crises of the "traditional" family home operate both as a critique of the narrowness of this ideal and as the occasion for increased vigilance about the porous borders of the family home and the nation it represents. Home invasions, of one kind or another, constitute a frequent plot device in stories involving romantic and business betrayals, class tensions, and various intrigues involving political corruption and social disruption. The interruption of the doorbell frequently heralds the arrival of an unwanted or dangerous new arrival to the community. These invasions

and arrivals, on *The Romance of Helen Trent, The Life of Mary Sothern, The Guiding Light,* and *Judy and Jane,* among others, threaten the
basic security of the domestic sphere and suggest larger national problems are at work: gambling rackets, corrupt businessmen, unstable
socioeconomic relationships, juvenile delinquency, shifting gender roles,
and the dislocations of the war.

On *Judy and Jane,* the women's cozy, cramped "little white house"
represents a haven from a series of big bad homes—each associated
with an oppressive domestic arrangement and unequal political, social,
and economic relations of power. The first and most significant is the
terrifying mansion inhabited by Jane's evil father-in-law, Father Sargent,
and—in another example of odd domestic pairings—his controlling
sister, Louella. Described as "that tomb they call a house," the big
house induces an inarticulate horror in Judy, Jerry, and Jane. The pairing of ailing, mutually contemptuous, but inseparable elderly siblings
and their "creepy" mansion recalls Poe's morbid and suspenseful tale
of incest, "The Fall of the House of Usher."[46] The most dramatic episode in the series's six-year run concerned their efforts to save Jane's
children from a custody battle with Louella that would have ended
with them living in the "creepy" mansion.[47]

In another exciting episode, Jane is taken against her will to the
home of gangster Charles Wilson, a mansion of gothic proportions,
guarded by a man with a tommy gun, hidden behind a long driveway,
complete with a vault hidden behind a working fireplace. There Jane
is nearly seduced by the lovely interior decor and Wilson's aggressive
propositions: "Won't you come into my parlor? said the spider to the
fly." The scene overflows with sexual tension and the stage directions
indicate that Jane's very presence, alone with a man in his home, should
exude a sense of indecency and danger. ("NOTE: PLEASE THREATEN
JANE'S VIRTUE AS MUCH AS POSSIBLE THROUGH INNUENDO. THE
LINES OF COURSE MUST BE INNOCENT" [February 10, 1937]). Jane
is, of course, saved at the last moment by Ben Feinberg, Judy, and
Jerry and whisked back home to the little white house.

Jerry is nearly seduced by a mansion-dwelling and vulgar socialite,
Patricia Van Cleve. Her millionaire father owns "Hopi Lodge," a
sprawling compound dedicated to his fetish for all things Native American. Patricia's contempt for the working class marks her as morally
corrupt in Judy's and Jane's eyes. Jane's only visit to Hopi Lodge, which
she undertakes ambivalently, starts poorly—the dinner conversation
turns on the merits of "the aristocracy of wealth" in the United States,

which is "just as grand" as European nobility—and ends worse, when her daughter spikes a fever and nearly falls victim to a terrible flu epidemic (March 5, 1937). This visit to the mansion spells the end of Jane's romance with Donald North, who reveals himself to be antidemocratic, snobbish, and, the last straw, domineering toward Jane. The only truly wholesome and constant love is that shared between Judy and Jane at the little white house they bought together. The transgressiveness of this relationship is underscored by the constant efforts of powerful elites to break them up financially, politically, and intimately. But the alignment of their domestic, political, and business relationships with social-justice causes, such as antiracketeering crusades, helps to guarantee that these transgressions will be endorsed, or at least forgiven, by their listeners. For Judy, Jane will forsake marriage. Despite the ardent attentions of Jerry, Judy seems completely uninterested in domestic companions other than Jane and her children.

The other key setting on the program is the Red Front department store, which Jane has been coerced to manage for her lazy, wealthy, and unwholesome in-laws. She surprises them with her successful business model, which involves hiring Ben Feinstein over their thinly veiled anti-Semitic opposition ("That fat little man!" Louella gasps), to bring his Hollywood creativity to bear on remaking the store (January 5, 1937). Jane and Ben decide to cater to a more working-class customer base, lowering prices and hosting parties and vaudeville shows at the store. The result is a big increase in sales and a dramatic shift in the clientele.

When Judy is framed by political rivals, Ben and Jane leverage the store's buying power, a Hollywood starlet's drive for publicity, and a charitable event for worthy children, to bribe and cajole the exculpatory truth to come out. The Red Front, the Petticoat Party, and the unorthodox family in the little white house are all inextricably entwined in the working out of the plot and the achievement of justice. The little white house, home to Judy, Jane, Jerry, and, at times, Ben, is also the hub around which a multiethnic political and social world revolves, bringing in immigrant farmers, husky longshoremen, and the other politically active women of the community. It is also a site for sociability, a place where gender roles are reversed, men cook for women, and, the announcer assures us, "gay" evenings abound (December 24, 1936).

Pepper Young's Family which ran, under various names, for twenty-seven years, was also one of the most popular soap operas—at one point it aired daily on all three networks, an unprecedented feat.[48] One of the four serial dramas to merit inclusion in the top ten programs that "most faithfully portrayed American life," it was also perhaps the most preoccupied with the moral contrast between small and large homes.[49] At the center of this Procter & Gamble–sponsored program's morality are the sanctity, cleanliness, and hospitality of the family home. But the Young household on Union Street seems to buzz with restless energy for much more, for collective action to solve a variety of thematically interrelated crises. Soon the preoccupation with good homes takes over the entire narrative and they begin proliferating across the town of Elmwood like the little green ones on a Monopoly board, resolving the social, economic, and romantic problems of all the main characters simultaneously.

By 1941, the Young family, a solidly middle-class, Middle Western clan, finds itself on the brink of homelessness. Patriarch Sam Young is out of work and in poor health and his family now rents the house they used to own. Curt Bradley, Sam's best friend and business partner, has moved to Chicago to look for work, leaving his son Biff to live with the Youngs. Worse, their landlord is looking to sell to another family. This all coincides with teenage daughter Peggy's engagement to the rich Carter Trent of Chicago. Just as their own tenancy in their house appears most tenuous, Peggy visits the Trents' enormous mansion, which repels her. She calls off the engagement, thereby reaffirming her allegiance to her own family and class, expressed exclusively in terms of her love for the Young home—which is cramped, unlike the cold "museum" of the Trents, where she got lost and where a maid had tried to remove her own dress for her after a dance. This affront is the last straw, breaking interrelated taboos of intimacy and class, and sending Peggy hurtling out of the big house and into the cold Chicago night.

Safe at home in Elmwood, Peggy sings the praises of their own small home, "where everyone is all sort of mixed together," and rails against the Trent house:

> It's not a house at all, I mean it's not a home at all. It's just one big enormous gigantic palace. It's an enormous huge hotel. You couldn't really live in a house like that. Or have fun. You'd just lose yourself. I never could find my way downstairs from my room. Carter always had to stop for me. Oh, it was so complicated, with rooms after rooms![50]

The resolution to the Youngs' intimate and financial problems begins with a deus ex machina common to the small-town world of the soaps:

Mysterious interests from the big city—New York, in this instance—
want to build a home for retarded children in a small Midwestern
town. But it must be the right kind of community, run by the right
sort of people. The Youngs' community-based values—epitomized by
Peggy's rejection of the Trent mansion, Sam's status as former mayor,
and Mary's willingness to adopt the retarded children as their own—
make the choice of Elmwood inevitable. The original plan was for one
central big house—another mansion—to house the children, but Sam
insists on converting some abandoned vacation cottages into myriad
little homes.

Sam will be its director (a modestly paid position) and Mary will
serve as matron (an unpaid honorary position). The salary provides just
enough for the Youngs to buy back their own house. Their new occupations—overseeing the creation of little homes for the homeless—
protect them from losing their own. To drive home this point, Sam and
Mary will reprise the gendered domestic economy of their own home—
and of the homes of many of their listeners—in their work at the Children's Center. This act of charity quickly spreads to all of Elmwood.
Within a matter of days, the Youngs have lobbied the entire town,
starting with its most public institutions, the newspaper and the town
hall, to rally fund-raising support to establish the money to begin rais-
ing roofs over the children's heads. At the symbolic center of the small
home, "where everyone is all sort of mixed together," related themes of
civic responsibility for the vulnerable and contempt for the wealthy
are a New Deal vision of a revitalized nation.

Carter's rejection of his own family home—the big house that is
the Trent mansion—convinces Peggy to renew their engagement; thus
marriage and still another modest home await while Carter enlists in
the military, another signal that he has chosen the collective good over
private wealth. Peggy's temporary return to the nuclear family—and
the sexual innocence of youth—coincides with the Youngs' purchase of
their home, and their new role at the center of a larger family institution.

Inevitably, however, there is a catch. With the stability of the Youngs'
home life secure, Biff Bradley, their young boarder, confronts his own
domestic crisis. Biff's father Curt—who has been forced to relocate to
Chicago in search of work—decides to remarry, throwing Biff's sense
of home into turmoil. Abandoned by his mother, and now by his father,
who shocks everyone by bringing his fiancée (a jealous Mary calls her
an "adventuress") into the Young home, Biff hides in the cold, dark,
abandoned Bradley home where no one has lived for months.[51] At the

Youngs' house there is great concern for Biff's fate amid the dust, cold, and vastness of an abandoned house—another crisis of domestic, romantic, and financial dislocation, another set of intimate public challenges for the Bradleys, the Youngs, and, as listeners will discover, the wider social world.

The resolution to these personal domestic crises—Biff's response to enlist in the military for wartime duty so as to make the world safe for his new blended family, while also conveniently avoiding it—almost invariably involves a turn toward collective institutions and, again, a symbolic link to a national ideal of security and service. In the process of securing their own domestic space, the out-of-place protagonists of soap operas find it necessary to become homemakers—makers of homes—on a broader community-wide scale.

In General Foods' *Portia Faces Life,* Portia's fight to retain custody of her son and their home coincides with her efforts to maintain her struggling law practice, and with her crusade for better conditions in the tenements of her city, exposing white-collar criminals who steal funds slated for housing improvements: "I've been in those tenements," Portia tells the district attorney, "they're (SHE GROPES FOR THE WORD)... unspeakable! Until you've seen them, you can't imagine how human beings can live in such conditions. There hasn't been any money spent on them in years."[52] The battles merge into a single mission to make and redeem imperiled homes.

We see a similar pattern in *The Life of Mary Sothern* from the late 1930s. Less popular and long-lived than *Pepper Young's Family, The Life of Mary Sothern,* in many ways, adheres even more closely to the soap-opera conventions: a strong woman, several fallible, unreliable men, cliff-hanger plots involving crime, jury trials, diseases, romantic entanglements, love triangles, and catastrophic fires.

But here too we have a town—Sanders—whose economic fortunes are central to the lives of the main characters. They, in turn, are only able to resolve the threats to their personal lives when they have conceived of them in terms of the common fate of Sanders. The fact that Mary Sothern's husband, Max Tilley Sanders, is the scion of the town's founder—a gangster who defrauded the town and left it teetering on bankruptcy—makes the connections between family and community prosperity explicit.

In the space of several months in the mid-1930s, Mary's life, that of her unborn child, as well as her reproductive health were linked to the success of a bottling works owned by the Sanders Springs Trust, an outfit of which she was the president.[53] In addition, the proceeds of the bottling works were to finance a childbirth clinic serving the unemployed and impoverished mill workers of Sanders. A prospective factory, to be located in Sanders by the proverbial big-city interests, becomes the means of resolving Max's pending criminal trial for racketeering, as well as his sister's paralysis—the result of difficult labor exacerbated by Max's criminal activities—and finally will redeem him and the town in the eyes of everyone.

If *Pepper Young's Family* centers on the multiple meanings of home, then *The Life of Mary Sothern* seems to focus on the interrelationship between different kinds of "labor." The centrality of work—good, honest work, as opposed to gambling—is ubiquitous. But this distinction is not nearly as straightforward as it sounds. While the announcer exults, "Work: the blessed remedy for our ills,"[54] the two central characters most closely aligned with entrepreneurial capitalism agree that "all business is gambling" (episode 17). This tension echoes through all of radio serialdom, as in *Judy and Jane* when the debate about the merits of honest work versus "being connected" at the Hopi Lodge dinner table leads to Jane and Donald's falling out.

Mary's capacity for work—she is a retired movie star, current president of Sanford's biggest going concern, and the mother of two children from a previous marriage—rather than merely her domestic stalwartness is what makes her the center of the show. Indeed, when the childbirth clinic is in desperate straits, Mary considers the merits of making a quick twenty-five thousand dollars in Hollywood (episode 22). Although she ultimately opts to stay in Sanders for the sake of her husband and children, it is clear that she is just as important to the town's economic and social institutions. Mary feigns modesty ("Who ever said running a company and running a family was easy?"), but even then she cannot help drawing attention to the ease with which she moves across traditional gendered boundaries of work (episode 23). As Hilmes points out, the more conventional resolution to such dilemmas almost always wins the day on serial dramas, but the days of suspense about Mary's decision challenged the notion that her domestic concerns automatically determined her identity. This point is underscored not so subtly by Mary's retention of the last name Sothern, rather than Sanders, which her housekeeper Viola reinforces when she says, "You're Mary Sothern to me and you'll always be Mary Sothern to me" (episode 11). In another telling scene, Max, who spends a fair amount of time unemployed or underemployed, boasts of his skill in tucking in his adopted twins while Mary tends to her business responsibilities: "When I put the twins to sleep they stay asleep!" (episode 7).

When trouble strikes Sanders, it threatens laborers—in the mill, the factory, and at the bottling works. But it also threatens women laboring to bring forth children. The clinic is verging on bankruptcy and dependent on the success of the bottled water enterprise. When the springs are poisoned just before Mary, as president of the bottling works, takes a celebratory first sip, the fate of the clinic, the water business, and Mary's own pregnancy hangs in the balance. Mary loses the child and nearly dies (episode 28). Max's response to Mary's illness and lost child is a revenge killing for which he is arrested and charged with murder. What follows is a sensational trial, complete with moving testimony and cliff-hanger verdict. When the judge, jury, and prosecutor learn of Mary's lost baby, any chance at conviction disappears and Max celebrates by inviting them all back to their house—described elsewhere as a "cottage"—for a party (episode 56). Freed from prison, but still reeling from Mary's poisoned labor, Max takes up with a gambling syndicate, throwing Mary's plans for a new child into question and bringing on yet another criminal trial. Subsequently, Max's sister Phyllis nearly dies in childbirth too, and ends up confined to a wheelchair, forcing her husband Danny into the mother role for their two children. It is not until an episode in which Mary creates a new job for Phyllis—magazine girl in the lobby of the Stratford Arms Hotel, built on the site of the springs—that Phyllis emerges from her nearly suicidal depression. The first half of this episode, which features the celebratory opening of the hotel, consists entirely of snippets of phone conversations interspersed with the announcer's enthusiastic account of the happy news circulating through the town, creating a web of relationships that all hinge on the financial success of this latest enterprise (episode 113).

But the women of The Life of Mary Sothern are not always ill or pregnant; they utilize their own networks of communication to organize the political events of the town, though not as overtly as do Judy and Jane in Honeycrest. In one series of episodes, Max's position as town manager, endangered by his rumormongering rivals, is saved when Mary organizes the wives of the angry mill workers to contrive to keep them all home the night of a crucial town meeting to vote him out (episodes 101–6).

Meanwhile, a Mr. Barton has come to town from Chicago—another big-city deus ex machina—and after weeks of nervous agitation, Max and Mary convince him to build a big factory in Sanders, bringing desperately needed jobs. Max and Mary will preside over the factory in much the same way that Sam and Mary Young preside over the home for retarded children in *Pepper Young's Family*: for him it's a job, for her another labor in the mothering of the community. In addition, Mr. Barton, moved by Phyllis's plight—his own wife died from a similar labor-related injury years before—pays for an expensive operation restoring her ability to walk and to mother (episodes 101–20).

And so goes the cycle of public and private labors. The collective benefits of fruitful labors are in constant tension with the collective peril caused by corruption and unemployment. The town of Sanders, even more than *Pepper Young's Family's* Elmwood, emerges as a separate character—crippled by economic loss, riven by ancient rifts and class antagonisms, yet always game for the next big chance. The stories of these towns, like the cottages and small homes at the center of them, serve as compelling symbols for the larger story of economic struggle and national renewal.

Public Reception

There has not been a great deal of fan mail preserved by producers of serial dramas, and what little there is often is less representative of a true cross section of audience response than it is revealing of what sorts of responses interested serial drama producers and their sponsors. As part of her defense of serial drama's realism and social significance, Irna Phillips preserved letters from dozens of community leaders all across the country. Heads of local chambers of commerce, ministers, educators, and scout leaders wrote in praising the program's "sermons" on Memorial Day, Mother's Day, and Independence Day in 1944 and asking for copies to share with their communities. "If possible I should like to get a copy of the script used in the speech on the May 30th... program of *The Guiding Light*.... We have an enrollment of over 1,000 pupils in our school and I should like to make sure they hear the speech given on this program."[55] Clearly, this kind of response was useful in Phillips's continual battle with serial drama's critics, which included doctors and politicians, as well as reporters for *Variety*. Given the general assumption of an exclusively female audience for daytime serial drama—an assumption that Phillips shared—it is interesting to note that of the letters of this kind preserved from the summer of 1944, more than a third were written by men.[56]

At times one can get a sense of how some listeners thought about soap operas from their letters to the networks and other programs. A woman writing to President Roosevelt after his first Fireside Chat in 1933 suggested that he broadcast "at the beginning of a weekday coast to coast program such as . . . the Chicago *Myrt and Marge* program when the whole country is turned on for their program. . . . I believe this will insure a greater audience."[57] This listener evidently did not see a conflict between Roosevelt's national, official address and the routine reception practices of daytime serial dramas, with their emphasis on the local, the commercial, the personal, and the feminine. In letters to NBC, soap operas come in for stinging criticism throughout the 1930s and 1940s. Once again, the handful of letters that have been preserved indicate much about what the network found important—and alarming—about listener response to serial drama, but not necessarily what the average letter writer had to say. In extant letters from the network's "Program—Criticism, 1938–1941" folder, for example, listeners complained about the vulgar references to "having babies," making clear how central sex and sexuality were to the characters in the serials.[58] A listener in Kansas complained of "an unending parade of gangsters, kidnappers, thieves, murders, etc. on the daily radio serials. . . . If the intelligence of the American public is no higher than these stories indicate, then we are not fit for self-government."[59] A North Dakota woman complained that "advertisers should realize we like something besides all these violent stories, noisy, painful and sad, some of them— a few funny at times."[60] Given the network's almost obsessive preoccupation with its public image, it is likely these letters were saved because they indicated a significant dissatisfaction not only with the serial dramas, but with radio sponsors and commercial radio's representation of "the American public," in effect, the system of broadcasting that NBC depended on for survival.

Fan mail for *The Story of Mary Marlin* has been well preserved, comparatively speaking.[61] These letters reveal an audience deeply invested in the story and characters and well aware of Procter & Gamble's desire for good publicity in connection with its sponsorship. Many fans emphasized their own real-life suffering and dramas as a reason for their appreciation of the program. Sad tales of lost loves, women dying in childbirth, and invalidism characterized many letters. Others wrote asking for synopses of missed programs; a U.S. soldier in France wrote his family asking for an update on Mary's adventures. Many wrote with specific requests for the direction of the plot, particularly regarding the volatile relationship between Mary and her inconstant husband, Joe. And many wrote with threats to Procter & Gamble to discontinue buying Kleenex if the story didn't take a particular turn or if the company pulled its sponsorship completely. In some instances, intense passions accompanied these plot suggestions. "If Joe is killed for Mary to marry David Post then the author has committed murder."[62]

A handful of the 194,000 responses to the murder trial of Bertha Schultz, from *Today's Children*, remain and they reveal similarly heated emotions.[63] These writers were convinced of Bertha's innocence in the murder of Tom Leaming and point the finger at a surprisingly wide array of other potential suspects.

The Soap-Opera Cultural Front?

Given the almost universal contempt with which soap operas have been regarded for the last seven or eight decades, it is tempting and relatively easy to string together an impressive list of evidence to show that soaps did more than merely transcend the stereotypes of maudlin, lachrymose women and feckless, impetuous men locked in interminable and tasteless affairs, and to argue that they also constituted an unlikely but potent "cultural front"; that is, taken together, there is ample evidence to make the case that the political alignments and commitments of a broad-based collection of leftists active in the mass entertainment industries of the 1930s and 1940s informed the production and circulation of daytime serial drama.

To make such an argument, one would point to the profusion of Popular Front and New Deal themes that these dramas featured from the early 1930s through the end of the war. Although the explicit philosophies of soap operas were always relentlessly apolitical and conventional, the most consistent plot tensions in the programs I have listened to pitted the people against powerful elite interests. In this dichotomous formula, the interests of the working and middle classes were elided and posed against those of the business and criminal organizations. Thus, small-town doctors and mill workers battled big-city bankers and gangsters. Further, the multiethnic ethos of the Popular Front obtained on many programs, with explicit references made to the solidarity of middle-class protagonists joining forces with immigrants and others in order to fend off the threats of domestic dislocation, or homelessness. The enormous number of free or reduced-fee clinics for the poor to receive medical and legal aid makes it clear that one of the easiest ways to generate affection for soap heroes or heroines was to associate them with a community project designed to bring relief to the poor, if not to create a model of socialized human services.

Many programs emphasized multiethnic communities of working-class immigrants including Jews, Italians, Poles, Swedes, Slavs, Germans, and Irish. For example, *The Guiding Light, The Right to Happiness, Judy and Jane,* and *Life Can Be Beautiful* each featured Jewish immigrants as central protagonists, a fairly remarkable move in the anti-Semitic popular and political culture of the 1930s. Furthermore, *Today's Children* was set in a Chicago neighborhood described by John Dunning as "a melting pot of hopes and nationalities."[64] Other serials focusing on working-class or underclass families include *Houseboat Hannah,* in which the family is displaced to a Shanty Fish Row houseboat in San Francisco Bay after Hannah's husband loses an arm in a cannery accident.[65] *Mrs. Wiggs of the Cabbage Patch* was based on a novel, which in turn was based on a real slum in Louisville, Kentucky.[66] *Central City* and *Painted Dreams* featured main characters whose backgrounds were decidedly blue-collar.

Of course, class tension was at the heart of the dozens of serials that featured working-class women marrying into wealthy families and the inevitable snobbery and uneasiness and heartache. And even for the sturdily middle-class families like those featured on *Pepper Young's Family, The Life of Mary Sothern,* and *Judy and Jane,* concerns about unemployment, eviction, failed businesses, contested property lines, lost deeds, and other financial crises were ubiquitous. Frank Hummert of the amazing Frank and Anne Hummert "soap factory," which was responsible for producing dozens of serial dramas, described their programs as "successful stories about unsuccessful people."[67] Even Folger's Coffee addressed the economic crisis frankly in its sponsorship of *Judy and Jane:* "Has the old Depression made your wardrobe about as bare as old Mrs. Hubbard's cupboard?" asked the announcer as part of a giveaway campaign for Easter clothes.[68] If the "average people" on these and other serials were financially unsuccessful, and if that led inevitably to marriage problems, is it fair to conclude that soap operas, as a genre, constituted a critique of the class system told through the language of popular romance?

It doesn't feel like much of a stretch to note that the "Slightly Read Bookstore" and the "Red Front" department store put one in mind of political puns. Both of these provocatively named businesses are run by idealistic Jewish immigrants and serve working-class and immigrant communities. The bookstore in *Life Can Be Beautiful* serves as a half-way house for a runaway girl and as a legal aid clinic. The department store in *Judy and Jane,* with its vaudeville shows and low prices, succeeds because it attracts the customers who fill the theaters, stores, and workplaces in Michael Denning's *The Cultural Front* and Lizabeth Cohen's *Making a New Deal.* And, of course, some of the serials targeted a large working-class audience for whom left-populist themes about workers and immigrants were most welcome. Audience research in the 1940s suggests that working-class, rural, less educated women made up a disproportionate percentage of the audience for *Stella Dallas,* whose eponymous heroine came from a similar background.[69]

One could compile a list of the soap-opera writers and actors who were associated with the Popular Front and the antifascist left starting with Mercedes McCambridge, Agnes Moorehead, Joe Julian, Burgess Meredith, and Melvyn Douglas. And, if it didn't feel too much like a House Committee on Un-American Activities–type question, one might inquire as to why Frank and Anne Hummert, the industry's biggest employers, ignored the postwar blacklist in their personnel decisions during the late 1940s and early 1950s.[70]

But this argument, entertaining as it would be to make, would obscure as much as it revealed, leaving us no closer to understanding the cultural work of soap operas than we had been earlier. Decoding the ideology of a medium as popular, multifaceted, and ephemeral as radio is difficult. Indeed, writing the cultural history of any popular-culture form runs the risk of making a procrustean bed, in which some details are stretched to fit while other, less useful ones are lopped off.[71] In this case, it would be exceedingly difficult to overlook the many instances when daytime serials reinforced conservative notions of domesticity that are so entwined with oppressive notions of class, race, and gender. Although many middle-class families like the Youngs or Max and Mary struggled with homelessness, they often did so surrounded by housekeepers, whose rough accents and folksy grammatical mistakes marked them as objects of humor and as reminders of the respectability, elegance, and beauty of the real woman of the house. For every factory, mill, and clinic planned, there were, as Arnheim suggested, very few voices of the folks who would labor in them. For every Jewish protagonist, there were, of course, dozens of WASP families reflecting, especially in the Hummert oeuvre, an overwhelming ethnic homogeneity. Even on *The Guiding Light,* Rose Kransky's Jewishness was not nearly as central to the plot as the Reverend Ruthledge's non-denominational yet stuffy Protestant piety. Papa David's Jewishness is often undermined by his admonitions to emulate the life of Jesus Christ.

Whereas Jews and other recent immigrants from Europe were occasionally featured sympathetically in prominent roles, the status of people of color is dismal. *Judy and Jane,* perhaps the most radical of the soaps—in its daring domestic arrangements, its provocative politics, and the unvarnished expressions of affection between Judy and Jane—leaned heavily on "Fees," a black maid from the minstrel tradition. The banter back and forth between Ben Feinberg (described by Jerry as "the whitest guy I know") and Fees (who is also known as "Mandy" for no clear reason) is unenlightened ethnic shtick right from the vaudeville stage.[72] The Native Americans who populated Mr. Van Cleve's mansion worked as silent, scantily clad servants. His fascination with them, and his mistaken assumption that Jerry is Native American, are presented as an affectation—if not a perversion—of the very rich. The notion of making common cause with Native Americans is seen as being as absurd and immoral as Van Cleve's claims for an American aristocracy. In *Life Can Be Beautiful,* the name of the lecherous villain, "Gyp Mendoza," economically elides stereotypes about Gypsies and Latinos. If there are models of alternative or transgressive community in these serials, it is clear that they have been sharply bounded—reinscribed—by race and class.

Embarrassingly protracted discussions of Ben Feinberg's generosity and his persecution by "greedy bankers" functioned both as a grand rebuke to Jewish stereotypes and as the return of the anti-Semitic repressed. Papa David's handy Torah and even handier Christian prayer seemed to cover similar ideological bases. The notion that any popular genre as large as radio serial drama could be reduced to a single coherent ideological charge is unrealistic.

This is not to say that I have merely imagined the left-populist themes and puns in these programs. It is instead to suggest that in order to become popular, soap operas had to engage the tensions and conflicts that were most gripping to their listeners. The economic distress felt by nearly every serial protagonist despite the upper-middle-class elegance of so many of their homes tapped into the complementary desires for both realism and fantasy on the part of listeners, who were becoming trained by advertising's "parable of the democracy of goods" to feel at home with such contradictions.[73] And if audiences for these shows resembled the mass audiences written about by Denning and Cohen, then it is safe to assume they tolerated the same race- and class- and ethnic-based prejudices and divisions promulgated by Hollywood, advertising, and national chain stores.

Representations of friendships among men were also the source of considerable ideological ambiguity. The collective solution to the economic and intimate problems in *Pepper Young's Family* could be used as another brief in the argument for a soap-opera cultural front. But the near total absence of competitive capitalism on this program, and elsewhere in soapland, leads in a less clear direction. When family patriarch Sam Young, unemployed for months, heads to Chicago to visit his best friend and former business partner Curt, the tension turns entirely on Curt's lying to Sam about having a job himself. The ostensible reason, repeated over and over again by several characters and announcer Martin Block, was that Sam's happiness for Curt was all that kept Sam going. And indeed, Sam's expressions of joy in his friend's fictional success knew no bounds. Days and days of protracted suspense followed—When would Sam discover Curt's lie? How would he bear up under it?—requiring that listeners suspend or disavow any familiarity with jealousy, competition, or masculine pride. Curt's concern for Sam's emotional state and Sam's unwavering support for Curt's business success suggest a marital partnership.[74] Curt, a widower, who has been mother and father to his son Biff, is also innocently in love with Sam's wife, Mary, who in turn has "adopted" Biff during Curt's absence. Curt represented hope to Sam, and this relationship, devoid of human frailties, represented a soapland fantasy that the combination of public and private, work, family, love, and friendship made for stronger emotional ties, not weaker ones.

It would also be both easy and misleading to make a case for serial drama's feminism. For every powerful Mary, Jane, Judy, or Claire, there were several Hummert heroines sobbing, fretting, and mewling over the latest heterosexual romantic crisis. More important, perhaps, even within programs we have been considering, there are frequent and extended passages that define extremely conservative boundaries around the proper sphere of women, and in particular the danger posed to the community when women abandon domesticity.

Mary Sothern counsels Phyllis to solve her marital conflicts by "giving in" to Danny: "A woman's greatest victory is turning what seems like defeat into victory." Calling this surrender "the psychological moment," Mary insists that men and marriage cannot function without wives' submission. Danny's and Max's success in business depends on their domination at home.[75] Passages like these, which are common on many of the serials I have examined, read like perfunctory lip service paid by writers and producers in order to humor sponsors, networks, critics, and conservative listeners. If the plots are really as subversive to this ideology as they often seem, such reassurances might well have been necessary to assure these forces that they, like Max and Danny, were really in charge. It is possible too that many listeners—women and men—came to expect this periodic ritual of redrawing the public/private boundary as one of the pleasures (or givens) of the soap-opera form.

Certainly, we have evidence from Hilmes and Horten that even powerful soap-opera auteurs such as Jane Crusinberry and Irna Phillips felt tremendous pressure to toe the network line on women's proper place.[76] In any case, these passages make clear again that the cultural work these programs perform is the negotiation of gendered boundaries connecting their intimate lives to their public ones. Even in the psychological moment of surrender, women's work is crucial to men's public success.

Claire Marshall's coverage of the "juvenile delinquency" problem in Five Points leads her toward the opinion that such problems require a community, even a national solution. But when *The Guiding Light* devotes nearly a full episode to an actual American Legion spokeswoman, the source of the problem is laid squarely on the shoulders of working mothers. Even Claire concedes that it is actually "parental [read maternal] delinquency" that is at the root of the problem.[77] Claire's coverage of this event provides an additional layer of perspective on the matter, complicating any easy ideological decoding. What is clear is that the proper place of women in Five Points is being struggled over. Rose Kransky's ill-fated affair with her married WASP boss provides an additional example. Although Rose's punishment for adultery and for stepping beyond the confines of her stifling immigrant ghetto is inevitable and harsh, it comes only after the protracted pleasure of the love affair, an event in which she gains our sympathies, and perhaps our admiration.[78] Either way, the character's popularity following this episode leads to her own spin-off program, *The Right to Happiness*.

Even on *Judy and Jane*, the rhetoric of women's domesticity is employed, although for obviously strategic reasons, as when Jane tries to use Father Sargeant and Louella's conservatism to convince them she belongs at home with her children rather than working at the store.

This again points to the radio soap opera as a medium where competing notions of women's place could be negotiated. As to the lesbian
subtext in *Judy and Jane,* it is difficult, from the vantage point of our
time, to know precisely how to read the signs. Suffice it to say that
there is more than enough material here to string together a compelling
conference paper. A scene in which Jane peers through the steam to
watch Judy bathe is noteworthy. Judy is coquettish about opening the
door; once in, Jane admires Judy's appearance as the steam dissipates,
watches as Judy clips her toenails, and teases her about how slowly
she dresses.[79] But, aside from this and several other "gay" moments,
the mere fact of their friendship, which is impervious to the usual jeal-
ousies, competitions, and misunderstandings that mark so many other
relationships among women on the soaps, represents a dramatic and
inescapably political innovation. Their partnership, sexual or otherwise,
is significant because, like Curt's and Sam's, its strength seems to derive
from its distribution along so many spheres of life.

If there is something to decode in these serial dramas, it is the
inevitability of women's struggles to find a legitimate social space to
call their own. Most often, their search leads them to a hypertrophied
domesticity—a solution that requires endless vigilance as other women
vie to take their places. But nearly as often, this uneasiness led serial
heroines to reach beyond the domestic sphere and to embrace a wider—
and more difficult—world. Often, such a move is the necessary pre-
condition for the show's premise. Women could not be counted on to
feel sufficiently out of place in the home. Their discomfort—and their
qualified victories—required a wider world.

Although no clear utopian social organization is being modeled in
these soap operas, the cultural labor of moving back and forth across
the boundaries of public and private life was presented as a new form
of "woman's work." And this gesture itself constitutes an important,
if ambivalent, concession. Women would have to reconcile the contradictions inherent in the twentieth-century version of the doctrine of
gendered spheres. But the power and pleasure involved in negotiating
the shifting lines of public and private could be performed on the radio
in ways that seemed, like Scheherazade's tales, necessary and endlessly
entertaining.

CHAPTER 4

The Shadow Meets the Phantom Public

> What is a network? In a way it is—strangely
> enough—almost nothing, a phantom.
> —*Eric Barnouw*, The Golden Web

Beginning in 1937, the Shadow haunted the evening airwaves, battling underworld masters of murder, racketeering, and the occult. The Shadow began each program with a haunting question: "Who knows what evil lurks in the hearts of men?" However, it was the evil lurking just *outside* the boundaries of the national and intimate spheres of American life that figured most centrally in the popular mystery stories of *The Shadow*. As the commercial network radio system helped create and spread the emergent national public culture of the 1930s, *The Shadow* evoked and assuaged fears of a phantom public, a dark and heterogeneous urban world marked by uncertain boundaries, a vulnerable citizenry, and a steady stream of "Oriental" national and racial outsiders.

As we saw with the Fireside Chats, *Vox Pop*, and soap operas, network radio's discourse of intimate publicity performed a paradoxical twin feat. On the one hand, it addressed its vast, indeterminate audience as a unified national public, irrespective of geographical and social boundaries; on the other hand, it constantly employed strategic distinctions in addressing and representing its national audience. On mystery-thriller programs like *The Shadow*, the promise and problems of a mass-mediated urban public became the self-conscious focus of suspenseful dramatic narratives. The city itself—diverse, bustling, and filled with public sites of mass entertainments—emerged as one of the show's central characters. The city's very publicness, its openness to difference, however, made it a site of constantly brewing crisis.

By evoking and assuaging fears of foreign invasion, mass manipulation, and the rising menace of totalitarianism, *The Shadow* emphasized the importance of maintaining and mobilizing traditional exclusions, hierarchies, and boundaries in the imagined community of the United States in the 1930s and 1940s. Often, these threats were most compellingly represented sexually; seduction of American women at the hands of foreign men became a handy code for critiquing the mixing of intimate and public space that radio, along with modern urban life, represented. At the same time, the show seemed to insist that public life, even amid the diversity and unruliness of the city, was something listeners could not do without. The Shadow himself was the symbol of this ambivalence toward the promiscuous mixing of privacy and publicity, Western science and Eastern mysticism, nationalism and cosmopolitanism, mass culture and elite control. In fact, his only purpose was to combine these opposites in order to prevent anyone else from doing so. In his hands, such mixing was thrilling, seductive, and necessary, and, in the logic of the program's introduction, *authorized* because such methods "may ultimately be used by all law enforcement agencies."

Debuting in 1937, a year before the Munich crisis and the infamous *War of the Worlds* broadcast, *The Shadow* seemed to anticipate the anxiety about the fate of democracy in a modern, mass-mediated world that would come to dominate the airwaves. From the series's inception until America's entry into World War II, as American radios crackled with the distressing news of war in Europe, renewed recession at home, and compelling parables of fascist invasion of American civic life, *The Shadow*'s evocation of constant danger was in tune with a broader set of historical anxieties. During the war, the Shadow continued without perceptible change to battle national outsiders in the name of national and sexual security in an era of penetrating radio waves and shadowy saboteurs from overseas. It was not until after the war that the program began to probe into threats of a more internal, psychological nature. Disgruntled employees, intellectual misfits, and garden-variety misanthropes were a constant source of danger from the program's inception in 1937, but the psychological dimensions of these sorts of villains, and the frequency of their appearance, increased dramatically in the late 1940s and early 1950s.

The early years of *The Shadow* illustrate how network radio's discourse of intimate publicity could attract a national mass audience at the same time that it dramatized the dangers that such an audience posed. Following a brief history of *The Shadow*'s origins in radio and pulp fiction, this chapter will examine several episodes from the first eight years of the series. In particular, it will focus on "The Hypnotized Audience," a typical episode from 1937, the show's first season. In this episode, the mystical threat of "Oriental culture" to white denizens of an urban sphere of popular entertainment becomes the means for dramatizing and resolving the interrelated crises of public space, mass culture, and national or racial outsiders. This episode is significant in the context of American anxiety about Asian immigration, crises at home and abroad, and the cultural changes being wrought by the media of communications and entertainment. The chapter concludes by comparing the world of *The Shadow* with Walter Lippmann's "phantom public," suggesting that the conservatism and pessimism of this conception of mass-mediated democracy was in tension with the optimism of the New Deal and wartime rhetoric of "the people"—in particular the people of the city—as the nation's bulwark against fascism and emasculation.

The Origins of *The Shadow*

The early history of *The Shadow* provides a good example of the web of relationships connecting early episodic radio, other popular culture forms, and the financial interests of their corporate sponsors, who, through their advertising agencies, came to have a larger role in the development and production of radio programming throughout the 1930s.[1] The Shadow debuted in 1930 as the omniscient voice of the mysterious narrator for CBS's *Detective Story Hour,* sponsored by Street and Smith, publishers of *Detective Story Magazine.*[2] This early Shadow was created to help promote the magazine, but the popularity of the radio narrator with the mirthless laugh inspired Street and Smith to develop a new magazine around a character named the Shadow, who solved mysteries while remaining a bit of one himself. As the first of radio's mysterious narrators, the Shadow inspired many programs featuring a mysterious, omniscient storyteller with a compelling voice, for example, *The Mysterious Traveler, The Whistler, Inner Sanctum,* and *Suspense.*[3]

The Shadow character, complete with multiple secret identities, supporting cast, and a dark urban mise-en-scène, was created by Walter

Brown Gibson for Street and Smith's *The Shadow Magazine*. As the first crime-fighting superhero with an alter ego, the Shadow of magazine and pulp novel fame represents an important precursor to, and inspiration for, Superman, Batman, and Captain America, and the runaway success of the print versions of the Shadow spawned a raft of similarly shadowy pulp heroes in *The Whisperer, Crime Buster, Doc Savage,* and *The Avenger,* the last two of which became radio programs as well.[4] Gibson also provided Lamont Cranston's origin story: a shadowy past and youthful pilgrimage to the Orient, where he learned "how to cloud men's minds." Cranston was only one of several alter egos and the Shadow's identity remained mysterious for years. Ultimately, it was revealed that his true identity, Kent Allard, World War I flying ace and spy, occasionally "borrowed" the identity of Cranston when the millionaire dilettante was out of the country.[5]

In the weekly magazine pulp novels, the Shadow inhabited a world of twisting city streets, convoluted plots, and foreign foes. This urban public setting was populated with a diverse cadre of amateur "agents," including a Jewish taxi driver, a reformed gambler, an Italian fruit vendor, a suicidal Wall Street investor, a Chinese American doctor, an African American doorman who also ran a Harlem employment agency, a female FBI agent who also assumed the identity of an Oriental spy, and many other blue- and white-collar denizens of the city whose loyalty the Shadow had won by having helped them in the past. Together, they formed a shadowy network of cooperation, a counterpublic often at odds with both criminals and the police. Despite apparent elements of a Cultural Front social formation, Gibson's pulp novels relied heavily on the theme of threats from the "Orient," frequently pitting the Shadow against the imperialist designs and telepathic powers of the Mongols, Afghans, and Tibetans constantly invading New York City. In the four-part series, *Golden Master* (1939), *Shiwan Khan Returns* (1939), *Masters of Death,* and *The Invincible Shiwan Khan,* the Shadow confronts wave after wave of invading, beastlike Oriental foes under the power of a master of mind control descended from Genghis Khan pillaging New York City for the weaponry he needs to take over the world.[6] The racist characterizations of these villains are strikingly vicious, even when taking into account the racism of the era.

The Shadow of the 1937 radio program, by contrast, relied less heavily on the diverse denizens of the city, working most often alone or with the help of his "constant aide and companion, Margot Lane." The Shadow's network of agents was considerably pared down and he was reduced to a single alter ego, Lamont Cranston, "wealthy young man about town," who moved in a narrow circle of elite cultural and official power.[7] Still, one of the show's main characters was the vibrant city, humming with the anonymous and heterogeneous sounds of the people in theaters and city streets. And Cranston was as well acquainted with the city's cab drivers and beggars as he was with its politicians, socialites, and scientific experts. Against the romantic backdrop of a city teeming with characters from all walks of life, the Shadow emerged as a hero of the people. This version of *The Shadow*, which aired on Sunday evenings at 5:30 p.m. on the Mutual Radio Network, quickly became one of the most popular programs on the air, maintaining its sponsorship by Blue Coal and high ratings throughout most of its seventeen-year run. The program hit its peak of popularity in 1942, when it dominated the all-important Hooper ratings with a 17.2 share, good for 55.6 percent of the listening audience and a new record for a commercial daytime program.[8] By 1940, the Shadow had become, according to Anthony Tollin, the first "multi-media phenomenon," with feature and short films, comic books, a daily newspaper cartoon strip, a monthly magazine with a circulation of 750,000, and a fan club with more than a million members, in addition to the pulp novels and the radio program.[9]

"The Hypnotized Audience"
Throughout the 1937–38 season, announcer Ken Roberts began each episode with an explanation of the program's purpose: "to demonstrate forcibly to old and young alike that crime does not pay." According to Roberts, the Shadow struck "terror into the hearts of sharpsters, law-breakers, and criminals," a list that may at first seem redundant, though it aptly conveys the program's preoccupation with the taxonomy of outsiders and the Shadow's long reach into every den of iniquity.

In *The Shadow*'s dark urban landscape, where outsiders and foreigners, especially Eastern mystics and Eastern European dissidents, constantly threaten the social order, the public sphere appears precarious, insubstantial, vulnerable—a phantom. The Shadow confronts hypnotists, telepaths, bombers, poisoners, and snipers, all of whom profess contempt for crowds. Many of these episodes feature long soliloquies by villains, revealing the inner workings of their sociopathic minds. A haughty contempt for the American masses is typical, based on the villains' greater intellectual powers or on racial or national difference. Showdowns take place in the city's subway tunnels, streets, arcades, theaters, and nightclubs—the physical and cultural infrastructure of the modern city. The vulnerable mass public, often figured as a "hypnotized audience," becomes a symbol for the chronic dangers and confusions of modern urban life and a rationale for the xenophobia and agoraphobia of official and popular forms of discourse in the years leading up to World War II.[10]

At the same time, the city is the one thing that the Shadow cannot do without. Its public spaces are highly vulnerable in part because of their significance: in all their unruly diversity, they are also the stages on which social distinctions are managed and represented. The Shadow's power depends on the city's heterogeneity, the multiple codes of the streets, and the centrality of mass communication and mass culture to the shape of city life. The plots, accents, and background noises emphasize this interdependence: climactic scenes invariably take place in large theaters, arcades, or public meetings. Unlike daytime serial dramas, *The Shadow* evoked a sense of public life through the unruly *sounds* of the city. Newsboys crying out the headlines, the hubbub of a theater crowd at intermission, the buzz of reporters' questions at a press conference—all of these sounds formed the background for the Shadow's strategic partnerships with diverse groups within the city, including the police, the press, corporate and scientific elites, and, in one episode, a highly organized group of beggars and peddlers who enable him to move more effectively through the city.

Thus it is important that *The Shadow*'s phantom public serves as the site where urban mass entertainments, especially theatrical ones, are figured as threats from national or racial outsiders. In "Can the Dead Talk?" (March 19, 1939), for example, Anton Proscovi, "the famous [Russian] anarchist" turned theatrical performer, reads the minds of an entire audience, discovers the Shadow's secret identity, and then asks the Shadow to join him in a hypnotic-telepathic venture to control the world. In "The Temple Bells of Neban" (1937), the Shadow is nearly swept off his feet by the lovely young Sadi Bel Ada, an "Oriental dancer" whose movements, chants, and bell ringing are in fact components of very powerful spells that she employs in the service of a complicated international heroin and kidnapping ring. Theatrical settings serve as the scene of a mass hypnotism or violent crime in "The Tenor with the Broken Voice" (1938), "The Green Man" (1940), "The Drums of Doom" (1942), "The Ghost without a Face" (1945), and many others. Murders take place in low-rent theatrical settings too, as when the dead body of a notorious gun moll is posed in a wax museum tableau in "Murders in Wax" (1938). In "The Tomb of Terror" (1938), a museum opening sets the scene for mass panic, when an Egyptian mummy's curse seems to be killing off the curious spectators.

Foreign, seductive threats to national security and sexual decency recur throughout the years 1937–45. In "Power of the Mind" (July 3, 1938), the tall, slender Countess Zara uses her feminine wiles—and torture—to steal "a new type of explosive, more powerful than any known to munitions makers anywhere in the world." In "Aboard the Steamship Amazon," Mrs. Todd, a deposed ruler of her Eastern country, seduces and kills as she smuggles munitions out of the United States, with the help of her unwitting stepson and her henchman, Tong Sui. "Night without End" (1938) features stolen military secrets, deadly gas, and the fiendishly foreign Dr. Zarov. An "Oriental plague" is the national security threat in "Murder on Approval" (August 21, 1938); the target is two hundred American soldiers with whom Margot has been flirting and dancing all evening. "The hidden menace to the armed strength of our country has been uncovered and destroyed," Lamont summarizes at the end of this episode, but the lingering sensation is one of vulnerability. The foreign general who hired the evil Dr. Kolanza to create the plague is still at large, and Margot and Lamont still frequent theaters, dances, and other public spectacles that make such perfect targets for terrorist attacks.

Margot Lane's frequent seductions by foreign masters of mind control pose particularly dramatic challenges to the Shadow's powers. In "The Bubbling Death" (1943), the patriarch of an unwholesome Louisiana bayou family, of the impoverished, decadent aristocracy type, returns from "South America" and uses mind control to send Margot on a nearly murderous rampage. In a truly horrifying episode, "The Gibbering Things" (1943), she is turned into "a human cow" by Professor Alexander Sergoff, a Russian who has created a race of blood-sucking monsters. In "The Man Who Dreamed Too Much" (1944), a Dr. Nightmare invades Margot's dreams, a seduction that is foreshadowed by her kitten's disturbing mewling. In "The Crystal Globe" (1943), a man known only as "Ahmed" charms Margot with the exotic furnishings in his home and then persuades her to shove Lamont Cranston off a subway platform, very nearly killing him.

"The Hypnotized Audience" (1937) illustrates the program's conflation of fears of foreigners, sexual seduction, mass culture, and the public sphere; it also shows how the Shadow's verbal and technical powers of mind control, surveillance, and persuasion simultaneously

Brett Morrison and Grace Matthews as the Shadow and Margot Lane.
Courtesy of the Library of American Broadcasting.

mirror and counteract the threats posed by alien forces. In this episode, the Shadow confronts "The Durga Khan," another "Oriental
dancer" whose mystical chants mesmerize an entire theater full of citizens, including the governor, the commissioner of police, and Margot
Lane, effectively and symbolically stopping the entire public and private worlds of Lamont Cranston in their tracks. A full minute of this
scene is dedicated to Lamont's attempt to rouse Margot from a deep
and rather sensual hypnotic stupor caused by Durga Khan's chanting

and gyrations—"Shame on you, Margot!" he finally hisses, in desperation. Then, under cover of mass hypnotism, Khan's henchmen kidnap the governor, dragging him from his box in the balcony as Lamont screams, "Wake up everyone! Listen to me! The governor has been kidnapped!"

At this, the hypnotized audience snaps out of it, erupting in howls of hysterical fear. The careful listener is not surprised by this turn of events, as Lamont has been waxing skeptical about the cultural value of Oriental dancing all evening. During the intermission at the Durga Khan's performance, Lamont bristles with disgust when overhearing a silly-sounding society woman gushing, "I just love Oriental culture." "Everything Oriental is perfect," Lamont responds sarcastically; he then launches into a scathing critique of "Oriental culture," linking Khan to Joseph Hakim, a brutal and notorious murderer scheduled to die that night in the electric chair. "Nobody cheered over *his* display of Oriental culture," Lamont sniffs. Hakim and the Durga Khan "are both the product of the Orient, from the same section and caste," Lamont notes significantly over Margot's blithe objections as he trudges back into the theater, wondering, rather superciliously, *why* the governor has left his office on the night of an execution and, rather ominously, *what* Durga Khan will do for an encore.

Despite yelling "The governor has been kidnapped!" in a crowded theater, Lamont fails to stop Khan's men; he quickly discovers that Durga Khan is in fact the brother of the murderer Joseph Hakim and that the kidnapping was an attempt to get the governor to order a stay of execution. What follows is a fairly virtuoso performance of technical and psychological wizardry, in which the Shadow and Margot use shortwave radios, tap into phone lines, impersonate telephone operators and prison officials, and finally, with the help of a timely radio news broadcast, turn Khan's sister-in-law against him and liberate the governor.

After intercepting Durga Khan's phone call to the prison warden, the Shadow outtalks the Durga Khan, and persuades Joseph Hakim's widow, Princess Zada, to turn on her brother-in-law, the Durga Khan, instead of shooting Governor Barnes.

THE SHADOW: Great is Durga Khan! He talks while his brother dies.
PRINCESS ZADA: His brother... dies?

DURGA KHAN: My brother lives! I saved him.

THE SHADOW: Princess Zada, this man, with his dreams of power, has deceived you. He has not saved Joseph Hakim.

DURGA KHAN: You must be mad.

THE SHADOW: Even now, your husband is dead.

DURGA KHAN: Wild talk, Shadow, and false!

THE SHADOW: You cannot stop the course of justice, by the power of your will. Hakim is dead. Your kidnapping was in vain.

DURGA KHAN: He lies, Zada. Shoot the governor.

THE SHADOW: Princess, wait.

DURGA KHAN: Zada, obey my orders!

THE SHADOW: *Listen, Princess!* Do you wish to know the truth about your husband?

PRINCESS ZADA: Yes, O voice!

DURGA KHAN: Oh, Zada!

THE SHADOW: *Listen!* Turn on the radio here. It's time for the news. *Listen,* and learn if Joseph Hakim was saved tonight or not. *Listen, Princess!*
(Click, sound of radio static)

RADIO ANNOUNCER: And that is the weather report for tonight.

THE SHADOW: *Listen, Princess!*

RADIO ANNOUNCER: And now we bring you a news flash which just arrived in the studio. Exactly two minutes ago, Joseph Hakim was executed at state prison for murder. Hakim walked to the death chamber unaided and he . . .

PRINCESS ZADA: (gasps)

DURGA KHAN: There must be some mistake.

PRINCESS ZADA: Durga Khan, you faithless one! You of so many promises! You, the fourth brother! The mistake was in my trusting you.

THE SHADOW: That was the mistake, Princess Zada.

DURGA KHAN: Zada, put that gun down. Zada, Durga Khan speaks!

PRINCESS ZADA: Durga Khan speaks for the last time!
(Gunshots, sound of body falling)[11]

In many ways, "The Hypnotized Audience" is emblematic of the episodes from the early years of the program. Most begin with a threat to the public order by a national outsider who has mastered some form of mass mind control; many end with the Shadow persuading his foes to shoot each other and/or themselves. And in between, most episodes feature the Shadow's descent into the invisible world of crime, where he manipulates information through various technical and rhetorical strategies in order to preserve the public order, if only until the next episode. J. Fred MacDonald has argued that the formulaic plots and quickly resolved crises of radio thrillers "supplied millions of Americans with understandable stories of achievement within a competitive, mass society," thereby providing "a paradigm for effective social existence." Hilmes suggests that the form's popularity stems from the twin pleasures of exploring and containing subversive ideas and actions, all within the space of a single episode.[12]

Michael Denning has focused on the mass media's "hypnotized audience" as a central source of ambivalence in the "allegories of antifascism" of Orson Welles starting in the mid-1930s in radio and theater and extending right through his film career and the 1950s. Welles used the conceit of the radio news announcer in Archibald MacLeish's radio plays *The Fall of the City* and *Air Raid,* both of which play on the threat of fascist invasions of one kind or another. In Welles's radio adaptation of *The Heart of Darkness,* his roles in MacLeish's play *Panic* and in the Mercury Theater's *Julius Ceasar,* and his films *Citizen Kane, Journey into Fear,* and *A Touch of Evil,* the antifascist allegory was hard to miss.[13] Welles, who played the Shadow/Cranston in the program's 1937 debut season in which the "The Hypnotized Audience" episode aired, was both drawn to and repulsed by the hypnotizing, magical power of theater, radio, and film. Although Welles maintained that "this kind of hypnosis is dangerous not only politically but esthetically and culturally," he returned again and again to roles and dramas in which he was the master mesmerist.[14] Perhaps the most famous example is the *War of the Worlds* radio broadcast, which terrified an estimated 1 million listeners and won Welles national attention and an unprecedented Hollywood contract.[15] "For Welles," Denning notes, "...the panic represented...the lure and danger of hypnotizing an audience." According to Denning, mass entertainment occupied an ambivalent social space for Welles: a repository of symbolic meanings for both "the showmanship of fascism" and the possibility of a democratic "People's Theater."[16]

In the fall of 1937, a full year before the famous *War of the Worlds* broadcast, Welles explored this same ambivalence as the Shadow/ Cranston. On *The Shadow,* however, it was theater and radio together that provided contradictory symbolism for the political potential of the urban mass audience. The passive audience present for the evening of Oriental dance joins the cultural and political functions of the public. Cranston's wake-up call to the crowd comes too late to save the governor, but the Shadow's subsequent use of the shortwave and broadcast radio, along with his own invisible voice, manages to rally public institutions such as the police, the press, and the penal system, while undermining the hypnotic and theatrical power of Khan.

Orientalism
The figure of the foreign, seductive, theatrical mesmerist recurs frequently on this program, perhaps because it is such a powerful symbol for the fear that the urban public, exposed to foreign influences and new media, and crammed into public spaces, was turning into an easily hypnotized audience. Overflowing theaters, nightclubs, arcades, and city streets are the most common scenes of public peril in *The Shadow,* providing a symbolic representation of the invisible, abstracted, and fragmented radio audience that broadcasters, regulators, and listeners themselves were in the process of imagining. The figure of the Durga Khan provides an ideal foil for the Shadow, whose powers are also a product of "Oriental culture." The Shadow calls their showdown "a battle of wills," but it also represents a struggle over the ambivalently defined turfs of mass culture, national identity, and American public space.

Indeed, many of the Shadow's villains possess almost identical powers. Using technology or "Oriental" knowledge, they pry into the privacy of their victims, turning public spectacles into sites of seduction, psychosis, or hypnotic control, or into a shadowy crime scene. In "The Touch of Death" (1943), Lucius Hawk returns to the United States after a decade in the Amazon with deadly powers that mirror the Shadow's. "We're Masters of the same art," the Shadow admits to the evil Dr. Dharma, in "The Hypnotic Death" (February 12, 1939), "but we apply it quite differently." In dozens of episodes, "Oriental" mystics use hypnotic and telepathic powers for evil ends. And garden-variety criminals team up repeatedly with naive or disgruntled scientists to produce technologies of surveillance that rival the Shadow's powers.

This preoccupation with the "Orientalist" myth of the criminally dangerous interloper from the East also speaks to some very specific anxieties circulating though official, popular, and literary discourses in the 1930s. As Edward Said has shown, such discourse has been crucial in the development of a range of Western civilization's literary and popular constructions of itself. Said argues that the interwar era was a particularly charged one for East–West relations, as rising political and economic demands for independence from Asian countries forced the West to rethink the meanings behind the "irreducibly opposed" Occident and Orient.[17] This new version of Orientalism responded to a powerful matrix of fears about cultural distinctions in the modern era: "the apocalypse to be feared was not the destruction of Western civilization but rather the destruction of the barriers that kept East and West from each other" (263). Said argues that the discourse of Orientalism is not as prevalent in the United States as it is in Europe (291–92); however, in "The Hypnotized Audience," "The Temple Bells of Neban," "Message from the Hills" (1938), "The Curse of Shiva" (1940), and "Voodoo" (1941), and in the origin story of the Shadow (which pops up in other episodes), the Shadow/Cranston epitomizes Said's account of the nineteenth-century Western Pilgrim attracted to and estranged from the sexual and sensual excesses of Oriental culture (166–97). Orson Welles's aristocratic, vaguely British rendition of Lamont Cranston in the first season emphasizes this association with colonialist tradition that Said describes. And, like the twentieth-century Orientalist Said describes, Cranston/Shadow is drawn back to the East as "the origin of European science," yet adamant that it is "a superseded origin" (251). The Shadow/Cranston is also given to making "summational statements" that conflate "one bit of Oriental material" with "the Orient as a whole," as when, for example, he links Khan's dancing with Hakim's "butchery" (255).

Historians of immigration and the 1930s have demonstrated that a virulent racist discourse about "Orientals" persisted in popular and official discourses from the 1882 Chinese Exclusion Act, the Immigration Act of 1924, the Tydings-McDuffie Act of 1934, right through to the internment of Japanese Americans during World War II. Bill Ong Hing argues that the passage of the Tydings-McDuffie Act of 1934, which granted the Philippines its independence from the United States in the name of a more total exclusion of all Asian immigration, "symbolized the peak of anti-immigrant power."[18] As Lisa Lowe has argued, these images and policies mark the contradictions surrounding the role that Asian immigrants and Asian Americans have played in the U.S. workforce, as citizens, and in the national imagination. Lowe suggests that "throughout the twentieth century, the figure of the Asian immigrant" reveals "a series of condensed, complicated anxieties regarding external and internal threats to the mutable coherence of the national body."[19] Jackson Lears observes a similar web of anxieties and anti-immigrant symbolism in the advertising copy of the 1920s and 1930s; in particular, he points to the "obsession with expelling 'alien' filth" in these ads, which captures the "connection between bodily and national purification: the eugenic dream of perfecting Anglo-Saxon racial dominance in the United States through immigration restriction." Lears also points out that since the nineteenth century, images of the Orient were linked to sexual rejuvenation, sensual excess, and ambivalent feelings toward the expanding world of consumer goods in general, and luxuries and patent medicines in particular. He argues that the patent-medicine peddler, precursor to the professional advertising executive of the 1920s and 1930s, was strongly associated with the mysterious, seductive powers of the Orient.[20]

Of the hundred episodes from 1937 through 1945 that I reviewed for this chapter, half featured national, racial, or ethnic outsiders as villains. A quarter featured a villain with supernatural or advanced scientific powers of telepathy, hypnotism, and/or mass mind control. Nearly one-third featured doctors, professors, or scientists as villains warped by their brilliance, social marginalization, and unnatural desire to control humanity and nature. The Shadow's weekly battles with national, racial, ethnic, and social outsiders presume a public mind susceptible to foreign, antidemocratic forces *and* unable to discern the crucial distinctions undergirding social and political hierarchies of race, gender, class, and ethnicity. This easily seduced public mind, often figured as feminine, is epitomized in "The Hypnotized Audience," first by the gullibility of the unnamed society woman's love of "Oriental culture" and then by Margot's breathy, moaning, hypnotic surrender to Khan, which Lamont is nearly powerless to overcome. The suggestion of Margot's sexual surrender to Khan is hard to miss: after nearly a minute of trying to rouse her from her blissful hypnotic state, Lamont scolds, "Shame on you, Margot!" These surrenders echo the governor's failure to estimate the danger of Joseph Hakim's "crime family" and his inability to resist the lure of the exotic theatrical entertainment that drew him away from his execution-night vigil at the statehouse. These twin failures, linked in Cranston's intermission attack on "Oriental culture," lead to the governor's kidnapping, torture, and near death at the hands of Princess Zada. The governor's reduction, first to culture vulture, then to hostage, enacts a symbolic decapitation of state authority in the face of a cultural public sphere marked by heterogeneity, permeable borders, and exoticism.

The particular form the Orientalist menace takes in "The Hypnotized Audience" is also connected to the peculiar features of radio itself, in particular its ability to render invisible the most common (that is, visual) markers of social difference, such as race, gender, or national identity. Michele Hilmes calls this "the basic transgressive quality of the medium itself."[21] Susan Douglas and Catherine Covert have pointed out the widespread ambivalence that radio waves inspired in the first decade of broadcasting, emphasizing the commonly expressed fears that radio's unseen words and sounds were the uncanny results of supernatural phenomena penetrating into public and private spheres.[22]

The Shadow's pattern of limning the dark, urban, phantom public frequently plays on these very fears of powerful disembodied voices transgressing important social boundaries. "The Hypnotized Audience" begins with a political, cultural, and personal disturbance at the theater largely brought about through aural means. Khan's hypnotic speech in the darkness of the theater effects the symbolic overthrow of state power, the virtual seduction of Margot Lane, and thus the emasculation of Lamont Cranston. "The Phantom Fingerprints" (October 29, 1939) begins with Lamont dithering over a line of dialogue in a play he is writing. "I am a woman," he says doubtfully, and then with increasing conviction over the course of several uneasy moments at the very start of the episode. Margot interrupts this odd performance and suggests that he might be losing his mind. Later, while he and Margot whisk Commissioner Westin off to see the play's opening night, a police veteran is murdered.

Technologies of communication, like theatrical settings, represent the danger of an exposed and vulnerable public sphere. Using "ultrasonic broadcasters," "television mechanisms," motion-picture cameras, and the gaudy lighting of theaters, foreign villains invade the privacy of citizens for the purposes of robbery, extortion, sabotage, and seduction. Many episodes use the peremptory shouts of newsboys calling out the headlines, radio newscasts, and panicked voices on the telephone to indicate the circulation of a public peril. "Society of the Living Dead" (January 23, 1938) begins with the sound of voices on the telephone and radio discussing news of an international "phony passport and identification ring," the details of which are never explained.

The radio announcer's most startling revelation—"Mr. and Mrs. Smith are not citizens!"—also goes unexplained, and we never hear of the Smiths again. Against this backdrop of anxiety about national identity circulating through the invisible voices of radio and other media, the Shadow confronts a world whose boundaries are so uncertain that the identity, to say nothing of the Americanness, of a "Mr. and Mrs. Smith" is left, figuratively and literally, up in the air.

Hilmes argues that the subversive potential of radio was met with a new preoccupation with articulating the *sounds* of difference. "Radio responded by...endlessly circulating and performing structured representations of ethnicity, race, gender, and other concentrated sites of social and cultural norms—all through language, dialect, and carefully selected aural context."[23] On *The Shadow,* racial, national, and gender differences are also marked aurally; by conflating foreignness, criminal activity, "feminization," and the occult, the program overdetermines what it means to be an outsider. The suspense of each episode consists in the fact that each of the Shadow's villains possesses mysterious powers of manipulation. Indeed, most episodes conclude, as does "The Hypnotized Audience," with a war of words between the Shadow and some dangerously articulate villain. Disdaining weapons, the Shadow intones to one terrified villain, "I prefer to defeat you with words." In the illustrated pulps, by contrast, stories tend to conclude in a spectacular hail of bullets, knives, and fists. The pulps' less verbal Shadow is also less *invisible* than his radio counterpart and thus is forced to defend himself physically.

By outtalking Durga Khan, the Shadow liberates the governor, restores the power of the state, and defends against the effeminizing, seductive, foreign influences threatening to undermine the cultural public sphere of urban entertainment. The Shadow achieves all this through the expert manipulation of speech and the communication devices designed to enhance its range, effects, and speed. In many episodes, the Shadow's success hinges on his ability to manipulate, understand, and transmit language, crack codes, and influence public opinion. In other episodes from 1937 through 1945, the Shadow employs shortwave radio, reedits the sound track on a surveillance film that has been tampered with, taps into a municipal public-address system, manipulates public opinion through the newspapers, and employs a state-of-the-art "headline machine" that flashes messages onto a giant electric light kiosk wrapped around the city's daily newspaper building. In the very first episode, the "Death House Rescue" (September 26, 1937), a hapless death-row innocent asks the Shadow if his mind-reading power is "like television."

He also "speaks" in the secret codes of an underground alliance of the city's homeless; masters the code used by an evil professor to control his deaf-mute henchman; and, as Lamont Cranston, is fluent in the cultural codes of the urban elite, among whom he circulates at all the finest restaurants, theaters, and nightclubs. Again and again, crises of the public sphere involve a loss of control of the means of communication, information, and entertainment, all of which have become hopelessly intertwined by mass-mediated consumer culture. Restoring a provisional order to this encoded, shadowy, noisy world requires nothing less than a technocratic magician, a master performer and communicator.

In the final confrontation scene with Durga Khan and Princess Zada, the Shadow's superior mastery of the power of speech makes the crucial difference between victory and defeat. The life-or-death struggle boils down to a contest over who can command Princess Zada's attention, who can persuade her to "listen" to the truth, and who can control the direction in which she aims her pistol. The Shadow asks the Princess to "listen" to him five separate times. His success here is a reversal of his first contest with Khan, when, as Lamont Cranston, he struggled to rouse Margot from a hypnotic stupor. In that encounter, he begged Margot to "listen" several times as well, before shouting, "Listen to me!" to the entire theater. It is a contest the Shadow wins handily, with cool, confident admonitions and the help of a well-timed radio news broadcast. In contrast, Durga Khan's speech is shrill, imperious, and grandiloquent; the foreignness of his voice, which had previously been so seductive in the theater, now sounds panicky compared to the Shadow's confident, authoritative, metallic voice (an authority reinforced by the breezily professional voice of the radio announcer who gives the definitive word that Joseph Hakim has been executed). The Shadow begins the confrontation by ridiculing the fact that Khan impotently "talks" while his brother dies. Durga Khan counters by accusing the Shadow of "wild talk," but it is *his* voice that seems out of control, interrupting, panicky, and finally, completely powerless. In response to his peremptory, "Zada, Durga Khan speaks!" she answers, "Durga Khan speaks for the last time!" Khan loses his life and the right to speak with one squeeze of the trigger. As in many episodes from this period, the Shadow talks the criminal into a corner and the system of law and order back into a tenuous, temporary equilibrium.

Wartime and Beyond

America's entry into World War II did little to change the terms in which *The Shadow* represented national security threats. The series anticipated the war effort's mobilization against "outsiders," and, in particular, it seemed to understand the tension between the urban, public ethos of the New Deal and the constraints on difference and dissent that threats to national security might entail. This tension is played out in the period 1937 through 1945 with remarkably little change to reflect the watersheds of Pearl Harbor and Hiroshima and Nagasaki. Just as television was prefigured, doomsday devices strikingly similar to the atomic bomb were a source of fear in episodes from the late 1930s.[24]

The continuity of Orientalist imagery throughout this period is demonstrated nicely in Alex Russo's examination of *The Green Hornet*. On this program, the faithful valet Kato, originally Japanese in the 1930s broadcasts, was quietly redesignated, in the war years, a Filipino. Kato's basic character—servile, mysterious, semiarticulate, and able to penetrate the mysterious crime dens of Chinatown on behalf of his white employer—remains the same, even if his country of origin has been conveniently transformed. Together, Kato and Britt Reid/ the Green Hornet cover the cultural territory of Cranston/the Shadow, endlessly evoking and assuaging fears of an apocalyptic blurring of the lines between East and West. And where *The Green Hornet* concerned itself primarily with civic corruption and the failure of local public institutions, *The Shadow* constantly linked such problems to insidious foreign threats.[25]

In the postwar years, *The Shadow*'s preoccupation with foreign interlopers gave way to plots revolving around garden-variety criminal gangs and, most of all, solitary criminals motivated by wild passions, insanity, and long-festering grudges against wealthy relatives or unappreciative employers. Spurned women kill their fickle lovers or their rivals, an insane young man kills his relatives to spare them the family trait of insanity, and society women team up with gangsters to pull off insurance scams.[26] Lonely misfits haunted by fears, passions, unrequited loves, and unslaked revenge turn so far inward they become psychological monsters, as when a simple zookeeper lets loose a violent gorilla after being driven mad by taunts about his resemblance to the ape.[27] Although villains from abroad made occasional appearances in the years 1946–54, they were far outnumbered by homegrown villains caught up in acts of passion or organized rackets. Of the postwar plots that do concern foreign foes, many of these resolve in surprising ways, as in "They Kill with a Silver Hatchet" (May 26, 1946), in which the evil Dragon Master is revealed at last to be "the wonderfully good-hearted" Mr. Andrews, whose drug use has made him both "Oriental" and insane. In "Trial of the Knifer" (1949), a young American woman kills the principals in a Broadway play in order to keep the play's story—about her Nazi father's atrocities—a secret. In both cases, the threat is less from abroad than from the private weaknesses and passions of Americans.

The Phantom Public?

In many ways, *The Shadow*'s vision of the modern city reflects the pessimism articulated by a generation of journalists, intellectuals, and bureaucrats between the world wars. In the 1920s, Walter Lippmann laid out a vision of an American public vexed by an unattainable ideal of civic competence and confused by the mass-mediated shadows of an increasingly complex world. Lippmann draws on Plato's parable of the cave for inspiration, and argues that the "pictures inside our heads" are mere shadows of "the world outside."[28] In what could be read as an allusion to Lippmann, the Shadow of the late 1930s eerily intones "I see the pictures inside your head" to many a lawbreaker. For Lippmann, the Shadow, and an emerging bureaucratic managerial class, understanding the problems posed by the phantom public begins with the assumption that the public is highly vulnerable to mass-mediated manipulation.[29]

In *Public Opinion,* Lippmann calls for a special knowledge class—an elite, highly specialized cadre of "intelligence workers"—to manage the difficulties posed by modern society.[30] This call was answered by the very forces from which Lippmann seemed to think the public needed protection: advertisers, pollsters, public-relations firms, and a press increasingly cynical about the nature of its audience.[31]

The Shadow represents, in many ways, an idealized version of Lippmann's intelligence worker, bringing psychology, surveillance, and communications technologies to bear on the problematic, invisible, and shadowy public world. And, like the network radio system of which he is a product, *The Shadow* helped to articulate a powerful prewar

sense of an imagined national community, bounded by important hierarchies, exclusions, and fears, and spoken in the accents of a new American form of speech that was both authoritative and intimate, broadly
accessible and yet highly useful for marking and policing multiple
forms of social difference. In his analysis of Hollywood films of the
1930s and 1940s, Lary May argues convincingly that the mobilization
of a national consensus narrative does not become dominant until
World War II. This consensus narrative marks a conversion away
from the themes of many 1930s films, including class and ethnic consciousness, New Deal values critical of monopoly capitalism, and support for "a multicultural republic . . . rooted in citizen action, pluralism,
and dreams of contemporary morals and abundance."[32] My analysis
of *The Shadow*'s transformation from Gibson's magazine stories to the
radio program of 1937–41 suggests that elements of this conversion
were already under way in other popular forms just prior to World War
II. As Lizabeth Cohen has noted, during the 1930s Americans came to
identify with national networks, national brands, and a national mass-
mediated culture in general, often at the expense of the local, class-
and ethnic-oriented patterns of identity.[33]

In his mastery of communication technology and public relations,
the Shadow bears a striking resemblance to Roosevelt, whose disembodied voice so powerfully embodied radio's promise to merge
public and private. Like Roosevelt, the Shadow of the late 1930s is a
"ganglion for reception, expression, transmission, combination, and
realization." His clipped, telegraphic speech, his penchant for repeating
phrases as if transmitting by Morse code, and the metallic sound of
his filtered voice all contribute to the sense that the Shadow speaks in
the idiom of electronic communication. An expert in the technologies
of communication and the psychology of the "mass mind," the Shadow
epitomizes the professional-managerial consciousness emerging in the
ranks of journalists, public-relations counsels, broadcasters, and advertising executives.[34] In his intimate knowledge of the hearts of men and
women and the trouble spots of the industrial city, he seems to range
over a territory as vast as that which Federal Communications Commis-
sion Chief Commissioner Anning Prall claims for radio itself in a 1936
address celebrating Mutual's first coast-to-coast broadcast: "a combination of the church, the public rostrum, the newspaper, the theater,
the concert hall—in fact all media."[35] In short, the Shadow knows.

His double identity represents his broad and flexible knowledge
of the public and private worlds whose inevitable collisions must be

managed so carefully. Lamont Cranston, "wealthy young man about town," inhabits a small, socially intensive world of face-to-face contacts and known quantities. The Shadow lurks in darkness and mystery, where he encounters foreign foes that are both interchangeable and inexhaustibly present. Cranston, amateur detective, must move back and forth between these two identities in order to protect the civic order from external threats; in that movement back and forth, he defines the borders of these worlds even as he transgresses them— from a crowded theater to a criminal's lair to a guilty conscience.

The Shadow was quickly followed by a raft of comic-book and radio imitators—Superman, the Green Hornet, Batman—crime fighters preoccupied with defending the modern city. These superheroes all came with alter egos (reporter Clark Kent, newspaper publisher Britt Reid, socialite Bruce Wayne) who, like Lamont Cranston, were influential intelligence workers in their own right. They shaped public opinion by day and policed the social boundaries of the city by night. *Boston Blackie,* which aired in 1944, adopted the Shadow's penchant for besting the police through his mastery of information technology and his perch in between the worlds of crime and law and order.[36] *The Green Hornet,* broadcast from 1935 to 1952, was the most blatant imitation of the Shadow, a remarkably faithful echo of *The Shadow*'s imperialist Orientalism and urban pluralism.[37]

Some have argued that, with the rise of the mass media and a bureaucratic welfare state, the terms "public" and "private" have ceased to refer to discrete entities.[38] But the terms continued to have meaning in the golden age of radio because of programs like *The Shadow,* which dramatized the dangerous play of outside and inside, foreign and domestic, unknown and known. At the end of the 1930s and the beginning of the 1940s, network radio shored up its ideological flanks against competing definitions of the public and the private. *The Shadow,* along with a growing number of daytime, evening, and prime-time serial and episodic dramas, helped to trace the contours of a new social space precariously situated in the uncanny borderlands between public and private. The public—perhaps always something of a phantom—became, in the idiom of intimate publicity, a rhetorical tool for policing the borders of national and racial difference and an imaginary landscape endlessly evoking and assuaging fears that radio's early national public was becoming a hypnotized audience.

America's Most Fascinating People

*The everywhere-ness, all-at-onceness, and
never-ending-ness of the media are powerful
barriers to understanding, or even
acknowledging their history.*
—*Daniel Czitrom,* Media and the American Mind

The man who gave voice to the Shadow in 1944 was born Ralph Bowman and only became "John Archer" through a process as strange as the one by which Lamont Cranston became the Shadow. Bowman won the name John Archer along with a movie contract with RKO Pictures in 1939 as a contestant on *Gateway to Hollywood,* a CBS radio talent show hosted by Hollywood producer Jesse L. Lasky, in which two contestants competed each week for specific names already made famous through the publicity machinery of the program.[1] In addition, the new John Archer received a membership in the Screen Actors Guild. The program's format of auditioning unknowns before a panel of well-known industry judges, a studio audience, and a massive audience at home—and the reward of instant celebrity and coveted professional credentials—may all sound familiar to fans of the contemporary Fox hit TV program *American Idol* and its myriad predecessors, spin-offs, and clones. *Gateway to Hollywood,* like *Major Bowes' Original Amateur Hour* before it, and dozens of radio and television programs since, was not able to resist taking "ordinary" people and turning them into stars, largely by providing the public arena in which to perform. And the process by which an ordinary person becomes a celebrity, in all its artifice and hype, was as mesmerizing as any Hollywood spectacle with its special effects and dazzling costumes.

Mark Andrejevec's analysis of the reality TV show *Extreme Makeover* applies, with modifications allowing for an aural rather than a visual medium, nearly as well to *Gateway to Hollywood*: "The logic is circular: The process of watching [listening to] the cast members as they are made over to look like [sound like] celebrities becomes the source of their fame. The referent—talent, genius, and so forth—has been eclipsed by this very circularity; one becomes famous by being made... to look [to sound] famous."[2]

Daniel Czitrom's warning about the difficulty of understanding the history of media seems especially apt when considering the popular and academic discourse buzzing around the spasm of "reality television" programs, whose origins in earlier forms of media have been obscured by their "everywhere-ness, all-at-onceness, and never-ending-ness." The persistence of this impulse—to bring ordinary people into contact with the publicity machinery of the electronic media—is almost as old as broadcasting itself, as we have seen. Informal chat shows began with radio hosts such as Roxy Rothafel and Arthur Godfrey in the mid-1920s. *The March of Time* pioneered the use of dramatized reenactments to tell the real news stories of the day in 1931. Advice shows began in the late 1920s with Dr. John R. Brinkley's *Medical Question Box* program, followed by *The Voice of Experience* in 1933 and the *Personal Column of the Air* in 1936. Doling out medical, spiritual, and relationship advice to an unseen audience that wrote in, these programs anticipated formats that continue in surprisingly unmodified forms to this day on the radio dial. Man-in-the street broadcasting began with Ted Husing during the 1932 presidential election, and soon thereafter became a regularly scheduled commercial program with the start of *Vox Pop*. Amateur performance shows began with Major Bowes in 1935. Public-affairs programs featuring audience participation began that same year with *America's Town Meeting of the Air*. In the postwar period, as radio began to develop new formats and new markets, programs like *So You Want to Be a Disc Jockey*, which offered amateur guests the chance to master the snappy, rhythmic patois of the DJ introducing "platters that matter," responded to this same impulse.

Studies of reality TV have sought to locate the appeal of "reality" in the first flickerings of the television tube in the years after World War II. Sean Baker traces a circuitous and idiosyncratic continuity from police shows such as *Dragnet*, which purported to dramatize "real crimes" in the 1950s, through *Candid Camera*, *The Partridge Family* (for reasons that remain unclear), *America's Funniest Home*

Videos, and *Unsolved Mysteries,* all the way up to contemporary reality shows like *Survivor.*[3] The meeting of "unscripted ingenuousness... of non-professional, 'average person' performers, next to the scripted formality of slicker program genres," in Wayne Munson's words, has been a reliable source of suspense, sympathy, titillation, and comedy for as long as there have been electronic media.[4]

In fact, Munson has argued that the preoccupation with participatory media forms dates back to "the birth of the eighteenth-century magazine, which followed the seventeenth-century emergence of the English coffeehouse as a salon-like setting for... an extra-parliamentary 'talk space'" (20). Munson traces this same impulse into the nineteenth century with the lyceum movement of the northeastern United States, and women's service magazines, and into the twentieth century with heterosocial and participatory "cheap amusements" such as the cabaret and the nightclub. With such varied examples of reality-based and/or participatory forms as *The Tatler, Godey's Ladies Book, So You Want to Be a Disc Jockey,* and *Extreme Makeover,* one begins to doubt the usefulness of such a category. It is important, however, to note that an important question threads its way through discourse about a great many of the media, amusements, and technological advances since the advent of the modern era: will they make for a more democratic nation and a more coherent community?

This question forms the center of debate about the value of every medium and cultural form since the printing press and continues to be debated in the most recent scholarship on reality TV. Munson identifies a powerful current of populism running from *The Tatler* to the cabaret, to radio programs such as *Reunion of the States, Pull Over Neighbor, Paging John Doe, Meet Joe Public, Breakfast Club,* and, of course, *Vox Pop.* In particular, Munson observes a nostalgic emphasis on "republican simplicity" and a distrust of elites and experts (27, 23).

As mentioned in the Introduction, critics such as Habermas view this same history less as the story of a continuous impulse and more as a narrative of decline, in which the rational critical discourse of the seventeenth-century coffeehouses and eighteenth-century magazines gave way to mere commercialized travesties, culminating in the radio and television talk show of the twentieth century. "Today," Habermas laments, "conversation itself is administered."[5]

In an essay titled "Chatter in the Age of Electronic Reproduction," Paolo Carpignano et al. offer a bold rethinking of the conventional wisdom that the mass media's absorption of the functions of the public sphere is "the reason for the degeneration of public life, if not its disappearance." The authors argue that the apparent degradation of the public sphere reveals the more important "crisis of the spectacle form itself, that is, a crisis of a communicative model based on the principle of propaganda and persuasion." In its place, they argue, a new political landscape emerges, marked by the collapse of the distinction between production and consumption, and the centrality of "social, personal, and environmental concerns," and circulated by new discursive practices beyond the control of formal institutions.[6] The epitome of these new discursive practices can be found in the television and radio talk show, which, for Habermas, signaled the complete hollowing out of rational-critical publicity. Mark Poster and Wayne Munson have also argued persuasively that mass-mediated forms like the talk show and the advertisement provide a bold new context for contemporary public and political discourse.[7] Joshua Meyrowitz, who draws on the work of Marshall McLuhan, Harold Innis, and Erving Goffman, argues that these electronic media blur older lines of social distinction and hierarchy based on a fixed "sense of place," ushering in a more egalitarian age in which people become "hunters and gatherers of information."[8] In this metaphor and in those of McLuhan ("global village," "tribal drum"), James W. Carey, and Bertolt Brecht, we see the longing for the cohesiveness of community associated with a primitive or biblical past.

In the twentieth century, the discourse circulating through media criticism, political theory, and the general public oscillated between utopian faith in the "technologies of freedom" and Orwellian fears of surveillance, propaganda, and, above all, unchecked corporate and government control of public discourse, or, in Habermas's phrase, administered conversation.[9] The crucial questions turn on the power of the electronic media to strengthen or weaken democratic processes. James Carey divides up the study of communications media into two competing models, one emphasizing social control and the other the power of media to create a ritual sense of "communitas."[10] Brecht imagined radio's interactive destiny as part of a bold new era of democratic freedom and as a fulfillment of some antediluvian promise humanity had made to itself and then forgotten. He also recognized its effective adaptability to fascist ends.[11] More recently, Michael Warner has described the process of the self-abstraction of entering Habermas's bourgeois public sphere as both a moment of "utopian universality" and a "major source of domination."[12] In a passage from 1927 that epitomizes this ambivalence from an administrative perspective with frightening bluntness, Harold Lasswell hails mass-mediated propaganda as the means by which modern society can recapture the tribal cohesion and centralized control of a primitive gemeinschaft:

> In the Great Society it is no longer possible to fuse the waywardness of individuals in the furnace of the war dance: a newer and subtler instrument must weld thousands and even millions of human beings into one amalgamated mass of hate and will and hope. A new flame must burn out the canker of dissent and temper the steel of bellicose enthusiasm. The name of this new hammer and anvil of social solidarity is propaganda.[13]

This ambivalence has, in fact, become so central to how the media of communication, entertainment, surveillance, and information are theorized, marketed, regulated, and consumed that it has become difficult to see them as part of everyday life, as expressions and negotiations of conflicts, hierarchies, and tensions in the broader social world. Typically, the argument has been that "participatory" media, with their emphasis on the inclusion of the untutored, often crude voices of ordinary people, were, by virtue of their popularity and seeming populism, inherently democratic. Criticism of such forms represented a species of elitist contempt for popular tastes and populist voices.

In the recent spasm of critical and popular discussion about the "impact" of reality television and in part because of the amnesia effect that Czitrom describes, it has also become difficult to see the ways that the reality impulse has become more than just a fad or a particular programming option.[14] It has come to permeate almost every part of the media landscape of the twentieth and twenty-first centuries. For several decades, we have heard it in the callers' voices on talk radio, and seen it on nightly newscast interviews with innocent bystanders, fans, and opinionated citizens. Much of broadcast television has depended on this impulse for at least part of its everyday programming: Jay Leno's comic encounters with astonishingly ignorant but good-natured Southern Californians recall the *Vox Pop* interview with Wilburn Gladsby on the streets of Houston in 1932. The canned laugh tracks on situation comedies, which have been "taped live" before small, carefully coached studio audiences, preserve the conceit of the participatory audiences of *America Calling*. Amateur and hidden-camera video programs, myriad vérité and reenactment-style crime programs, recall *Candid Microphone* and *The March of Time*. *Law and Order's* "ripped from the headlines" topicality recalls *Dragnet's* claims of authentic story lines.[15] Special television broadcasts of "bloopers," or outtakes—some situation comedies run such hilarious miscues at the end of each episode, while the credits run—are a reminder of the program's status as both a live performance and a seamlessly edited commercial product. On a 1999 episode of NBC's news magazine, *Dateline*, viewers were invited to vote via the Internet for the innocence or guilt of a murder suspect, whose story the show covered.[16] This display of interactive democracy represents an early example of the interactive innovation that *Big Brother* formatted soon thereafter. But it puts me in mind of the trial of Bertha Schultz on *Today's Children* in 1944, a trial that was decided by audience mail and whose live audience functioned as a kind of jury during commercial breaks, opining as to Schultz's guilt or innocence. On Baltimore's CBS news affiliate, WJZ-TV, the eleven o'clock news begins each night with coanchor Denise Koch's breathless greeting, "Good evening. Here's what people are talking about tonight." The attempt to portray the news as that which has already entered into the informal networks of community and orality speaks to the nostalgic impulse for simpler forms of community, despite the Doppler radar, remote broadcasting equipment, and satellite video feeds that make such a presentation possible. The conceit that broadcast speech was merely a wider circulation of the kinds of speech already circulating over the back fence, at the town square, or, more recently, the water cooler, dates back to the earliest chat-style programs of the 1920s.

But John Caldwell has dubbed such self-consciousness "televisuality," a newfound preoccupation, beginning in the 1980s, with "increasingly sophisticated references to lived reality" and "an extreme self-consciousness of style."[17] Dramatic programs that simulate newscasts, for instance, recall the documentary techniques of Orson Welles and his radio collaborators Archibald MacLeish, Norman Corwin, and others who used the conceit of a newscast to tell stories. This documentary style, borrowed from *The March of Time* and, in theater, from the "living newspapers," called attention to the role that specific media play in how the people come to know about their world. With the Internet, smart VCRs, satellite radio and TV, MP3 file sharing, and the marketing trend in everything from automobiles to online news sites toward "customization," the everywhereness of "participatory" media has only intensified along with oscillating utopian and dystopian predictions for their impact on democratic community.

In his analysis of reality TV, Andrejevec argues that "we find ourselves caught between the promise of an empowering form of interactivity and the potential of an increasingly exploitative one."[18] Specifically, he brings critical attention to the fact that the utopian hopes of
interactivity to liberate us from an oppressive "one-way, top-down,
mass-media" culture industry that render us "passive spectators" requires that we submit to ever finer, ever more pervasive forms of moni-
toring or surveillance.[19] Rather than liberating us, he suggests, such a
process actually intensifies the very hold that large media corporate
interests have on consumers. In this model, the sense of individuality
lost with the rise of the culture industries of the twentieth century is
recovered through the process of customization. From Amazon.com
and Netflix's strategy of matching consumer choices of millions of customers to predict desired products, to Toyota's Scion's offer of dozens
of distinct options to assure buyers of the almost snowflake-like unique-
ness of their car, examples of such customization abound. The popular
CBS franchise *Big Brother,* a reality TV program that incorporated
twenty-four-hour Internet surveillance, for example, repositions interactivity and surveillance as necessary conditions for self-expression
and authentic experience.[20] Such a repositioning, Andrejevic observes,
matches the rhetoric of utopian futurists such as Bill Gates and Nicholas
Negroponte, not to mention the endless commercial hype that attends
each new technology of freedom.[21]

The promise of interactivity is the "dedifferentiation of the boundaries between production and consumption," work and leisure, and the
social spaces in which these activities traditionally take place.[22] The
blurring of the social boundaries of workplace, leisure, and domestic
space brings with it, as we have seen, both utopian promises of greater
equality and freedom and the likelihood of a reinscription of social
boundaries, perhaps ones even more effective at removing these practices from critical public scrutiny. As Wayne Munson has put it, "when
transgression is commodified, modern oppositionalism is folded back
into the very political economy it pretends to oppose" (28). Because
the origins of the electronic media are so easily forgotten, it is tempting to overemphasize the powerful lines of continuity that link today's
burst of reality TV to radio of the 1930s and 1940s. I do not mean to
argue that there is nothing new under the sun. But I find the contemporary debates about the meaning of "reality TV" to be, in some key
ways, a distillation of the central concerns and preoccupations that

first arose during radio's network era. Like radio's soap operas, crime thrillers, quiz shows, and presidential addresses, contemporary reality television programs seek to simulate intimacy, the real, and to engage audiences in participatory relationships that promise a fantasy of mobility (boundary crossing or "dedifferentiation") and that often deliver an intensified experience of hierarchical boundaries and distinctions.

At the heart of dedifferentiation is the impetus to "get real," in the phrase made famous by MTV's *The Real World*. But Arild Fetveit suggests that the seemingly opposed developments of digital video manipulation and reality TV—one a discourse of making believe, the other ostensibly a discourse of truth—actually share a common urge for fantasy, escape, and simulation.[23] What seems at first to be the revolutionary truth-telling and dedifferentiating capacity of reality TV becomes, instead, yet another technology for "compartmentalizing" social worlds, insulating viewers from social undesirables such as criminals and the poor. The thrilling power of communication technology to collapse social worlds works just as effectively to recompartmentalize them, a lesson *The Shadow* taught its audience in the late 1930s: portable videocams in the back of police cars on *COPS*, in the savanna where "animals attack," or in the streets and towns and homes where disasters are routinely "caught on tape"; reenactments in the hunt for criminals in *America's Most Wanted;* and the casting and editing of outlandish "characters" that reinforce stereotypical characterizations of racial and sexual minorities.

The appeal of reality TV has also been widely ascribed to the intensely competitive nature of contemporary life. Programs like Mark Burnett's *Survivor* evoked comparisons to the office politics of corporate life, where survival requires strategic alliances and the unsentimental realization that, in a "flexible" downsizing and outsourcing economic regime, coworkers are ultimately competitors. Burnett's subsequent hit, *The Apprentice,* with its irresistible tagline, "You're fired," made this metaphoric interpretation literal. Indeed, programs such as these were often interpreted as providing information and strategies for use by workers in competitive workplaces. Writing in *Psychology Today,* a psychology professor and his graduate student argue that such shows appeal to particularly competitive people:

> One aspect that all of the reality TV shows had in common was their competitive nature: contestants were vying with one another for a cash prize and were engaged in building alliances and betraying allies....

It makes sense, then, that fans of both *Survivor* and *Temptation Island* tend to be competitive—and that they are more likely to place a very high value on revenge than are other people.[24]

These interpretations help to construct a vision of the audience for such programs as disproportionately high-achieving and masculine— welcome news to producers and networks who hope to lure sponsors to shows that draw such coveted viewers. Such interpretations challenge the common assertion that reality TV is, in essence, merely another species of soap opera, a charge that has been leveled at professional wrestling as well. A fan-generated Web site called "A Soap Kind of Reality" bears out the ways in which audiences have made this connection their own. This site is dedicated to documenting plot developments and audience response to a dozen soap operas along with reality shows like *Big Brother* and *The Amazing Race*.[25] It is not difficult to see that these competing understandings of reality TV's audience turn on still-dominant notions of gender and programming that consign women to daytime, low-prestige formats like soap opera, and that prize men's viewing as more prestigious, socially useful, and, of course, economically significant, both for sponsors and for the larger economic system in which men function (it is assumed) more productively than women.

Kristen Hatch's work on daytime televised congressional hearings in the 1950s reveals how the ideology of the gendered broadcast schedule, first elucidated by Michele Hilmes, trumped even the sacrosanct profit motive or technological determinism in deciding what sorts of programming would be made regularly available to a largely female daytime audience. The popularity among women viewers of hearings led by Sen. Estes Kefauver into links between the government and organized crime and the more famous Army–McCarthy hearings sparked anxiety about women entering political life. Comparing women's reception of the hearings to that of soap operas, critics of the day were not making the point I make in chapter 3—that the soaps, like the hearings, provided a forum to talk about common political problems. Instead, they sought to discredit women's burgeoning interest in politics by denigrating the form—daytime television—in which it was presented.[26]

Forty years later, much the same process accompanied the widespread interest in the O. J. Simpson murder trial, another daytime television sensation. This time, however, it was women, unemployed men, and the indolent in general who were scorned for their unproductive and voyeuristic interest in the soap-like trial. Television's revolutionary potential, to lay bare the machinations of justice for all to see—especially the persistent power of racial and gender and socioeconomic inequities to shape the judicial process—was counterbalanced by a steady drumbeat of derision of its audience as slack-jawed soap-opera fans entranced by a media circus, the sparkle of celebrity, and the coarse details of a gruesome crime. The murder case against Scott Peterson in 2004 occasioned comparisons to the O. J. Simpson trial and its audience.[27] And all of this reminds one of the radio and newsreel coverage of the Bruno Hauptmann kidnapping and murder trial of 1932, which Wilburn Gladsby weighed in on thanks to *Vox Pop*. The trial, which made radio coverage of live events massively popular in 1935, created a new class of celebrity journalists, such as Walter Winchell, whose nearly constant coverage helped to convey a sense of urgency and immediacy to the proceedings in a Los Angeles courtroom.[28] Even as such coverage brought a national public together into an almost ritualized hush of rapt attention, it also generated uneasiness about the kind of person who listens in on such melodrama (a private vice) to the exclusion of productive labor (a public virtue). Just as Gladsby's inadvertent performance of an irrational consumer of information and products epitomized a complicated and ambivalent portrait of the identity and status of radio's new mass audience, so too does the contemporary discourse surrounding reality TV remind us, again and again, that the electronic media continue to serve as important cultural sites in the ongoing "crisis" over public and private speech and space. As public and private continue to operate as codes for unstable social identities in a society marked by steep structural hierarchies, and as their collapse, the one into the other, continues to represent the ambivalent circulation of these hierarchies through new technological forms of communication, entertainment, and surveillance, radio, television, the Internet, and other media forms will continue to embrace endless variations on the intimate public.

Notes

Introduction

1. See Ray Barfield, *Listening to Radio, 1920–1950* (Westport, CT, and London: Praeger Press), 68; Rita Barnard, *The Great Depression and the Culture of Abundance* (Cambridge and New York: Cambridge University Press, 1995), 15; Jim Cox, *The Great Radio Soap Operas* (Jefferson, NC, and London: McFarland & Company, 1999), 2; Madeleine Edmondson and David Rounds, *From Mary Noble to Mary Hartman: The Complete Soap Opera Book* (New York: Stein and Day, 1976), 27.

2. In the 1920s and early 1930s, radio's installation into family and community life was often greeted with profound ambivalence. Barfield provides accounts of radio listeners who remember the intersection of telephone lines and intercoms with radio waves, creating shared mini-networks of reception that blurred the lines of public and private in often unsettling ways. Of course, he also records many idyllic memories of shared reception around a receiving set in department stores, on a neighbor's porch, and at outdoor community gatherings (Barfield, *Listening to Radio*, 3–14, 51–53).

3. Robert S. Lynd and Helen Merrel Lynd, *Middletown in Transition: A Study in Cultural Conflicts* (Harcourt, Brace and World, 1937), 144, quoted in Rita Barnard, *The Great Depression and the Culture of Consumption, Kennth Fearing, Nathaniel West, and Mass Culture in the 1930s* (Cambridge: Cambridge University Press, 1995), 27.

4. Many writers have treated radio's "illusion of intimacy"; for a particularly good discussion, see Wayne Munson, *All Talk: The Talkshow in Media Culture* (Philadelphia: Temple University Press, 1993), 23, 153–54.

5. See ibid., 28, on the "effective popularization and commodification of transgression" that takes place in the early radio talk shows such as *Arthur Godfrey's Talent Scouts.*

6. See Carolyn Marvin, *When Old Technologies Were New: Thinking about Electric Communication in the Late Nineteenth Century* (New York: Oxford University Press, 1988).

7. I have in mind here the ironic turn of Foucault's analysis of the "repressive hypothesis" of Victorian notions about sexuality. See Michel Foucault, *The History of Sexuality,* vol. 1, *An Introduction* (New York: Vintage Books, 1980), 15–35.

8. Jeffrey Weintraub and Krishan Kumar, eds., *Public and Private in Thought and Practice: Perspectives on a Grand Dichotomy* (Chicago: University of Chicago Press, 1997), 1.

9. Nancy Fraser, "Sex, Lies, and the Public Sphere: Some Reflections on the Confirmation of Clarence Thomas," *Critical Inquiry* 18 (spring 1992): 597.

10. Ibid.

11. See Michele Hilmes, *Radio Voices: American Broadcasting, 1922–1952* (Minneapolis: University of Minnesota Press, 1997); Margaret T. McFadden, "America's Boy Friend Who Can't Get a Date: Gender, Race, and the Cultural Work of the Jack Benny Program, 1932–1946," *Journal of American History* 80 (June 1993): 113–34; Allison McCracken, "Scary Women and Scarred Men: Suspense, Gender Trouble, and Postwar Change, 1942–1950," in *Radio Reader: Essays in the Cultural History of Radio,* ed. Michele Hilmes and Jason Loviglio (New York: Routledge, 2002), 183–208; Matthew Murray, "'The Tendency to Deprave and Corrupt Morals': Regulation and Irregular Sexuality in Golden Age Radio Comedy," in Hilmes and Loviglio, *Radio Reader;* Barbara D. Savage, *Broadcasting Freedom: Radio, War, and the Politics of Race, 1938–1948* (Chapel Hill: University of North Carolina Press, 1999); Susan J. Douglas, *Listening In: Radio and the American Imagination* (Minneapolis: University of Minnesota Press, 2004).

12. Catherine L. Covert, "We May Hear Too Much: American Sensibility and the Response to Radio, 1919–1924," in *Mass Media between the Wars: Perceptions of Cultural Tension, 1918–1941,* ed. Catherine L. Covert and John D. Stevens (Syracuse, NY: Syracuse University Press, 1984).

13. For the history of this period in terms of regulation, see Robert W. McChesney, *Telecommunications, Mass Media, and Democracy: The Battle for the Control of U.S. Broadcasting, 1928–1935* (New York: Oxford University Press, 1993); and Susan Smulyan, *Selling Radio: The Commercialization of American Broadcasting, 1920–1934* (Washington, DC: Smithsonian Institution Press, 1994).

14. Hilmes, *Radio Voices,* 1.

15. Jürgen Habermas, *The Structural Transformation of the Public Sphere: An Inquiry into a Category of Bourgeois Society* (Cambridge: MIT Press,

1989); E. J. Hobsbawm and Terence Ranger, eds., *The Invention of Tradition* (Cambridge: Cambridge University Press, 1992); Richard Sennet, *The Fall of Public Man* (New York: W. W. Norton, 1992); Hannah Arendt, *The Human Condition* (Chicago: University of Chicago Press, 1958).

16. Habermas, *The Structural Transformation,* 160.

17. Bruce Robbins, "Introduction," Nancy Fraser, "Rethinking the Public Sphere: A Contribution to the Critique of Actually Existing Democracy," and Michael Warner, "The Mass Public and the Mass Subject," in *The Phantom Public Sphere,* ed. Bruce Robbins (Minneapolis: University of Minnesota Press, 1993); Weintraub and Kumar, *Public and Private;* Craig Calhoun, ed., *Habermas and the Public Sphere* (Cambridge: MIT Press, 1992).

18. For Nancy Fraser, Habermas's overly narrow and static public sphere is a useful starting point for introducing the concept of "counterpublics," smaller spaces where groups historically excluded from the supposedly universal liberal public sphere and marginalized in various ghettos of "privacy" could constitute their own political identities (Fraser, "Rethinking the Public Sphere").

19. Jeff Weintraub, "The Theory and Politics of the Public/Private Distinction," in Weintraub and Kumar, *Public and Private,* 4–7.

20. Warner, "The Mass Public and the Mass Subject," 383, 377.

21. Ibid., 382.

22. Ibid., 385.

23. Lisabeth Cohen, *Making a New Deal: Industrial Workers in Chicago, 1919–1939* (Cambridge: Cambridge University Press, 1991); Michael Denning, *The Cultural Front: The Laboring of American Culture in the Twentieth Century* (London and New York: Verso, 1996); Roland Marchand, *Advertising the American Dream: Making Way for Modernity, 1920–1940* (Berkeley: University of California Press, 1985); Lary May, *The Big Tomorrow: Hollywood and the Politics of the American Way* (Chicago: University of Chicago Press, 2000); Warren Susman, *Culture as History: The Transformation of the American Society in the Twentieth Century* (New York: Pantheon Books, 1984).

24. Denning, *The Cultural Front,* 126.

25. Lawrence W. Levine, "Hollywood's Washington: Film Images of National Politics during the Great Depression," *Prospects* 10, ed. Jack Salzman (New York: Cambridge University Press, 178).

26. Walter Lippmann, *Public Opinion* (New York: Macmillan, 1922, 1960) and *The Phantom Public* (New York: Harcourt, Brace & Co., 1925); Raymond Seidelman, *Disenchanted Realists: Political Scientists and the American Crisis, 1884–1984* (Albany: State University of New York Press, 1985); Elton Mayo, "The Irrational Factor in Human Behavior: The 'Night-Mind' in Industry," *Annals of the American Academy of Political and Social Science* (November 1923): 117–30; Walter T. Shepard, "Democracy in Transition," *American Political Science Review* 29:1 (February 1935): 1–20.

27. On the importance of "the people" as the central symbol of the Popular Front, see Kenneth Burke's address to the American Writers Congress in 1935 and Michael Denning's discussion of its significance, in *The Cultural Front*, 124–36. For a discussion of the link between the symbol of "the people" and an essentially conservative vision of Americanism, see Warren Susman, "The People's Fair: Cultural Contradictions of a Consumer Society," in *Culture as History*, 211–29.

28. Warner, "The Mass Public and the Mass Subject," 236.

29. For information on Brinkley, see Gene Fowler and Bill Crawford, *Border Radio: Quacks, Yodelers, Pitchmen, Psychics, and Other Amazing Broadcasters of the American Airwaves* (New York: Limelight Editions, 1987), 13–46, and recordings of Doctor Brinkley's radio program at the Radio Program Archive at the University of Memphis, Memphis, Tennessee (http://www.people.memphis.edu/~mbensman/welcome.html). For a discussion of Will Rogers, see May, *The Big Tomorrow*, 11–54.

30. Leila Sussman suggests that other factors, such as expanding literacy and education rates and the advent of the New Deal itself, were also responsible for the explosion of political letter writing that swept the Congress and the White House in the 1930s (*Dear FDR: A Study of Presidential Letter-Writing* [Totowa, NJ: Bedminster Press, 1963], xvi). See also Marchand, *Advertising the American Dream*, 93, 353–57, quoted in Joy Elizabeth Hayes, "Radio Broadcasting and Nation Building in Mexico and the United States, 1925–1945," Ph.D. dissertation, University of California, San Diego, 1994, 9.

31. See Denning, *The Cultural Front*, 115–18, for a discussion of "Ballad for Americans." The comedy of late-night television talk programs such as *The Late Show with David Letterman* and *The Tonight Show with Jay Leno* still relies heavily on this highly derivative form of the host chatting spontaneously with members of the audience or with men and women encountered on the street. This man-in-the-street interview form dates from the early 1930s, with Ted Husing in Chicago and then with *Vox Pop* in Texas, about which more later.

32. John Dunning, *On the Air: The Encyclopedia of Old-Time Radio* (New York: Oxford University Press, 1998), 30–31.

33. *Town Hall Tonight*'s opening bit—a parade through the "town's" streets to the Town Hall led by the Mighty Allen Art Players—plays on the ideal of a small, coherent, and inclusive public, a world that radio promised to resurrect. As the parade moves through the streets, we hear snippets of the voices of the people engaged in various public and private activities, peremptorily adjourning their business because "It's *Town Hall Tonight!*" This scene recalls Bellow's sense of radio reception as a universal community ritual, blurring public and private, taking over the streets, and, in its immediacy, bringing together all of the social activities of the people. For more on Fred Allen and his fictional townspeople, see Hilmes, *Radio Voices*, 200–12, Alan Havig, *Fred*

Allen's Radio Comedy (Philadelphia: Temple University Press, 1990), and Arthur Frank Wertheim, *Radio Comedy* (New York and London: Oxford University Press, 1979), 157–88, 335–52.

34. Denning, *The Cultural Front*, 362–402.

35. Hilmes, *Radio Voices*, 151–82.

1. The Fireside Chats and the New Deal

All letters to Roosevelt mentioned in this chapter, unless otherwise noted, can be found in the president's Personal File 200 (PPF200), Franklin D. Roosevelt Library, Hyde Park, New York.

1. Frederick Bixler, New York, to Franklin D. Roosevelt, March 13, 1933.

2. Frank Cort, Sunnyside, CA, to Franklin D. Roosevelt, May 7, 1933.

3. J. E. Baudo, Brooklyn, NY, to Franklin D. Roosevelt, March 13, 1933.

4. Charles Johnson, Englewood Cliffs, NJ, March 13, 1933.

5. The image of domestic space transformed by broadcasting into a quasi-theatrical space is one that Lynn Spigel sees as central to television's installation into the home in the 1950s. She argues that postwar television oscillated between the promise of domesticating public space (bringing the outside world in) and whisking the viewer out of the domestic space and into the wide world. Both possibilities were fraught with ambivalence, but, Spigel concludes, the forms of programming that became dominant in this period tended to strike a compromise between the two, creating a self-conscious space neither wholly public nor private. The television sitcom, like nineteenth-century "parlor theatricals" and even early Hollywood cinema, in its self-conscious representations of family life, sent the message that, in Karen Haltunnen's words, "middle-class social life was itself a charade" (*Confidence Men and Painted Women: A Study of Middle-Class Culture in America, 1830–1870* [New Haven: Yale University Press, 1986], 184–85). Given the radio origins of the soap opera and the situation comedy, it is surprising that Spigel neglects radio's role in the development of these self-conscious representations of theatrical domesticity (Lynn Spigel, *Make Room for TV: Television and the Family Ideal in Postwar America* [Chicago: University of Chicago Press, 1992], 162).

6. Edward Miller, *Emergency Broadcasting and 1930s American Radio* (Philadelphia: Temple University Press, 2003), 79.

7. *Broadcasting,* December 1, 1931, 7.

8. Fans wrote fondly of their evening ritual of "visiting with the Goldbergs," starting in 1930. See Donald Weber, "The Jewish-American World of Gertrude Berg: The Goldbergs on Radio and Television, 1930–1950," in *Talking Back: Images of Jewish Women in American Popular Culture,* ed. Joyce Antler (Hanover, NH: University Press of New England, 1998).

9. In 1924, When Samuel L. "Roxy" Rothafel and the cast of AT&T's proto-network "Roxy and His Gang" traveled to towns where the show was

broadcast, they were "addressed . . . by name just as intimately as though they had been friends for years." Listeners protested in 1925 in record numbers when "Roxy," in response to orders from WEAF executives, abruptly formalized the folksy "radio family" quality of the program. Michele Hilmes demonstrates in this and other examples the conflicting impulses felt by commercial broadcasters toward popularity, on the one hand, and high-brow respectability, on the other (*Radio Voices: American Broadcasting, 1922–1952* [Minneapolis: University of Minnesota Press, 1997], 61–63). See also Bruce Bliven, "How Radio Is Remaking Our World," *Century* 108 (July 1924): 147, quoted in Susan Smulyan, *Selling Radio: The Commercialization of American Broadcasting, 1920–1934* (Washington, DC: Smithsonian Books, 1996), 55.

10. Anthony Slide, ed., *Selected Radio and Television Criticism* (Metuchen, NJ: Scarecrow Press, 1987), 36.

11. Leila Sussman, *Dear FDR: A Study of Presidential Letter-Writing* (Totowa, NJ: Bedminster Press, 1963), xvi. See also Roland Marchand, *Advertising the American Dream: Making Way for Modernity, 1920–1940* (Berkeley: University of California Press, 1985), 93, 353–57, quoted in Joy Elizabeth Hayes, "Radio Broadcasting and Nation Building in Mexico and the United States, 1925–1945," Ph.D. dissertation, University of California, San Diego, 1994, 13.

12. Sussman, *Dear FDR*, 1–18, 60.

13. Mr. S. E. Kemp, Blair, NE, to Louis Howe, March 28, 1933.

14. There is general agreement about which broadcasts were considered Fireside Chats and which were not. For a discussion of the handful of broadcasts about which there has been some disagreement, see Russell D. Buhite and David W. Levy, *FDR's Fireside Chats* (Norman: Oklahoma University Press, 1992), xv.

15. Frequent guests to the White House for the broadcasts of the chats emphasize Roosevelt's deep concentration on the visual and aural aspects of his performance: his smiling face, nodding head, and reassuring gestures along with his crisp, clear tone of voice, his careful pronunciation, and his deep concentration on the radio audience at home. See Doris Kearns Goodwin, *No Ordinary Time: Franklin and Eleanor Roosevelt: The Home Front in World War II* (New York: Simon and Schuster, 1994), 57–60; Buhite and Levy, *FDR's Fireside Chats*, xviii.

16. Robert T. Oliver, "The Speech That Established Roosevelt's Reputation," *Quarterly Journal of Speech* (October 1945): 274, quoted in Earnest Brandenburg and Waldo W. Braden, "Franklin D. Roosevelt's Voice and Pronunciation," *Quarterly Journal of Speech* (February 1952): 23–24.

17. Brandenburg and Braden, "Franklin D. Roosevelt's Voice and Pronunciation," 23–30.

18. Waldo W. Braden, "The Roosevelt Wartime Fireside Chats: A Rhetorical Study of Strategy and Tactics, in *The Presidency and National Security*

Policy Proceedings 1:1 (1984): 141. These performances were the result of hours of rehearsal and careful attention to the aesthetics of radio and public speaking. Roosevelt's closest aide, Harry Hopkins, regularly listened to the chats on the radio in his own room in the White House in order to hear them exactly as the rest of the country did. When it was discovered that a small gap between Roosevelt's front teeth produced a slight whistle on the air, he had a special removable dental bridge made, to be worn only during the broadcasting of the chats (Grace Tully's memoir, *FDR: My Boss* [New York: Charles Scribner's Sons, 1949], 100, quoted in Goodwin, *No Ordinary Time,* 58).

19. All the others were delivered within weeks of major elections, congressional votes, or implementation of laws or policies. Most important, Roosevelt resisted the thousands of letters pleading with him to make the chats a weekly program; he averaged four chats a year, partly because they were so time- and labor-intensive, but mostly because he wanted them to maintain the status of a national media event and not become commonplace.

20. Waldo W. Braden and Earnest Brandenburg, "Roosevelt's Fireside Chats," in *Speech Monographs* 22 (November 1955): 292.

21. Sussman, *Dear FDR,* 9.

22. Robert K. Merton, "Introduction," in ibid., xv. As part of his campaigns for governor and the presidency, Roosevelt began a nationwide letter-writing campaign to thousands of national and local political operators, including every delegate to the 1924 Democratic National Convention and numerous state and county chairmen, candidates for Congress, and others who had written to him. In an early version of his fireside appeals for public participation in national affairs, these letters were part of Roosevelt's growing quest for data about how to quantify and direct the course of public opinion: "I am anxious to obtain the views of men and women representing every part of our country who are recognized as having an abiding faith and interest in the Democratic Party" (Sussman, *Dear FDR,* 27–29).

23. See, for instance, William E. Leuchtenberg, *Franklin Roosevelt and the New Deal* (New York: Harper and Row, 1963), 44–45, quoted in Hayes, "Radio Broadcasting and Nation Building." For a nice collection of letters attesting to the broadcast's success, see Lawrence W. Levine and Cornelia R. Levine, eds., *The People and the President: America's Conversation with FDR* (Boston: Beacon Press, 2002), 34–35.

24. Buhite and Levy, *FDR's Fireside Chats,* 12.

25. Edward Miller has shown how Roosevelt used shifting pronouns to play with the boundaries of inclusion and exclusion in these broadcasts (*Emergency Broadcasting,* 93). Hayes found this pronominal shifting in letters to the president from his Fireside Chat listeners ("Radio Broadcasting and Nation Building," 243).

26. Buhite and Levy, *FDR's Fireside Chats,* 13. Subsequent references are given in the text.

27. Michael Warner calls polls "a performative genre. They do not measure something that already exists as public opinion; but when they are reported as such they are public opinion" ("The Mass Public and the Mass Subject," in *The Phantom Public Sphere*, ed. Bruce Robbins [Minneapolis: University of Minnesota Press, 1993], 236). The rise of the opinion poll captures the ambivalence of the new preoccupation with the people. On the one hand, polls represented the triumph of an immediate democracy, a new attention to the centrality of the people's voice and choice. On the other hand, they seemed to represent the triumph of the administrative strategy of channeling the people's voice into acceptable opinions. Warren Susman argues that "the polls themselves became a force, an instrument of significance, not only for the discovery and molding of dominant cultural patterns, but also for their reinforcement" (*Culture as History: The Transformation of American Society in the Twentieth Century* [New York: Pantheon Books, 1984], 158). See also Hayes's discussion of "rhetorical presidency" ("Radio Broadcasting and Nation Building," 6–8).

28. Edward Miller notes a similar moment in a speech on the topic "Democracy, Justice, and Freedom" when Roosevelt says, "I can hear your unspoken wonder as to where we are headed in this troubled world," implying that he has "access to the interiority of his citizenry" (*Emergency Broadcasting,* 92), much like the Shadow, discussed in chapter 4. See also Hayes on this same passage, which, she argues, makes Roosevelt seem "spiritually present" in the homes of his listeners ("Radio Broadcasting and Nation Building," 16).

29. Sussman, *Dear FDR,* 113.

30. The ill-fated and short-lived NRA, ruled unconstitutional in 1935, exemplified the New Deal's masterful use of public relations, public spectacle, and the discourse of nationalism. Using the analogy of soldiers in battle, Roosevelt introduced the NRA's logo, the Blue Eagle, with its motto, "we do our part," as a badge of honor, promising "to keep posted in the post office of every town, a roll of honor of all those who join with me" (Buhite and Levy, *FDR's Fireside Chats,* 35).

31. Sussman, *Dear FDR,* 99.rem

32. These figures from a Hooper ratings chart are in Betty Houchin Winfield, *FDR and the News Media* (New York: Columbia University Press, 1990), 120 n. 20.

33. As Doris Kearns Goodwin has pointed out, the ratings giants of the day, *Amos 'n' Andy, The Goldbergs,* Jack Benny, and so on, were considered to have monstrously good ratings with 35 percent of the listening audience (*No Ordinary Time,* 240).

34. Ibid., 195, 238.

35. Richard W. Steele, "Preparing the Public for War: Efforts to Establish a National Propaganda Agency, 1940–1941," *American Historical Review* 75:6 (October 1970): 1640–53. See also Gerd Horten, *Radio Goes to War:*

The Cultural Politics of Propaganda during World War II (Berkeley: University of California Press, 2002), 41–65.

36. See William E. Leuchtenburg, "The New Deal and the Analogue of War," in *The FDR Years: On Roosevelt and His Legacy* (New York: Columbia University Press, 1995).

37. As many historians of labor and of the Roosevelt administration have pointed out, despite the seeming parity of his injunction in the chats to both labor and management to "get along," the war mobilization works out in ways that are highly favorable to capital and often extremely difficult for labor, especially miners. See, for example, Nelson Lichtenstein, *Labor's War at Home: The CIO in World War II* (Cambridge: Cambridg University Press, 1983).

38. Janice Peck provided thoughtful and insightful assistance to my argument.

39. "My Day," May 27, 1941, quoted in Goodwin, *No Ordinary Time,* 239.

40. Hayes notes that "over a quarter of [the letters] specifically requested that FDR give more frequent talks to the people" ("Radio Broadcasting and Nation Building," 36).

41. Chester E. Bruns, Chicago, to Franklin D. Roosevelt, March 13, 1933.

42. Charles Barrell, New York, to Franklin D. Roosevelt, March 13, 1933.

43. R. H. Adams, Minneapolis, to Franklin D. Roosevelt, May 9, 1933.

44. Mrs. P. Branson, Chicago, to Franklin D. Roosevelt, December 30, 1940.

45. B. Kurlander, to Franklin D. Roosevelt, March 16, 1933.

46. Ann B. Clapp, Duluth, MN, to Franklin D. Roosevelt, May 8, 1933; emphasis added.

47. Jacob Miller, Philadelphia, to Franklin D. Roosevelt, March 13, 1933.

48. J. M. Curran, Saint Paul, MN, to Franklin D. Roosevelt, May 28, 1941.

49. F. W. Meyers, Iowa City, to Franklin D. Roosevelt, March 13, 1933.

50. Robert E. Reid, Long Island, NY, to Franklin D. Roosevelt, June 28, 1934.

51. Letter from Faye Clement, Woodsville, NH, May 30, 1941. PPF Radio Speech, May 27, 1941 (Pro C).

52. Alfred D. Cookson, Green Bay, WI, to Franklin D. Roosevelt, May 28, 1941.

53. William D. Carr, New York, to Franklin D. Roosevelt, June 3, 1941; Chester E. Bruns, Chicago, March 13, 1933; R. L. to Franklin D. Roosevelt, March 1933.

54. Perry Morgan, Syracuse, NY, to Franklin D. Roosevelt, March 15, 1933.

55. Henry E. Steinbrenner et al., Chicago, to Franklin D. Roosevelt, April 1938.

56. Frank Cort, Sunnyside, CA, to Franklin D. Roosevelt, May 7, 1933.

57. Michael Cornwall, Garfield, NJ, to Franklin D. Roosevelt, July 14, 1934.

58. H. L. Boyer, Geneva, NY, to Franklin D. Roosevelt, March 14, 1933; Chester E. Bruns, Chicago, to Franklin D. Roosevelt, March 13, 1933; Frederick H. Bixler, New York, to Franklin D. Roosevelt, March 12, 1933; Wilbur E. Bender, Boston, to Franklin D. Roosevelt, January 1, 1941; J. J. Crawley, Baltimore, to Franklin D. Roosevelt, May 8, 1933.

59. Name unintelligible, Cleveland, OH, March 1933.

60. Marie Barrell, New York, to Franklin D. Roosevelt, March 13, 1933; R. H. Adams, Minneapolis, to Franklin D. Roosevelt, May 9, 1933; Irving Aronowitz, Brooklyn, NY, to Franklin D. Roosevelt, May 10, 1933; H. Wade Shepard, Jersey City, NJ, to Franklin D. Roosevelt, March 13, 1933; F. W. Meyers, Iowa City, to Franklin D. Roosevelt, March 13, 1933.

61. See, for example, the letter from Mabel and Vern Clark, Sioux City, IA, May 28, 1941.

62. N. L. Patch, Lakeview, OH, to Franklin D. Roosevelt, May 29, 1941.

63. Mabel and Vern Clark, Sioux City, IA, May 28, 1941. PPF 200B, May 27, 1941 (Pro-C).

64. Name and city unintelligible, to Franklin D. Roosevelt, May 29, 1941.

65. Mary Chatin, Larchmont, NY, to Franklin D. Roosevelt, June 1, 1941; A. B. Cox, Long Beach, CA, to Franklin D. Roosevelt, May 29, 1941.

66. A. B. Cox, Long Beach, CA, to Franklin D. Roosevelt, May 29, 1941.

67. Kathleen Cheney to Franklin D. Roosevelt, May 29, 1941.

68. Frank H. Canaday, Chicago, to Franklin D. Roosevelt, May 28, 1941.

69. Russell D. Baker, Decorah, IA, to Franklin D. Roosevelt, December 30, 1940.

70. Andrew S. Draper, Tarrytown, NY, to Franklin D. Roosevelt, December 30, 1940.

71. Maureen H. Beasley, *Eleanor Roosevelt and the Media* (Urbana and Chicago: University of Illinois Press, 1987), 189.

72. Scripts for Simmons Broadcast, September 25, 1934, Box 3027. Speech and Article File, Eleanor Roosevelt Papers, p. 5, quoted in ibid., 73.

73. James T. Howard, "Males Squirm at First Lady's Parley," clipping, *PM*, September 28, 1943; Ruby A. Black Papers, Franklin D. Roosevelt Library, quoted in Beasley, *Eleanor Roosevelt*, 159.

74. Beasley, *Eleanor Roosevelt*, 173, 183.

75. Helen Essary, "Dear Washington," clipping, *Washington Times-Herald*, September 28, 1943, quoted in ibid., 159.

76. Beasley, *Eleanor Roosevelt*, 74–75, 132.

77. Ibid., 120–21, 133, 137, 190.

78. See Michele Hilmes, "Rethinking Radio," in *Radio Reader: Essays in*

the Cultural History of Radio, ed. Michele Hilmes and Jason Loviglio (New York: Routledge, 2002), 1–20.

79. Beasley, *Eleanor Roosevelt,* 74–75.

80. I am indebted to Michele Hilmes for this insight. Personal communication, August 27, 2004.

81. Beasley, *Eleanor Roosevelt,* 34.

82. Ibid., 34–35.

83. Ibid., 72.

84. The Eleanor Roosevelt Speech and Article File Finding Aid, FDR Library.

85. Beasley, *Eleanor Roosevelt,* 31–36, 72–76, 159–60, 132.

86. Ibid., 113, 131, 76.

87. The Eleanor Roosevelt Speech and Article File Finding Aid, FDR Library.

88. Ibid.

89. Beasley, *Eleanor Roosevelt,* 172–73.

90. Ibid.

91. The Eleanor Roosevelt Speech and Article File Finding Aid, FDR Library.

92. Ibid.

93. *Pan-American Coffee Hour,* September 28, 1941. Eleanor Roosevelt: Recorded Speeches and Interviews, 1933–62, FDR Library.

94. Ibid.

95. Ibid., October 5, 1941.

96. Ibid., September 28, 1941.

97. Ibid., October 5, 1941.

98. Ibid., October 26, 1941; October 19, 1941.

99. Ibid., October 12, 1941.

100. Ibid.

101. Elmo Roper, "After the War: Portrait of Gloom," public opinion survey prepared for Franklin D. Roosevelt, November 12, 1941.

102. *Pan-American Coffee Hour,* October 5, 1941.

103. Beasley, *Eleanor Roosevelt,* 167.

104. Goodwin, *No Ordinary Time,* 325; Beasley, *Eleanor Roosevelt,* 140–52; and *Pan-American Coffee Hour,* February 22, 1942.

105. Goodwin, *No Ordinary Time,* 325.

106. *Pan-American Coffee Hour,* February 22, 1942.

107. Ibid.

108. The Eleanor Roosevelt Speech and Article File Finding Aid, FDR Library.

109. Beasley, *Eleanor Roosevelt,* 150; *Pan-American Coffee Hour,* March 15, 1942; February 22, 1942.

110. Beasley, *Eleanor Roosevelt,* 137; Eleanor Roosevelt, *You Learn by Living* (New York: Harper, 1960), 77, 82, quoted in Beasley, *Eleanor Roosevelt,* 182.

111. *Pan-American Coffee Hour,* February 22, 1942.

2. Vox Pop

Unless otherwise noted, all *Vox Pop* broadcasts referred to can be found in the *Vox Pop* Collection (VPC) at the Library of American Broadcasting (LAB), College Park, Maryland.

1. Wayne Munson, *All Talk: The Talkshow in Media Culture* (Philadelphia: Temple University Press, 1993), 28.

2. For a discussion of audience-participation radio programs and the broader ethos of "republican simplicity" running through participatory media forms, see ibid., 19–62.

3. Lisabeth Cohen, *The Consumer's Republic: The Politics of Mass Consumption in Postwar America* (New York: Vintage Books, 2003).

4. The Sammis and Bisch articles from *Radioland* can be found in the Radioland Collection (RLC) at the Library of American Broadcasting (LAB).

5. Michael Denning, *The Cultural Front: The Laboring of American Culture in the Twentieth Century* (London and New York: Verso, 1997).

6. According to Bill Johnson, Parks Johnson's son, Ted Husing, a radio announcer in Chicago, first began interviewing people on the street about their choice for president in the upcoming 1932 presidential election. See Bill Johnson and M. F. Johnson, "*Vox Pop:* 1932–1949 and Parks Johnson, Its Originator" (Sabino Ranch, TX: Sabino Publishers, 1997), 11, VPC.

7. For a broad variation on this argument, see Lisabeth Cohen, *Making a New Deal: Industrial Workers in Chicago, 1919–1939* (Cambridge: Cambridge University Press, 1991); Gerd Horten, *Radio Goes to War: The Cultural Politics of Propaganda during World War II* (Berkeley: University of California Press, 2002); Lary May, *The Big Tomorrow: Hollywood and the Politics of the American Way* (Chicago: University of Chicago Press, 2000); and Robert W. McChesney, *Telecommunications, Mass Media, and Democracy: The Battle for the Control of U.S. Broadcasting, 1928–1935* (New York: Oxford University Press, 1993).

8. Denning, *The Cultural Front;* Lary May, "Making the American Consensus: The Narrative of Conversion and Subversion in World War II Films," in *The War in American Culture: Society and Consciousness during World War II,* ed. Lewis A. Ehrenberg and Susan E. Hirsch (Chicago and London: University of Chicago Press, 1996), 71–102. See also May, *The Big Tomorrow;* Paula Rabinowitz, *They Must Be Represented: The Politics of Documentary* (London: Verso, 1994); Warren Susman, *Culture as History: The Transformation of American Society in the Twentieth Century* (New York: Pantheon Books, 1984).

9. See the letter from Parks Johnson to Niles Trammell, undated, and the letter from Niles Trammell to Parks Johnson, September 22, 1939. VPC series I, box 20, folder 26.

10. David K. Grant, "The Rise of Audience Participation Programs," *Advertising and Selling* (June 1946).

11. John Dunning, *On the Air: The Encyclopedia of Old-Time Radio* (New York: Oxford University Press, 1998), 47, 341–42, 37.

12. Ibid., 25–26, 30–31; Munson, *All Talk*, 30–31.

13. Dunning, *On the Air*, 25–26, 538.

14. The urgency and dramatic power of documentary film and photography during the 1930s has been well noted; however, less attention has been paid to the importance of the documentary impulse in radio's representation of social and political realities of the Depression. Some recent examples of scholarship that does begin to acknowledge this impulse include Barbara Dianne Savage, *Broadcasting Freedom: Radio, War, and the Politics of Race, 1938–1948* (Chapel Hill: University of North Carolina Press, 1999), and Howard Blue, *Words at War: World War II Era Radio Drama and the Postwar Broadcasting Industry Blacklist* (Lanham, MD: Scarecrow Press, 2002).

15. Dunning, *On the Air*, 261–69, 478, 425–29; 43–47; 510, 114–17.

16. Willard Rowland, "The Meaning of 'The Public Interest' in Communications Policy, Part I: Its Origins in State and Federal Regulation," *Communication Law and Policy* 2:3 (summer 1997): 321–25.

17. See McChesney, *Telecommunications, Mass Media, and Democracy.*

18. May, *The Big Tomorrow*, 30, 17.

19. Chuck Howell and Mike Mashon's interview with Bill Johnson, October 25, 1995. VPC series II, box 3, folder 72.

20. January 11, 1935, broadcast. VPC series III.

21. Ibid.

22. Ibid.

23. Ibid. See also VPC series I, subseries 2, box 1, folders 22–25, interview questions.

24. Indeed, Roosevelt's timing of the Fireside Chats to coincide with addresses to Congress, announcements of new administrative initiatives, and official proclamations made clear how he intended to use them as a way of enlisting public opinion to support his efforts to influence Congress (see chapter 1).

25. Walter Lippmann, *Public Opinion* (New York: Macmillan, 1922, 1960) and *The Phantom Public* (New York: Harcourt, Brace & Co., 1925); Raymond Seidelman, *Disenchanted Realists: Political Scientists and the American Crisis, 1884–1984* (Albany: State U Press, 1985); Elton Mayo, "The Irrational Factor in Human Behavior: The 'Night-Mind' in Industry," *Annals of the American Academy of Political and Social Science* (November 1923): 117–30; Walter T. Shepard, "Democracy in Transition," *American Political Science Review* 29:1 (February 1935): 1–20.

26. Munson, *All Talk,* 19.

27. Lawrence Levine has identified a similar ambivalence vis-à-vis "the people" in the Hollywood movies of the period: "Hollywood evinced a pervasive ambivalence concerning the American people who were constantly referred to as the cure and hope of the state but who were depicted again and again as weak, fickle, confused sheep who could be frightened, manipulated, and controlled" ("Hollywood's Washington: Film Images of National Politics during the Great Depression," *Prospects* 10, ed. Jack Salzman (New York: Cambridge University Press, 1985), 169–95.

28. The cause of the Depression was understood, by some in business and government, to be "a buyer's strike." A return to consumerism, therefore, could return the nation to economic prosperity. See Rita Barnard, *The Great Depression and the Culture of Abundance: Kenneth Fearing, Nathanael West, and Mass Culture in the 1930s* (Cambridge: Cambridge University Press, 1995).

29. Michele Hilmes, *Radio Voices: American Broadcasting, 1922–1952* (Minneapolis: University of Minnesota Press, 1997), 151–82.

30. Parks Johnson, VPC series III, box 3, folder 6, interview questions.

31. Ibid. and VPC series I, subseries 2, box 1, folders 22 and 23, interview questions.

32. Munson, *All Talk,* 32.

33. Ibid. and VPC series I, subseries 4, general, box 2, folders 1–2, Parks Johnson notebook 1.

34. Script for July 7, 1935, and August 18, 1935. VPC series I, subseries 5, scripts, box 2, folder 13, May 6, 1935–November 17, 1935.

35. Parks Johnson notebook, VPC series I, subseries 4, general, box 2, folder 1, #1, June 28, 1935.

36. VPC series I, subseries 5, scripts, box 2, folder 14, January 26, 1936—April 28, 1936.

37. Munson, *All Talk,* 42. Television "bloopers" are also examples of this same appeal, though with the seven-second tape delay in the 1970s, live broadcasting became more of a "feeling" than a reality.

38. VPC series I, subseries 3, box 1, folders 31–33, searches; and series I, subseries 1, box 1, folders 6–8, correspondence.

39. 1938 memo, unsigned. VPC series I, subseries 11, business files and correspondence. NBC box 20, folder 26.

40. Memo from Nate Tufts to Parks Johnson, July 31, 1939. VPC series I, subseries 11, business files and correspondence. NBC box 20, folder 34.

41. Memo from Nate Tufts to Parks Johnson, September 28, 1939. VPC series I, subseries 11, business files and correspondence. NBC box 20, folder 34.

42. Parks Johnson notebooks, VPC series 1, subseries 4, general, box 2, folders 1 and 2.

43. VPC series I, subseries 4, general, box 1, folder 44.

44. Warren Susman, *Culture as History: The Transformation of American Society in the Twentieth Century* (New York: Pantheon Books, 1984), 184–210.

45. Christopher H. Sterling and John M. Kittross, eds., *Stay Tuned: A Concise History of American Broadcasting* (Belmont, CA: Wadsworth Publishing Co., 1978), 189–92. See also Richard W. Steele, "The Great Debate: Roosevelt, the Media, and the Coming of the War, 1940–1941," *Journal of American History* 71 (June 1984), and "Preparing the Public for War: Efforts to Establish a National Propaganda Agency, 1940–1941," *American Historical Review* 75 (1970). See also Hilmes, *Radio Voices,* 230–70.

46. *Vox Pop* garnered ratings of 19 or higher during the first three months of 1944; VPC series I, subseries 11, business files and correspondence. NBC box 21, folder 38.

47. November 15, 1943, broadcast, VPC series III.

48. Maureen Honey, *Creating Rosie the Riveter: Class, Gender, and Propaganda during World War II* (Amherst: University of Massachusetts Press, 1984), 23, quoted in Wendy Kozol, *Life's America: Family and Nation in Postwar Photojournalism* (Philadelphia: Temple University Press, 1994), 66.

49. Allison McCracken, "Scary Women and Scarred Men: Suspense, Gender Trouble, and Postwar Change, 1942–1950," in *Radio Reader: Essays in the Cultural History of Radio,* ed. Michele Hilmes and Jason Loviglio (New York: Routledge, 2001).

50. Letter from Gordon Hines, dated February 23, 1942. VPC series I, subseries 1, correspondence, box 1, folder 10.

51. Letter from Mrs. Margaret Miller, dated April 17, 1945. VPC series I, subseries 1, correspondence, box 1, folder 13.

52. Hilmes, *Radio Voices,* 235. Savage argues that "a coalition of African American activists, public officials, intellectuals, and artists struggled in the World War II era to access and use the mass medium of national radio to advocate a brand of American freedom that called for an end to racial segregation and discrimination" (*Broadcasting Freedom,* 5).

53. *Vox Pop* broadcast transcription, March 23, 1942. VPC series III.

54. March 23, 1942, entry. VPC series I, subseries 4, general, Parks Johnson's notebooks, box 2, folder 2.

55. Letter from Pfc. Monticello J. Howell, Mac Dill Field, FL, to CBS, August 15, 1945, "The Negro Problem, 1945." VPC series I, subseries 11, business files and correspondence. NBC box 21, folder 29.

56. Letter from Mrs. L. B. O'Neal, Long Island City, NY, to *Vox Pop,* 1945, "The Negro Problem, 1945." VPC series I, subseries 11, business files and correspondence. NBC box 21, folder 29.

57. Interdepartment correspondence, from Wm. Burke Miller to Mr. John F. Royal, June 18, 1939, "Programs-Criticism 1938–1941." NBC Files, box 430, Library of Congress.

58. Letter from James L. Stewart to *Vox Pop*, March 20, 1945, "The Negro Problem, 1945." VPC series I, subseries 11, business files and correspondence. NBC box 21, folder 29.

59. For a few examples, see the letters from H. W. Monsell, St. Lambert, Quebec, to Parks Johnson, January 18, 1943, and Mrs. D. J. Paolini, Syracuse, NY, to Parks Johnson, August 11, 1943, both in VPC series I, subseries 1, correspondance, box 1, folder 11; and Mrs. Dorothy P. Fowlker, Norfolk, VA, to Parks Johnson, February 23, 1944. VPC series I, subseries 1, correspondence, box 1, folder 12.

60. Excerpts from letters, circa 1942. VPC series I, subseries 1, correspondence, box 1, folder 10.

61. Unsigned letter, Norfolk, VA, February 20, 1946, to Parks Johnson. VPC series I, subseries 1, correspondence, box 1, folder 14.

62. Donald Horton and R. Richard Wohl, "Mass Communication and Para-Social Interaction: Observations on Intimacy at a Distance," in *Drama in Life: The Uses of Communication in Society,* ed. James E. Combs and Michael W. Mansfield (New York: Hastings House, 1976), 212–28.

63. Letter from Marian Sears, Kansas City, KS, October 17, 1946, to Parks Johnson, "Special Letters." VPC series I, subseries 11, business files and correspondence. NBC box 21, folder 42.

64. Letter from Ed Overend, Coronado, CA, October 30, 1946. VPC series I, subseries 1, correspondence, box 1, folder 14.

65. Letter from "A BUNCH OF YOUNG BOYS BACK FROM THE WAR," Saint Petersburg, FL, March 7, 1946, to Parks Johnson. VPC series I, subseries 1, correspondence, box 1, folder 14. "According to the National Housing Agency, at least 3.5 million new houses were needed in 1946 just to provide veterans with decent housing, yet there was only enough material and labor to build 460,000 units" (Wendy Kozol, *Life's America: Family and Nation in Postwar Photojournalism* [Philadelphia: Temple University Press, 1994], 80).

3. Public Affairs

1. The popularity of the interminable O. J. Simpson trial, which captivated daytime television audiences in the summer of 1995, was perceived less as an expression of civic interest in law, race, and domestic violence than as another variation on the soap-opera phenomenon. Televised professional wrestling has widely been labeled "soap opera for men." Most recently, the term has been applied to "reality television" programs such as *The Bachelor.* For good discussions of the historical origins of this attitude toward daytime broadcasting, see Michele Hilmes, *Radio Voices: American Broadcasting, 1922–1952* (Minneapolis: University of Minnesota Press, 1997), 151–82, and Kristen Hatch, "Kefauver, McCarthy, and the American Housewife," in *Reality Squared: Televisual Discourse on the Real* (New Brunswick, NJ: Rutgers University Press, 2002), 75–91.

2. There has been some wonderful scholarship on soap opera in the past two decades, almost all of it focusing primarily on the television era. See especially Robert Allen, *Speaking of Soap Operas* (Chapel Hill: University of North Carolina Press, 1985); Hilmes, *Radio Voices*; Gerd Horten, *Radio Goes to War: The Cultural Politics of Propaganda during World War II* (Berkeley: University of California Press, 2002); Tania Modlieski, *Loving with a Vengeance: Mass-Produced Fantasies for Women* (London and New York: Routledge, 1984); Kathy Newman, *Radio Active: Advertising and Consumer Activism, 1935–1947* (Berkeley: University of California Press, 2004); Elayne Rapping, "Daytime Utopias: If You Lived in Pine Valley, You'd Be Home," in *Hop on Pop: The Politics and Pleasures of Popular Culture,* ed. Henry Jenkins, Tara McPherson, and Jane Shattuc (Durham, NC: Duke University Press, 2002), 47–65; and Jennifer Wang, "Clubwomen vs. Drudges: The Battle to Define the Daytime Audience," paper presented at "The Radio Conference: A Transnational Forum," July 31, 2003, Madison, WI.

3. Rudolph Arnheim, "The World of the Daytimes Serial," in *Radio Research, 1942–1943,* ed. Paul F. Lazarsfeld and Frank N. Stanton (New York: Duell, Sloan, and Pearce, 1944), 47.

4. James Thurber, "Ivorytown, Rinsoville, Anacinburg and Crisco Corners," in *The Beast in Me and Other Animals* (New York: Harcourt, Brace & World, 1948), 210.

5. Jim Cox has counted the number of serial dramas bearing this central premise of cross-class romance. He comes up with an even dozen that fit the precise formula of "marrying an ordinary girl to wealth or prominence," which is, I think, a conservative estimate. He concedes that there are many more that practice some kind of modification on this formula but keep the central class tension. See Jim Cox, *The Great Radio Soap Operas* (Jefferson, NC, and London: McFarland & Company, 1999), 301.

6. Thurber, *The Beast in Me,* 210.

7. Gerd Horten's otherwise excellent *Radio Goes to War: The Cultural Politics of Propaganda during World War II* (Berkeley: University of California Press, 2002) relies a bit too heavily on this notion of the 1930s as an oasis of progressivism that disappears with the outbreak of World War II. For a review of Horten's book and two others that investigate the complicated politics of radio during World War II, see Jason Loviglio, "Radio in Wartime: The Politics of Propaganda, Race, and the American Way in the Second World War," *American Quarterly* (December 2004): 1079–87.

8. The term "parasocial intimacy" comes from Donald Horton and R. Richard Wohl, "Mass Communication and Para-Social Interaction: Observations on Intimacy at a Distance," in *Drama in Life: The Uses of Communication in Society,* ed. James E. Combs and Michael W. Mansfield (New York: Hastings House, 1976), 212–28.

9. Hilmes, *Radio Voices,* 177. Soap-opera auteur Irna Phillips also claims

that her attempts to take on "public" issues such as race relations were censored by the network (ibid., 160). For another account of Phillips's frustration with overbearing network and sponsor interference, see Horten, *Radio Goes to War*, 153–54, 157–61, 172–73.

10. "Soap Opera," *Fortune* (March 1946): 119–24, 146–48, 151–52, quoted in Allen, *Speaking of Soap Operas*, 15.

11. Arnheim, "The World of the Daytimes Serial," 41.

12. Cox, *The Great Radio Soap Operas*, 243.

13. My thanks to Michele Hilmes for help in refining the ideas in this paragraph.

14. Thurber, *The Beast in Me*, 251–52.

15. Cox, *The Great Radio Soap Operas*, 28.

16. Wendy Kozol, *Life's America: Family and Nation in Postwar Photojournalism* (Philadelphia: Temple University Press, 1994), 79. Thanks to Patrice McDermott for help in refining my discussion here.

17. I have also referred to criticism of the soap-opera genre as a whole, when in fact the academic literature on radio soaps is rather scarce, compared to work on television soaps. However, it is true that the most strident critics of daytime serials have made virtually identical cases against the radio and television versions. And most recent revisionist work on the soap opera has tended to focus on television, casually including radio forms too, without much attention to the differences. The result has been a lack of critical attention to the radio soap-opera form. A few exceptions, discussed in the following paragraphs, merit mention because of their influence on my analysis.

18. Hilmes, *Radio Voices*, 151–82.

19. Allen, *Speaking of Soap Operas*, 69–81.

20. This line is excerpted from the introduction to *The Guiding Light* in the summer of 1944, delivered by Ed Prentiss, announcer for *The Guiding Light* and host of *The General Mills Hour*.

21. See, for example, Arnheim, "The World of Daytime Serials," 41, and Horton and Wohl, "Mass Communication and Para-Social Intimacy."

22. See, for example, *The Life of Mary Sothern*, episode 12, private collection of Ryan Ellett. See http://www.geocities.com/ryanellett/.

23. *Our Gal Sunday* began each broadcast with this question from 1937 to 1959. See John Dunning, *Tune in Yesterday: The Ultimate Encyclopedia of Old-Time Radio, 1925–1976* (Englewood Cliffs, NJ: Prentice Hall, 1976), 460.

24. Cox, *The Great Radio Soap Operas*, 106.

25. Herta Herzog, "What Do We Really Know about Daytime Serial Listeners?" in Lazarsfeld and Stanton, *Radio Research, 1942–1943*, 24–25, 28–29.

26. Ibid., 3–33.

27. *Radio Mirror*, February 1947, 41, quoted in Cox, *The Great Radio Soap Operas*, 91.

28. Hobe Morrison, "Analyzing the Daytime Serials," *Variety,* August 18, 1943, 34, in box 63, correspondence, Irna Phillips Papers, Wisconsin Historical Society Broadcasting Archives (hereafter IPP).

29. Letter to Hobe Morrison, August 23, 1943, box 63, correspondence, IPP.

30. Untitled manuscript, box 63, correspondence, IPP.

31. Ibid.

32. "Painted Dreams Outline and Pitch, Painted Dreams," box 4, IPP.

33. Lynn Spigel, *Make Room for TV: Television and the Family Ideal in Postwar America* (Chicago: University of Chicago Press, 1992), 162.

34. Horten, *Radio Goes to War,* 171–72.

35. *The Guiding Light,* June 16, 1944, DAT recording, Motion Picture, Broadcasting, and Recorded Sound Division, Library of Congress (hereafter LOC).

36. Ibid.

37. *The General Mills Hour,* June 13, 1944, DAT recording, Motion Picture, Broadcasting, and Recorded Sound Division, LOC.

38. *The Guiding Light,* June 23, 1944, DAT recording, Motion Picture, Broadcasting, and Recorded Sound Division, LOC. See also *Judy and Jane,* December 12, 1936, in which the announcer invites an anonymous "woman, a housewife," to talk about the virtues of making drip coffee using Folgers (*Judy and Jane,* continuity, December 1936, LOC).

39. See, for instance, *The Guiding Light,* January 5, 1944: "Dear Lord . . . Grant thy protection to our sailors and soldiers; . . ." DAT recording, Motion Picture, Broadcasting, and Recorded Sound Division, LOC.

40. *Today's Children,* June 15, 1944, DAT recording, Motion Picture, Broadcasting, and Recorded Sound Division, LOC.

41. See, for example, the testimony of Emma Puschner, director of the National Welfare Division of the American Legion, on *The Guiding Light,* June 13, 1944, DAT recording, Motion Picture, Broadcasting, and Recorded Sound Division, LOC.

42. See Paul Rhymer, *The Small House Half-Way Up in the Next Block: Paul Rhymer's Vic and Sade* (New York: McGraw-Hill, 1972), a wonderful collection of the radio scripts from *Vic and Sade* from the 1930s and 1940s.

43. *Life Can Be Beautiful,* continuity, November 23, 1938, Collections of the Manuscript Division, LOC.

44. *The Guiding Light,* June 20, 1944, DAT recording, Motion Picture, Broadcasting, and Recorded Sound Division, LOC.

45. *Portia Faces Life,* October 1940, General Foods Corporation Radio Script Collection, Collections of the Manuscript Division, LOC; *Judy and Jane,* continuity, December 23, 1936, LOC. For a complete synopsis of the plot developments in the show's first year on the air, see Doctor John Ruthledge,

The Guiding Light (Chicago: Guiding Light Publishing Co., 1938), 105 (LOC). *The Romance of Helen Trent*, episode title: "Helen to Lose Gil," circa 1946, private collection of Ryan Ellett. See http://www.geocities.com/ryanellett/.

46. *Judy and Jane*, continuity, December 4, 1936, LOC.

47. It is hard to find accurate data to confirm how long *Judy and Jane* was on the air. John Dunning's *On the Air: The Encyclopedia of Old-Time Radio* (New York: Oxford University Press, 1998) gives its dates as 1932–35, but I have seen script continuities dated as late as 1938. Also, in 1937, frequent references to the show's five years on the air suggest that Dunning is correct in giving its start date as 1932, which makes it one of the very earliest soaps on the air. Because *Judy and Jane* aired only in the Midwest, it has not received as much scholarly or archival attention as national programs.

48. For an account of the long, complicated history of *Pepper Young's Family* and its several names and networks, see Dunning, *On the Air,* 539; and Cox, *The Great Radio Soap Operas,* 157–69.

49. See *Radio Mirror,* February 1947, 41, quoted in Cox, *The Great Radio Soap Operas,* 91.

50. *Pepper Young's Family,* episode 49, circa 1940, private collection of Ryan Ellett. See http://www.geocities.com/ryanellett/.

51. *Pepper Young's Family,* episode 61, circa 1940, private collection of Ryan Ellett. See http://www.geocities.com/ryanellett/.

52. *Portia Faces Life,* June 12, 1941, continuity, from the Collections of the Manuscript Division, LOC.

53. I have not been successful in getting precise dates for the episodes that are extant. According to Dunning *(On the Air),* the show aired between 1934 and 1938. My references to *The Life of Mary Sothern* all come from recordings in the private collection of Ryan Ellett. See http://www.geocities.com/ryanellett/.

54. *The Life of Mary Sothern,* episode 113, private collection of Ryan Ellett.

55. Letter from Elwood B. Mason, "Fan Mail: *The Guiding Light* and *Today's Children,*" box 46, IPP.

56. Of the twenty-three letters in the folder praising speeches and sermons from the spring and summer of 1944, nine were written by men. See "Fan Mail: *Guiding Light* and *Today's Children,*" box 46, IPP. For Phillips's insistence on an exclusively female audience, see "NBC Press Conference, New York, May 29, 1945," correspondence, box 63, IPP.

57. Miss Virginia Miller, Sierra Madre, CA, to Franklin D. Roosevelt, March 13, 1933.

58. May Brannan, Washington, DC, to NBC, May 9, 1938.

59. Florence Pulver, Osborne, KS, to NBC, March 18, 1938.

60. Elsie N. Bliss, Minot, ND, to NBC, February 23, 1938.

61. For a wonderful analysis of *The Story of Mary Marlin,* and audience response to it, see Hilmes, *Radio Voices,* 151–82.

62. Letter from May 1, 1941; author's name unintelligible. "*The Story of Mary Marlin*—Fan Mail," box 3, folders 9 and 10, Jane Crusinberry papers, Wisconsin Historical Society Broadcasting Archives.

63. See "Fan Mail: *The Guiding Light* and *Today's Children*," box 46, IPP.

64. Dunning, *On the Air*, 674.

65. Jim Cox, *Frank and Anne Hummert's Radio Factory: The Programs and Personalities of Broadcasting's Most Prolific Producers* (Jefferson, NC, and London: McFarland & Company, 203), 164.

66. Dunning, *On the Air*, 462.

67. Rocky Clark, "They Started Radio Serials—Can You Blame Them?" *Bridgeport Sunday Post*, October 8, 1939, sec. 3, p. 1, quoted in Cox, *Frank and Anne Hummert's Radio Factory*, 102.

68. *Judy and Jane*, continuity, March 3, 1937, LOC.

69. Helen J. Kaufman, "The Appeal of Specific Daytime Serials," in Lazarsfeld and Stanton, *Radio Research, 1942–1943*, 91–93.

70. Madeleine Edmondson and David Rounds, *From Mary Noble to Mary Hartman: The Complete Soap Opera Book* (New York: Stein and Day, 1976), 47.

71. Jason Loviglio, "Radio in Wartime: The Politics of Propaganda, Race, and the American Way in the Second World War," review essay, *American Quarterly* (December 2004): 1079–87.

72. *Judy and Jane*, continuity, December 23, 1936, and January 13, 1937, LOC.

73. Roland Marchand, *Advertising the American Dream: Making Way for Modernity, 1920–1940* (Berkeley: University of California Press, 1985), 217.

74. *Pepper Young's Family*, episode 24, circa 1940, private collection of Ryan Ellett. See http://www.geocities.com/ryanellett/.

75. *The Life of Mary Sothern*, episode 25, private collection of Ryan Ellett.

76. Hilmes, *Radio Voices*, 160; and Horten, *Radio Goes to War*, 172–73.

77. *The Guiding Light*, June 13, 1944, and June 14, 1944, LOC. For a different interpretation of the American Legion episode, see Horten, *Radio Goes to War*, 170.

78. Ruthledge, *The Guiding Light*, 68–104.

79. *Judy and Jane*, continuity, December 8, 1936, LOC.

4. *The Shadow* Meets the Phantom Public

Unless otherwise noted, all episodes quoted from are from Ryan Ellett's personal collection. See http://www.geocities.com/ryanellett/.

1. For more on the relationship between radio programming and other popular cultural forms, see Eric Barnouw, *A Tower in Babel: A History of Broadcasting in the United States*, vol. 1 (New York: Oxford University Press, 1966), 273–83, and Michele Hilmes, *Radio Voices: American Broadcasting, 1922–1952* (Minneapolis: University of Minnesota Press, 1997), 82–86.

Marshall McLuhan suggests that the "content" of a new medium is "always another medium" (*Understanding Media: The Extensions of Man* [Cambridge: MIT Press, 1994], 80–93, 305). For more on the tensions and conflicts surrounding the relationships between networks, sponsors, advertising agencies, and a broader public debate over the direction of radio, see Eric Barnouw, *The Golden Web: A History of Broadcasting in the United States,* vol. 2 (New York: Oxford University Press, 1968), 9–44; Hilmes, *Radio Voices,* 97–129; and Robert W. McChesney, *Telecommunications, Mass Media, and Democracy: The Battle for the Control of U.S. Broadcasting, 1928–1935* (New York: Oxford University Press, 1993).

2. Anthony Tollin, *The Shadow: The Making of a Legend* (New York: Conde Nast Publications, 1996), 4.

3. See ibid., 4–7.

4. Ibid., 14–15.

5. See ibid., 14, and *The Shadow in Review* Web site: http://www.spaceports.com/~deshadow/.

6. See Walter Gibson, *The Golden Master* and *Shiwan Khan Returns* (New York: Conde Nast Publications, 1967). See "The Shadow Pulp Reviews," a fan Web site with hundreds of reviews of Shadow pulp novels, revealing that a majority of the plots turn on threats from "Oriental outsiders" (http://www.spaceports.com/~deshadow/reviews/index.html).

7. *The Shadow* of the 1940s and 1950s, in turn, explored an increasingly psychological and sociological landscape of fears, featuring as villains isolated madmen or organized crime syndicates. For a discussion of the more formulaic nature of the plots and the more dilettantish character of Lamont Cranston in *The Shadow* of the 1940s, see Tollin, *The Shadow,* 32–35.

8. By the late 1940s, the program was heard on nearly three hundred stations nationwide, with an unusual split-sponsor setup: Blue Coal in the East, Carey Salt in the Midwest, Balm Barr in the South, and the U.S. Air Force over the Don Lee Pacific Coast network. Blue Coal stopped sponsoring the show in 1950 because of a collapse in the anthracite market, not because of popularity ratings. After that the program had several different sponsors and one season of "sustaining" (i.e., unsponsored) broadcasts. See ibid., 26–54.

9. Ibid., 35.

10. For a discussion of the ways in which prime-time "prestige" dramas *(The Fall of the City, War of the Worlds)* expressed the domestic and international crises of the 1930s, through stories of the city in peril, see Barnouw, *The Golden Web,* 66–70, 74–89.

11. Emphasis added.

12. J. Fred MacDonald, *Don't Touch That Dial! Radio Programming in American Life from 1920 to 1960* (Chicago: Nelson-Hall, 1979), 159, quoted in Hilmes, *Radio Voices,* 112, 110–13.

13. Michael Denning, *The Cultural Front: The Laboring of American Culture in the Twentieth Century* (London and New York: Verso, 1996), 362–84.

14. Ibid., 365.

15. Hadley Cantril, *The Invasion from Mars: A Study in the Psychology of Panic* (Princeton, NJ: Princeton University Press, 1947), 47, 58.

16. Denning, *The Cultural Front*, 365.

17. Edward Said, *Orientalism* (New York: Pantheon Books, 1978), 248–57. Subsequent references are given in the text.

18. Bill Ong Hing, *Making and Remaking Asian America through Immigration Policy, 1850–1990* (Stanford, CA: Stanford University Press, 1993), 35–36. See also John W. Dower, *War without Mercy: Race and Power in the Pacific War* (New York: Pantheon Books, 1986), 38–45. For a discussion of the ways that radio demagogues such as Father Charles Coughlin exacerbated and articulated nativist fears of immigration; racial, religious, and ethnic outsiders; and international trade, see Alan Brinkley, *Voices of Protest: Huey Long, Father Coughlin, and the Great Depression* (New York: Alfred A. Knopf, 1982); and Donald Warren, *Radio Priest: Charles Coughlin, the Father of Hate Radio* (New York: Free Press, 1996).

19. Lisa Lowe, *Immigrant Acts: On Asian American Cultural Politics* (Durham, NC: Duke University Press, 1996), 101.

20. Jackson Lears, *Fables of Abundance: A Cultural History of Advertising in America* (New York: Basic Books, 1994), 166, 45, 63–88.

21. Hilmes argues that radio's "ability to escape visual overdetermination had the potential to set off a virtual riot of social signifiers. While the peculiar effects of radio's aurality have not been studied in much depth, there is a considerable literature on the broader transgressive nature of electronic media, particularly their ability to blur and reorder social hierarchies" (*Radio Voices*, 20). For Marshall McLuhan, electronic media create a "tribal" sense of connectedness across boundaries of individual bodies, and geography, by extending the human "sensorium" (*Understanding Media: The Extensions of Man* [New York: McGraw-Hill, 1964]). Similarly, for Joshua Meyrowitz, who draws on the work of McLuhan, Harold Innis, and Erving Goffman, these electronic media blur older lines of social distinction and hierarchy based on a fixed "sense of place," ushering in a more egalitarian age in which we are "hunters and gatherers" of information. (*No Sense of Place: The Impact of Electronic Media on Social Behavior* [New York: Oxford University Press, 1985], 131–83; 315–17).

22. See Susan J. Douglas, *Inventing American Broadcasting, 1899–1922* (Baltimore: Johns Hopkins University Press, 1987), 292–314, and Catherine L. Covert, "We May Hear Too Much: American Sensibility and the Response to Radio, 1919–1924," in *Mass Media between the Wars: Perceptions of Cultural Tension, 1918–1941*, ed. Catherine L. Covert and John D. Stevens (Syracuse, NY: Syracuse University Press, 1984), 199–220.

23. Hilmes, *Radio Voices,* 21. Hilmes cites the centrality of exotic and familiar racial stereotypes in important early network programs like *Amos 'n' Andy, The Cliquot Club Eskimos, The A&P Gypsies,* and *The Goldbergs.*

24. See, for example, "Night without End" (October 16, 1938), "The Power of the Mind" (July 3, 1938), and "Murder on Approval" (August 21, 1938).

25. See Alex Russo, "A Dark(ened) Figure on the Airwaves," in *Radio Reader: Essays in the Cultural History of Radio,* ed. Michele Hilmes and Jason Loviglio (New York: Routledge, 2002), 257–76.

26. For these plots, see *Dreams of Death* (1946), *Monkey Woman* (1949), *The Bride Wore Black* (1946), and *Etched with Acid* (1946).

27. *The Spider Boy* (1945), *The Gorilla Man* (1946), *The Werewolf of Hamilton Mansion* (1947).

28. Walter Lippmann, *Public Opinion* (New York: Macmillan, 1922), 3–32.

29. See Covert, "We May Hear Too Much," 207–10, and Michael Kirkhorn, "This Curious Existence: Journalistic Identity in the Interwar Period," in Covert and Stevens, *Mass Media between the Wars,* 127–40.

30. Lippmann, *Public Opinion,* 379–97.

31. Edward L. Bernays's *Crystallizing Public Opinion* (New York: Boni and Liveright, 1923) is often regarded as the first primer on how to be a "public-relations counsel" for private interests. Bernays draws extensively on the insights of Lippmann's *Public Opinion,* published the year before.

32. Lary May, *The Big Tomorrow: Hollywood and the Politics of the American Way* (Chicago: University of Chicago Press, 2000), 99.

33. A more exhaustive analysis of popular radio dramas of the period, paralleling May's analysis of a sample of more than 240 films, has not, to my knowledge, been conducted, but would be very useful in exploring this issue in greater depth. See Lary May, "Making the American Consensus: The Narrative of Conversion and Subversion in World War II Films," in *The War in American Culture: Society and Consciousness during World War II,* ed. Lewis A. Ehrenberg and Susan E. Hirsch (Chicago: University of Chicago Press, 1996), 71–102.

34. See Kirkhorn, "This Curious Existence," for a discussion of the narrowing gap between journalists' and advertisers' cynical views of the "mass mind" in the interwar period; Bernays, *Crystallizing Public Opinion,* for a discussion of the emergence of the public-relations counsel; and Lears, *Fables of Abundance,* 137–260, on the development of an ethos of managerial-industrial efficiency in the early modern advertising industry.

35. See Michele Hilmes and Jason Loviglio, "Introduction," in Hilmes and Loviglio, *Radio Reader.*

36. See, for example, "The Phonograph Murder" (April 15, 1947), in which Boston Blackie and his loyal, sexless companion, Mary Wesley, tinker with recording machines to solve a murder mystery ("Old-Time Radio's 60 All-Time Favorites," compact disc collection, Radio Spirits). See also John Dun-

ning, *On the Air: The Encyclopedia of Old-Time Radio* (New York: Oxford University Press, 1998), 110.

37. For a comparison of the Green Hornet and the Lone Ranger, see Dunning, *On the Air,* 297–99.

38. As mentioned in the Introduction, Jürgen Habermas, *The Structural Transformation of the Public Sphere: An Inquiry into a Category of Bourgeois Society* (Cambridge: MIT Press, 1989), and Richard Sennett, *The Fall of Public Man* (New York: W. W. Norton, 1992), make versions of this argument.

Conclusion

1. Anthony Tollin, *The Shadow: The Making of a Legend* (New York: Conde Nast Publications, 1996), 43; John Dunning, *On the Air: The Encyclopedia of Old-Time Radio* (New York: Oxford University Press, 1998), 279–80.

2. Mark Andrejevec, *Reality TV: The Work of Being Watched* (Lanham, MD: Rowman and Littlefield, 2003), 10.

3. Sean Baker, "From *Dragnet* to *Survivor:* Historical and Cultural Perspectives on Reality Television," in *Survivor Lessons: Essays on Communication and Reality Television,* ed. Matthew J. Smith and Andrew F. Wood (Jefferson, NC: McFarland & Company, 2003), 57–70.

4. Wayne Munson, *All Talk: The Talkshow in Media Culture* (Philadelphia: Temple University Press, 1993), 33. Subsequent references are given in the text.

5. Jürgen Habermas, *The Structural Transformation of the Public Sphere: An Inquiry into a Category of Bourgeois Society* (Cambridge: MIT Press, 1989), 164. Habermas has since acknowledged the "strong influence of Adorno's theory of mass culture" in shaping his pessimism here: "At the time, I was too pessimistic about the resisting power and above all the critical potential of a pluralistic, internally much differentiated mass public whose cultural usages have begun to shake off the constraints of class" (Jürgen Habermas, "Further Reflections on the Public Sphere," trans. Thomas Burger, in *Habermas and the Public Sphere,* ed. Craig Calhoun [Cambridge, MA: MIT Press, 1992], 438).

6. Paolo Carpignano et al., "Chatter in the Age of Electronic Reproduction: Talk Television and the 'Public Mind,'" in *The Phantom Public Sphere,* ed. Bruce Robbins (Minneapolis: University of Minnesota Press, 1993), 118.

7. Mark Poster, *The Mode of Information: Poststructuralism and Social Context* (Chicago: University of Chicago Press, 1990), 43–68; Munson, *All Talk,* 149–56.

8. Joshua Meyrowitz, *No Sense of Place: The Impact of Electronic Media on Social Behavior* (New York: Oxford University Press, 1985), 315.

9. The term "technologies of freedom" comes from Ithiel de Sola Pool, *Technologies of Freedom* (Cambridge: Harvard University Press, 1983), quoted in Lloyd Morrisett, "Technologies of Freedom?" in *Democracy and New*

Media, ed. Henry Jenkins and David Thorburn (Cambridge: MIT Press, 2003), 21–32.

10. James W. Carey, *Communication as Culture: Essays on Media and Society* (New York and London: Routledge, 1988), 37–68.

11. Bertolt Brecht, "Radio as a Means of Communication," in *Communication and Class Struggle 2: Liberation, Socialism,* ed. Armand Mattelart and Seth Siegelaub (Bagnolet, France: International Mass Media Research Center, 1983), 169–71.

12. Michael Warner, "The Mass Public and the Mass Subject," in Robbins, *The Phantom Public Sphere,* 382.

13. Harold D. Lasswell, *Propaganda Technique in the World War* (New York: Alfred A. Knopf, 1927), 220–21, quoted in Melvin L. De Fleur and Sandra J. Ball-Rokeach, *Theories of Mass Communication* (New York: Longman, 1989), 161.

14. Daniel Czitrom, *Media and the American Mind from Marx to McLuhan* (Chapel Hill: University of North Carolina Press, 1982), xi.

15. James Friedman, *Reality Squared: Televisual Discourse on the Real* (New Brunswick, NJ: Rutgers University Press, 2002), 11.

16. Andrejevic, *Reality TV,* 44–45.

17. John Caldwell, *Televisuality: Style, Crisis, and Authority in American Television* (New Brunswick, NJ: Rutgers University Press, 1995), 4, quoted in Friedman, *Reality Squared,* 10.

18. Andrejevic, *Reality TV,* 7.

19. Ibid., 106, 111.

20. Andrejevic, *Reality TV,* 152.

21. Ibid., 41.

22. Ibid., 45.

23. Arild Fetveit, "Reality TV in the Digital Era: A Paradox in Visual Culture?" in Friedman, *Reality Squared,* 131.

24. Steven Reiss and James Wiltz, "Why America Loves Reality TV" *Psychology Today,* September 1, 2001. See also Jennifer Thackaberry, "Mutual Metaphors of Survivor and Office Politics: Images of Work in Popular Survivor Criticism," in *Survivor Lessons,* ed. Matthew J. Smith and Andrew F. Wood (Jefferson, NC, and London: McFarland & Company, 2003), 153–81.

25. See the Web site for "A Soap Kind of Reality": http://www.aimoo .com/forum/whoson.cfm?id=589997.

26. Kristen Hatch, "Daytime Politics: Kefauver, McCarthy, and the American Housewife," in Friedman, *Reality Squared,* 75–91.

27. See the discussion logs for "Scott Peterson" at H-Amstdy listserv Web site: http://www.h-net.msu.edu/~amstdy/.

28. See Neil Gabler, *Winchell: Gossip, Power, and the Culture of Celebrity* (New York: Vintage, 1995).

Index

Jason Loviglio is assistant professor of American studies and director of the Certificate in Communications and Media Studies at University of Maryland Baltimore County, where he teaches courses in media, popular culture, and multiculturalism. He is coeditor, with Michele Hilmes, of *Radio Reader: Essays in the Cultural History of Radio.*